Distinguished Dissertations

Springer
London
Berlin
Heidelberg
New York
Barcelona
Hong Kong
Milan
Paris
Singapore
Tokyo

Other titles published in this Series:

Extensional Constructs in Intensional Type Theory
Martin Hoffman

Search and Planning Under Incomplete Information: A Study Using Bridge Card Play
Ian Frank

Theorem Proving with the Real Numbers
John Harrison

Games and Full Abstraction for a Functional Metalanguage with Recursive Types
Guy McCusker

Hardware Evolution: Automatic Design of Electronic Circuits in Reconfigurable Hardware by Artificial Evolution
Adrian Thompson

Models of Sharing Graphs: A Categorical Semantics of ***let*** *and* ***letrec***
Masahito Hasegawa

Large Scale Collaborative Virtual Environments
Chris Greenhalgh

Radu C. Calinescu

Architecture-Independent Loop Parallelisation

Springer

Radu C. Calinescu, DPhil, MSc
Oxford University Computing Laboratory, Wolfson Building, Parks Road, Oxford, OX1 3QD, UK

Series Editor

Professor C.J. van Rijsbergen
Department of Computing Science, University of Glasgow, G12 8RZ, UK

ISSN 1439-9768

ISBN-13: 978-1-4471-1197-9 Springer-Verlag London Berlin Heidelberg

British Library Cataloguing in Publication Data
Calinescu, Radu C.
Architecture-independent loop parallelisation.-
(Distinguished dissertations)
1.Parallel processing (Electronic computers)
I.Title
004.3'5
ISBN-13: 978-1-4471-1197-9

Library of Congress Cataloging-in-Publication Data
Calinescu, Radu., 1968-
Architecture-independent loop parallelisation / Radu C. Calinescu.
p. cm. -- (Distinguished dissertations)
Includes bibliographical references and index.

ISBN-13: 978-1-4471-1197-9 e-ISBN-13: 978-1-4471-0763-7
DOI: 10.1007/978-1-4471-0763-7

1. Parallel processing (Computer science) 2. Computer architecture. I. Title. II. Distinguished dissertations (Springer-Verlag)
QA76.58.C34 2000
004'.35--dc21 00-037369

Softcover reprint of the hardcover 1st edition 2000

Typesetting: Camera-ready by author

34/3830-543210 Printed on acid-free paper SPIN 10760296

Preface

This book addresses the automatic parallelisation of regular loop computations involving dense data structures. In order to achieve parallel code which is architecture-independent, scalable and of analytically predictable performance, scheduling in the bulk-synchronous parallel model of computation is considered.

Our parallelisation approach combines two types of scheduling in a novel way. A class of parallelisation techniques termed template-matching scheduling is used to build the parallel version of certain loop computations starting from predefined, highly optimised schedule skeletons. A more complicated technique called generic loop nest scheduling tackles the parallelisation of nested loops whose structure matches none of the recognised computation templates.

A collection of template-matching parallelisation methods is developed in the book. This collection builds on recent advances in automatic parallelisation and architecture-independent parallel programming, and includes two categories of scheduling techniques. The subset of techniques belonging to the first category is dedicated to the parallelisation of uniform-dependence perfect loop nests. The second category of techniques addresses the parallelisation of several loop constructs that appear frequently in imperative programs and comprise non-uniform dependences.

We also introduce a new scheme for the parallelisation of generic, untightly nested loops. This scheme comprises four steps: data dependence analysis, potential parallelism identification, data and computation partitioning, and communication and synchronisation generation. Due to the new algorithms employed in its last three steps, the scheme is able to identify coarse-grained potential parallelism, and to map it efficiently on the processor/memory units of a general purpose parallel computer.

The effectiveness of architecture-independent loop parallelisation is assessed through a series of case studies addressing the parallelisation of several scientific computing problems. For each problem, the best known parallel solution is compared with the one obtained using the automatic scheduling techniques, as well as with the parallel schedule generated by a research tool that implements a subset of these techniques. This study reveals that the new parallelisation approach is feasible, and can be successfully applied to many scientific computations involving dense data structures.

Except for a few minor corrections, this book represents the author's University of Oxford D.Phil. thesis.

Acknowledgements

I would like to express my gratitude to Bill McColl, my supervisor; he has provided invaluable advice and encouragement throughout the development of this thesis. I am also indebted to Alex Gerbessiotis, Constantinos Siniolakis, Stephen Donaldson, Alexandre Tiskin, Fabrizio Petrini, Jonathan Hill, Ronald Sujithan and all other current and former members of the Oxford BSP group for their comments on my work.

Special thanks are due to David J. Evans, Mike Giles, and Dan Stefanescu for their suggestions at various moments during my D.Phil. course, and to Stephen Donaldson and Tom Costello for proof-reading parts of the thesis.

Gaétan Hains and Fabrizio Petrini kindly accepted to examine this work, their valuable comments having led to several improvements in the final version of the thesis. I am also grateful to my examiners for suggesting that my thesis should be submitted to the Distinguished Dissertation competition.

To a great extent, this thesis represents the result of over twenty years of formal education in my life. I owe my success over all these years to many remarkable teachers. I am especially indebted to Octav Pastravanu for introducing me to the challenging world of research.

I am deeply grateful to my parents, Rodica and Dumitru, and to my wife, Ani, for their love, support and understanding; and to little Maria for reminding me that there is much more to life than computer science.

This work was funded by an Overseas Research Studentship, a Dulverton Scholarship, and an Oxford Overseas Bursary.

Contents

Glossary of Notations

Arithmetic

$\lvert x \rvert$	the absolute value of x
$\lceil x \rceil$	the ceiling of x ($y \in \mathbf{Z}$ such that $y-1 < x \leq y$)
$\lfloor x \rfloor$	the floor of x ($y \in \mathbf{Z}$ such that $y \leq x < y+1$)
$\gcd(x_1, x_2, \ldots, x_n)$	the greatest common divisor of $x_1, x_2, \ldots, x_n$
$\min\{x_1, x_2, \ldots, x_n\}$	the minimum of $x_1, x_2, \ldots, x_n$
$\max\{x_1, x_2, \ldots, x_n\}$	the maximum of $x_1, x_2, \ldots, x_n$
$x \bmod y$	the remainder of the integer division of x by y

Sets

$\{\}$	the empty set
$\{x_1, x_2, \ldots, x_n\}$	the set containing elements $x_1, x_2, \ldots, x_n$
$\#X$	the number of elements in set X
$A, B, C, \ldots$	sets
$\mathbf{N}$	the set of natural numbers ($\{0,1,2,\ldots\}$)
$\mathbf{Z}$	the set of integer numbers ($\{\ldots,-2,-1,0,1,2,\ldots\}$)
$x \in X$	set membership
$\{x \in T \mid P(x)\}$	set comprehension (the set of all x in T such that $P(x)$ holds)
$\mathbf{P}A$	the powerset of A ($\{X \mid X \subseteq A\}$)
$x..y$	the set $\{k \in \mathbf{Z} \mid x \leq k \leq y\}$, where $x, y \in \mathbf{Z}$
$X \subseteq Y$	set inclusion ($\forall x \in X \bullet x \in Y$)
$X \setminus Y$	set difference ($\{x \in X \mid x \notin Y\}$)
$X \cup Y$	set union ($\{x \mid x \in X \vee x \in Y\}$)
$X \cap Y$	set intersection ($\{x \in X \mid x \in Y\}$)
$X \times Y$	the Cartesian product of sets X and Y ($\{(x,y) \mid x \in X \wedge y \in Y\}$)

Logic

$\neg x$	negation (not x)
$x \vee y$	disjunction (x or y)
$x \wedge y$	conjunction (x and y)

$x \Rightarrow y$	implication (if x, then y)
$\forall x \in X \bullet pred$	universal quantification ($pred$ holds for all $x \in X$)
$\exists x \in X \bullet pred$	existential quantification ($pred$ holds for at least one $x \in X$)

Linear Algebra

$\mathsf{A}, \mathsf{B}, \mathsf{C}, \ldots$	matrices
$\mathsf{A} = [\mathbf{a}_1, \mathbf{a}_2, \ldots, \mathbf{a}_n]$	matrix A has columns $\mathbf{a}_1, \mathbf{a}_2, \ldots, \mathbf{a}_n$
$\mathsf{A} = [a_{i,j}]$	matrix A has elements $a_{i,j}$
A^{T}	the transpose of matrix A
$\det \mathsf{A}$	the determinant of matrix A
$\operatorname{rank} \mathsf{A}$	the rank of matrix A
I_n	the $n \times n$ identity matrix
$\mathbf{u}, \mathbf{v}, \mathbf{x}, \ldots$	vectors
$\mathbf{x} = [x_1, x_2, \ldots, x_n]^{\mathrm{T}}$	the n-dimensional vector $\mathbf{x}$ has elements $x_1, x_2, \ldots, x_n$
$(x_1, x_2, \ldots, x_n)$	the point of coordinates $x_1, x_2, \ldots, x_n$ in an n-dimensional space
$\operatorname{diag}(x_1, x_2, \ldots, x_n)$	the matrix $\mathsf{I}_n[x_1, x_2, \ldots, x_K]^{\mathrm{T}}$
$\operatorname{span}\{\mathbf{v}^1, \mathbf{v}^2, \ldots, \mathbf{v}^n\}$	the vector space spanned by the vectors $\mathbf{v}^1, \mathbf{v}^2, \ldots, \mathbf{v}^n$
$\mathbf{N}^x$	the vector space of x-dimensional vectors with natural elements

Asymptotic Notation

$O(f(n))$	$\{g(n) \mid \exists (c > 0, n_0 > 0) \bullet \forall n \geq n_0 \bullet g(n) \leq cf(n)\}$
$o(f(n))$	$\{g(n) \mid \forall c > 0 \bullet \exists n_0 > 0 \bullet \forall n \geq n_0 \bullet g(n) \leq cf(n)\}$
$\Omega(f(n))$	$\{g(n) \mid \exists (c > 0, n_0 > 0) \bullet \forall n \geq n_0 \bullet cf(n) \leq g(n)\}$
$\omega(f(n))$	$\{g(n) \mid \forall c > 0 \bullet \exists n_0 > 0 \bullet \forall n \geq n_0 \bullet cf(n) \leq g(n)\}$
$\theta(f(n))$	$\{g(n) \mid \exists (c_1 > 0, c_2 > 0, n_0 > 0) \bullet \forall n \geq n_0 \bullet c_1 f(n) \leq g(n) \leq c_2 f(n)\}$

Automatic Parallelisation and the BSP Model

$a, b, c, \ldots$	arrays
$\mathbf{d}, \mathbf{d}^1, \mathbf{d}^2, \mathbf{d}^3, \ldots$	distance vectors
$\operatorname{footprint}(a)$	the footprint of array a
g	the BSP communication parameter
$\mathcal{G}$	dependence graph
$i, i_1, i_2, i_3, \ldots$	loop indices
$\mathbf{i}$	the index vector of a perfect loop nest ($\mathbf{i} = [i_1, i_2, \ldots, i_K]^{\mathrm{T}}$) or an iteration point of a perfect loop nest ($\mathbf{i} = (i_1, i_2, \ldots, i_K)$)
I	the iteration space of a perfect loop nest
K	the number of loops in a perfect loop nest
$l, l_1, l_2, l_3, \ldots$	loops in a computer program
L	the BSP synchronisation parameter
$\mathcal{L}$	loop nest

p	the number of processor/memory units of a BSP computer
$S, S_1, S_2, S_3, \ldots$	statements in a computer program
$S_1 \delta S_2$	flow data dependence between statements S_1 and S_2
$S_1 \bar{\delta} S_2$	data antidependence between statements S_1 and S_2
$S_1 \delta^o S_2$	output data dependence between statements S_1 and S_2
$S_1 \delta^* S_2$	generic data dependence between statements S_1 and S_2
$\mathbf{v}, \mathbf{v}^1, \mathbf{v}^2, \mathbf{v}^3, \ldots$	direction vectors

List of Figures

1. Introduction

'Where shall I begin, please your Majesty' he asked.
'Begin at the beginning,' the King said, gravely, 'and go on till you come to the end: then stop.'

Lewis Carroll – *Alice's Adventures in Wonderland*

1.1 Motivation

We are living in an age when developments in sequential computing, while rapidly approaching the ultimate limits of physical performance, are constantly surpassed by unprecedented demands for more computing power. Under these circumstances, many computer applications of practical importance rely entirely on the use of parallel computers, and will probably continue to do so.

Despite this powerful incentive, parallel computing has striven unsuccessfully to become a dependable and affordable commodity for more than two decades. The main causes of failure are the lack of a unitary approach to parallel architecture and application design, and the prohibitive costs of parallel software development.

In an attempt to address the lack of unity in parallel hardware and software design, a number of realistic models of parallel computation have been proposed over recent years. These models encompass many of the features that made the von Neumann paradigm so successful in the realm of sequential computing, and include the bulk-synchronous parallel (BSP) model of Valiant [1], the LogP model of Culler et al. [2], and the weakly coherent PRAM (WPRAM) model of Nash et al. [3].

The parallel software development costs have also received close scrutiny, leading to an ever increasing interest in the automatic parallelisation of existing sequential code. As a result, the past twenty years or so have witnessed remarkable advances in areas such as data dependence analysis [4–12], code transformation [13–19], and potential parallelism identification [20–27]. Based on these theoretical advances, many architecture-specific parallelising compilers and tools have been devised within the last decade [28–33].

While each of the above research areas tackles one of the two problems faced by parallel computing, this book builds on recent developments in these areas to provide a global solution to both problems. In order to achieve this global solution, we address the architecture-independent parallelisation of imperative sequential code in the BSP model of computation.

We have chosen the BSP model as the target platform for our automatic parallelisation techniques for two reasons. Firstly, due to its generality, simplicity and elegance, this model represents one of the most powerful theoretical frameworks for the design of both portable parallel algorithms and scalable parallel architectures [34, 35]. Secondly, the recent release of the BSP programming library BSPlib [36], and of a BSP application development toolset [37, 38] has turned BSP into a remarkably effective approach to parallel software development. As a result of this choice, the parallelisation methods proposed in this book generate real parallel code which is scalable, portable and whose performance is predictable analytically.

A few other frameworks are currently used to design portable parallel applications. The most noteworthy are the Parallel Virtual Machine (PVM) system [39], and the Message Passing Interface (MPI) standard [40]. Unlike BSP, neither of these parallel programming paradigms is based on a simple, compositional cost model. Hence, the only way of evaluating the performance of an application developed within these frameworks is through experiment. Furthermore, due to the intricacy of their underlying programming models, the practical implementations of the two systems mentioned are significantly more complicated to use than BSPlib. Consequently, parallel programs built on these platforms are more difficult to develop, debug and maintain than BSP applications. Finally, the BSP programming discipline yields more efficient implementations on many parallel systems than the other approaches [41].

Since imperative programs spend most of their computation time performing loop calculations, we concentrate on the automatic parallelisation of loop constructs. Nevertheless, many of the results in the book can be readily extended to entire sequential procedures regarded as sequences of loop nests and simple statements, and, given appropriate inter-procedural analysis techniques, to whole sequential programs.

1.2 Parallelisation Approach Proposed in the Book

The loop nest parallelisation techniques developed to date fall into two broad classes. The first class includes techniques that address the parallelisation of a specific computation pattern (e.g. the parallelisation of uniform-dependence perfect loop nests [18, 23, 26, 42–44]), and are referred to in this book as *template-matching scheduling*. After a step in which they analyse the data dependences of the sequential loop nest, these techniques build its parallel version starting from a predefined, highly optimised schedule. They therefore offer the advantage of generating efficient parallel code inexpensively. However, when faced with the parallelisation of a nested loop whose structure does not resemble the computation pattern they address, template-matching scheduling techniques are unable to deliver any parallel schedule whatsoever.

The second class of techniques deals with the *automatic parallelisation of generic loop nests* [28–30, 45–47]. Consequently, the techniques belonging to this class provide a means of parallelising any nested loop structure. Nevertheless, generic loop nest scheduling has its own disadvantages. Firstly, it typically comprises several distinct steps beyond the data dependence analysis (e.g. data and computation partitioning, and communication and synchronisation generation), and is therefore very intricate and computationally intensive. Secondly, generic parallelisation techniques are inclined to yield sub-optimal schedules even when dealing with very simple nested loops.

In this book, we address both types of scheduling, and propose an entirely new approach to automatic parallelisation. This novel approach takes advantage of the benefits of both classes of parallelisation techniques, by employing a hybrid, two-phase strategy for the parallelisation of nested loops. In the first phase of this strategy, the application of template-matching scheduling is attempted. If this attempt is successful, the parallelisation is completed, and an efficient schedule of the nested loop is obtained with low cost. Otherwise, generic loop nest scheduling is employed in the second phase of the strategy to generate a parallel version of the original loop nest.

Based on a communication cost analysis framework introduced in the book, we provide an extensive collection of techniques for the template-matching scheduling of nested loops. Some of these techniques are BSP extensions of existing parallelisation methods, while others are completely new. For each parallelisation technique, we give a detailed analysis of the schedules it produces, clearly indicating in which circumstances it can be used to generate efficient parallel code.

We also devise a new scheme for the BSP parallelisation of generic, untightly nested loops. The scheme comprises four steps—data dependence analysis, potential parallelism identification, data and computation partitioning, and communication and synchronisation generation—and the book presents new algorithms for each of the last three steps.

The novel parallelisation strategy introduced in the book is implemented within a new research tool for the computer-assisted scheduling of nested loops. This scheduling tool accepts as input a generic nested loop described in some simple pseudocode, and produces its parallel version. For the sake of readability, the parallel schedule is initially described in pseudocode, but the tool is able to convert it into real parallel code, ready to be incorporated into an architecture-independent parallel application.

1.3 Organisation of the Book

The remainder of the book is organised as follows. Chapter 2 offers an overview of the bulk-synchronous parallel model of computation. It includes details on the BSP programming and cost model, as well as a presentation of the pseudocode used to describe the various algorithms and examples of BSP schedules in the book. In Chapter 3, we briefly survey data dependence analysis and code transformation results related to our work. These two chapters provide background information, introducing concepts and notations used throughout the rest of the book.

In Chapter 4, we develop a thorough theoretical framework for the analysis of the communication overheads associated with the architecture-independent parallelisation of nested loops. Next, in Chapter 5, we devise a collection of template-matching scheduling techniques for the BSP model. Given the importance of perfect loop nests with uniform data dependences, we begin the chapter with a set of techniques that addresses their automatic parallelisation. We then study the template-matching scheduling of several computation patterns that appear frequently in imperative programs and comprise non-uniform dependences (e.g. reductions and recurrences).

Our scheme for the BSP parallelisation of generic loop nests is presented in Chapter 6. Each of its four steps is described in detail, and new algorithms are devised for the last three steps. In addition, we provide a straightforward algorithm for the performance analysis of the schedules generated by the parallelisation scheme.

Based on the scheduling methods described in Chapters 5 and 6, Chapter 7 introduces our new loop parallelisation strategy, and presents the implementation of a research tool that employs this strategy. The effectiveness of architecture-independent parallelisation is then assessed in Chapter 8, where we study the application of our scheduling approach to a set of scientific computing problems. Finally, in Chapter 9 we conclude the book with a summary of contributions and a discussion of future research directions.

2. The Bulk-Synchronous Parallel Model

When we mean to build,
We first survey the plot, then draw the model;
And when we see the figure of the house,
Then must we rate the cost of the erection.

William Shakespeare – *King Henry IV. Part II*

2.1 Introduction

The bulk-synchronous parallel (BSP) model of computation was introduced by Valiant [1] in the early 1990s, and further developed over the ensuing years [34, 35, 41, 48–50]. Its primary purpose is to act as a "bridging model" [1] mitigating the discrepancies between parallel architectures and the software executed on them. In other words, BSP is intended to be a universal model of parallel computing, capable of providing a reliable underlying framework for the design of both scalable parallel architectures and portable parallel applications [34].

While BSP started largely as a realistic theoretical model for devising and analysing parallel algorithms, recent developments have turned it into a model that is also capable of supporting the implementation of real, architecture-independent parallel software. Indeed, the novel emergence of a BSP programming library standard [36] permits the development of real parallel code which is scalable, portable, and whose performance is predictable analytically. Furthermore, the newly released BSP application development toolset [37, 38] is capable of assisting and guiding the parallel software designer in the profiling and tuning of this parallel code for best performance.

2.2 Bulk-Synchronous Parallel Computers

A bulk-synchronous parallel computer is defined [1] as a system comprising three elements: a set of processor/memory units, a communication network permitting point-to-point message delivery between pairs of units, and a mechanism for the efficient barrier synchronisation of the processors. No special broadcasting or combining facilities are assumed. The only requirement is that the communication network provides uniformly efficient non-local memory access, and this requirement can typically be satisfied by using two-phase randomised routing [51]. This definition is general enough to describe all existing and future types of parallel computers, a feature that parallels the most important characteristic of the von Neumann sequential computing model. At the same time, the definition clearly specifies the basic building blocks that, in one form or another, must be included into any feasible parallel computer [35].

A bulk-synchronous parallel computer is fully characterised by four parameters:

- s, the processor speed;
- p, the number of processor/memory units;
- L, the synchronisation parameter;
- g, the communication parameter.

The parameter s gives the speed of the processors in floating point operations (or *flops*) per second. The parameter L was originally defined as the *synchronisation periodicity* or the minimum distance between successive barrier synchronisations [1, 34]. However, due to its role in assessing the cost of a BSP algorithm, L is largely viewed nowadays as the cost of performing a barrier synchronisation of all processors. In order to express this cost in a way which is coherent with the cost of the local computations, the parameter L is normalised with respect to s, i.e. it is measured in flops rather than in real-time units. Typically, the hardware of the parallel computer imposes a lower bound on the value of L, which may or may not be met by the software layer.

The communication parameter g can also be defined in several equivalent ways. Firstly, g can be regarded [34] as the ratio between the total number of local operations performed by all processors in a time unit and the total number of words delivered by the communication network in a time unit. This interpretation of g indicates that any efficient algorithm must perform at least g local operations for each data transfer. Accordingly, g can also be viewed as a measure of the throughput of the communication network.

However, we prefer the definition in [1], which relates g to the cost of realising a so-called h-relation. An h-relation is a communication pattern in which any processor sends and receives at most h items of data (or words); for conformity with the definition of L, we shall assume that the length of a word is that of a floating point scalar. Under these circumstances, the cost of realising an h-relation is $g\max\{h, h_0\}$, where h_0 is a threshold value accommodating the start-up cost of the communication. In other words, if $h \geq h_0$, the implementation of an h-relation costs gh. This feature shows that in order to achieve efficient communication, the size of the exchanged messages must be larger than the threshold h_0. The parameter g is also normalised with respect to s, i.e. it is expressed in flops per floating point word.

As shown in [35], any parallel architecture can be regarded as a BSP machine, and represents a point in the (p, L, g) space of BSP computers. As we shall see in the following sections, it is this abstraction from the hardware details of the computing system which allows the development of parallel software which is scalable, portable and whose performance is predictable analytically.

2.3 The BSP Programming Model

A BSP computation consists of a sequence of *supersteps* (Figure 2.1). The processors proceed asynchronously through each superstep, and barrier synchronise at the

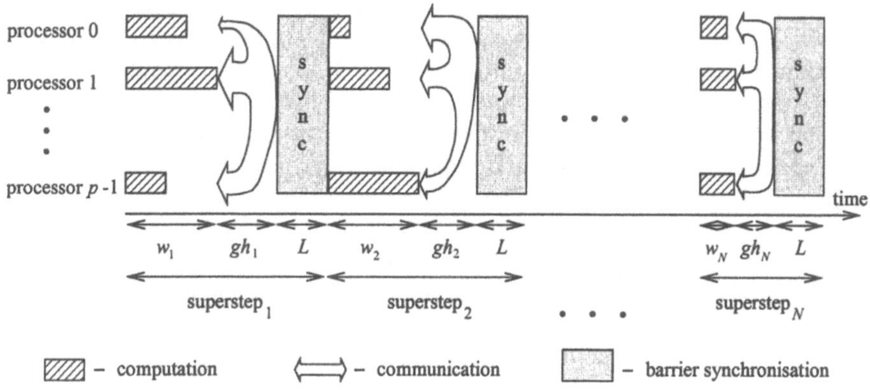

Figure 2.1: A bulk-synchronous parallel computation.

end of the supersteps—hence the name of "bulk-synchronous" parallelism. Within a superstep, the processors may execute operations on locally held data and/or initiate read/write requests for non-local data. However, the non-local memory accesses initiated during a superstep take effect only when all the processors reach the barrier synchronisation which ends that superstep.

The crucial benefit of this programming model is the separation of the three main components of a parallel application, namely computation, communication and synchronisation [1, 35]. As a result, the cost of each of the three components can be assessed independently and analytically.

2.4 The BSP Cost Model

The BSP cost model is compositional: the cost of a BSP program is simply the sum of the costs of its constituent supersteps. Several equivalent expressions have been proposed for the cost of a single superstep. Thus, in [52], the authors adopt the expression

$$cost(i) = \max\{L, w_i, gh_i\}$$

for the cost of superstep i, $1 \leq i \leq N$, of a N-superstep BSP program, where w_i denotes the maximum number of local operations executed by any processor in superstep i, and h_i is the maximum number of words sent or received by any processor in superstep i. This formulation of the BSP cost accounts for a desired overlapping of computation and communication, and considers one of the synchronisation mechanisms proposed in [1], namely that in which the system checks the termination of a superstep every L time units.

A more conservative alternative is to charge a cost of

$$\max\{L, w_i + gh_i\}$$

for the execution of superstep i of a BSP computation [48]. This cost is consistent with the fact that real parallel computers are often unable to fully overlap computation and communication. Indeed, as pointed out in [53], on many computers the most costly communication operation is the transfer of data from the operating system to the application buffers, and this operation typically requires processor participation.

Since a specialised mechanism for processor synchronisation is seldom available on the existing parallel computers, barrier synchronisations are usually implemented through inter-processor communication. As a result, it is often the case that the situation in Figure 2.1 arises, i.e. that the cost of synchronisation must be charged in addition to the computation and communication costs. Accordingly, the cost of superstep i, $1 \leq i \leq N$, is given by

$$cost(i) = L + w_i + gh_i, \tag{2.1}$$

with L representing a measure of the latency of the communication network. It is this expression of the cost of a superstep that we shall use throughout the book. Nevertheless, all the expressions of the BSP cost presented in this section are equivalent within a small multiplicative constant. Therefore, the consistent use of any of them in analysing the efficiency and relative merits of the parallel schedules derived in the book would lead to similar results.

So far we considered that irrespective of the value of h_i—the maximum number of words sent or received by any processor during superstep i—the contribution of communication to the cost of superstep i is gh_i. This is apparently against the requirement that h must be greater than or equal to a threshold value h_0 for the cost of an h-relation to be gh. The explanation is that the parameter L is large enough to cover for the start-up cost of an h-relation (i.e. $L \geq gh_0$). Therefore, it is always safe to consider that the realisation of an h-relation within a superstep brings a contribution of gh to the cost of that superstep.

2.5 Assessing the Efficiency of BSP Code

The standard way of assessing the efficiency of parallel algorithms is to compare them with the best (known) sequential algorithm that solves the same problem. This strategy also applies to BSP algorithms. Assume, for instance, that the sequential cost of solving a given problem of size n is $T(n)$, and the cost of an N-superstep BSP algorithm solving the problem is

$$NL + \sum_{i=1}^{N} w_i + g\sum_{i=1}^{N} h_i = N(n,p)L + W(n,p) + gH(n,p). \tag{2.2}$$

Several ways of evaluating the efficiency of BSP code have been proposed so far. Valiant [1] considers that a BSP algorithm achieves optimality if its overall cost has order O(T(n)/p), and gives the constraints under which the algorithms he describes in [1] are optimal. In [35], a BSP algorithm is considered to be efficient if $W(n,p) = T(n)/p$, and $N(n,p)$ and $H(n,p)$ are as small as possible. Also, in [48], two performance metrics, $\pi = pW(n,p)/T(n)$ and $\mu = gH(n,p)/(T(n)/p)$ are defined, and a BSP algorithm is regarded as optimal if $\pi = 1 + o(1)$ and μ is small (e.g. $\mu \leq 1$).

We shall examine the effectiveness of the BSP schedules generated by the parallelisation techniques introduced in this book in a similar way. Thus, we shall say that a BSP schedule is k-optimal in computation, $k \geq 1$, if

$$pW(n,p)/T(n) = k + o(1). \tag{2.3}$$

Similar to [1], a schedule will be deemed optimal if in addition to being k-optimal in computation, its communication and synchronisation overheads do not exceed the computation time; the values of L and g for which optimality is achieved will be specified.

Additionally, we introduce a new performance metric denoted n_ε, and we shall endeavour to compute its value, or a non-trivial upper bound for it, whenever the expression of the schedule cost is simple enough. For any $\varepsilon > 0$, n_ε is defined as the smallest integer value such that for all $n \geq n_\varepsilon$

$$W(n,p) \geq \frac{N(n,p)L + gH(n,p)}{\varepsilon}.$$

In other words, for problem sizes larger than or equal to n_ε, the schedule cost is upper bounded by $(1+\varepsilon)W(n,p)$, and the practical implementation of a schedule which is k-optimal in computation is expected to attain at least $(1+\varepsilon)^{-1}p/k$ speedup.

2.6 The Development of BSP Applications

Two approaches to BSP application development have been envisaged in [1]. The first approach, called *automatic mode programming*, consists of writing the program in a PRAM style (i.e. without explicitly addressing the memory and communication management issues) and simulating the resulting code on the target BSP computer. Techniques for the optimally efficient BSP simulation of PRAMs have been devised for this purpose [1, 51]. The second approach, called *direct mode programming*, allows the programmer to retain control of the memory and communication management. As emphasised in [1], this approach "avoids the overheads of automatic memory management and may exploit the relative advantage in throughput of computation over communication that may exist".

Despite the solid theoretical results underlying PRAM simulation, practical BSP implementations of PRAM simulation are still in their infancy [54]. Direct BSP algorithms and applications, on the other hand, have been extremely successful from the early days of the BSP model [1, 34, 51, 52, 55, 56]. Initially due to the simplicity of designing and analysing direct BSP algorithms, this success has been boosted by the emergence of powerful environments for the development of BSP software. These environments include the Oxford BSP Library [57] and the Green BSP Library [58], culminating with the recent implementation of the standard BSP programming library

BSPlib [36]. All these libraries comprise a small number of functions that can be called from C, Fortran and other imperative languages with a similar memory model.

Although this book addresses the automatic BSP parallelisation of sequential computer code, all the parallelisation methods we develop are targeted at the direct mode programming. Indeed, our parallelisation techniques aim at automatically generating BSP schedules that are entirely similar to the direct BSP code produced by a human programmer, and should not be confused with the automatic mode programming.

2.7 BSP Pseudocode

The scheduling algorithms devised in this book, as well as the sequential code they parallelise and the resulting BSP schedules, are described in pseudocode. This section presents the conventions used in our pseudocode.

Firstly, for the sake of brevity, variables are not explicitly declared. Instead, we assume that loop indices are integers, and other variables and array elements are of floating point type, unless otherwise specified. Secondly, indentation is used to indicate block and procedure limits instead of begin/end or similar constructs. Thirdly, for all functions that appear in an algorithm or block of code, we consider that function parameters are scalars passed as values, function executions have no side effects, and functions return a scalar value. In the few situations when this is not the case, we shall explicitly describe the function characteristics that do not obey these rules. Finally, less important and simple parts of an algorithm or schedule are sometimes described informally rather than being specified in detail.

When pseudocode is used to describe either sequential or parallel computer code, vectors and matrices are represented as arrays of appropriate dimensionality. Thus, a matrix element $a_{i,j}$ is represented in pseudocode as $a[i,j]$ and, in general, $x^{i_1,i_2,\ldots,i_n}_{j_1,j_2,\ldots,j_m}$ is represented as $x[i_1,i_2,\ldots,i_n,j_1,j_2,\ldots,j_m]$. The mathematical notation, however, is maintained in the description of the various algorithms introduced in the book.

The pseudocode uses three broad classes of statements: assignments, conditional statements, and repetitive statements. All three types of statement have the same interpretation as in a typical imperative programming language, such as C or Fortran. The generic form of an assignment statement is

variable = *expression*

where *expression* is an expression whose type coincides with that of the variable on the left-hand side of the assignment. A conditional statement has the generic form:

if *condition* **then**
  statement-list
else
  statement-list

where *condition* is a boolean expression, and the else part is optional. Three types of repetitive statements are used. The first two,

for *index=lower_bound,upper_bound,step* **do**
statement-list

and

while *condition* **do**
statement-list

describe sequential for and while loops, respectively; the *step* parameter of a for loop is not specified when equal to 1. The third type of repetitive statement is used to describe parallel for loops, i.e. loops whose iterations can be executed concurrently, without any synchronisation or communication:

forall *index=lower_bound,upper_bound* **do in parallel**
statement-list

As the BSP schedules considered in this book are single-program multiple-data (SPMD) applications, we shall present them by providing the code assigned to a generic processor. This will be the processor with identifier *me*, $0 \leq me < p$ or, when the processors are organised into a logical $p_1 \times p_2 \times \cdots \times p_m$ array with $m > 1$ and $\prod_{i=1}^{m} p_i = p$, the processor with coordinates $(me_1, me_2, \ldots, me_m)$ in this array, where $0 \leq me_i < p_i$ for all $1 \leq i \leq m$.

For increased readability, all parallel schedule descriptions consider that the data space on each processor coincides with that of the associated sequential code. Accordingly, any array element is accessed using the same subscripts as in the sequential version of the schedule. Nevertheless, we always assume that, in the practical implementation of a schedule, storage is allocated only for the smallest rectangular array blocks comprising all locally used array elements. The array subscript adjustments that need to be performed when translating BSP pseudocode into real parallel code are discussed in Section 7.4.6.

In addition to the types of statement mentioned so far, the pseudocode of a parallel schedule comprises BSP primitive calls. The ends of supersteps are marked by **bsp_sync** calls, while the BSP communication primitives **bsp_get** and **bsp_put** are used for remote memory reads and remote memory writes, respectively. The generic form of the two communication routines is

bsp_get *variable* **from processor** *pid-source*

and

bsp_put *variable* **on processor** *pid-destination*

where *variable* denotes a scalar or an array block, and *pid-source* and *pid-destination* are expressions that evaluate to a valid processor identifier (or processor coordinate when the processors are organised into a logical array).

The first routine copies the contents of the location(s) addressed by *variable* from the memory of processor *pid-source* into the local memory (i.e. into the memory of the processor that issued the primitive call); conversely for the execution of the second routine. In accordance with the similar functions from the standard BSP library BSPlib [36], the data transfers take place after the completion of all local computations in the current superstep, and before the end of the barrier synchronisation that ends this superstep.

3. Data Dependence Analysis and Code Transformation

No bird soars too high, if he soars with his own wings.

William Blake – *The Marriage of Heaven and Hell*

3.1 Introduction

This chapter provides the theoretical background for the parallelisation methods devised in the book, introducing concepts and notations employed by these methods. In automatic parallelisation, different statements from a sequential program or block of code are scheduled for concurrent execution on the processors of a parallel computer. As two statements can be executed in parallel only if they are independent, we first address the important issue of data dependence. Then, we provide a brief overview of the vast and rapidly growing area of code transformation techniques, paying special attention to those techniques which are used in different stages of our work.

In addressing the two topics, we employ the following terminology. Two loops that surround the same block of statements are called *perfectly* (or *tightly*) *nested*. In a similar way, an entire loop nest is termed a *tightly nested loop* or a *perfect loop nest* if its constituent loops surround the same block of simple (i.e. non-repetitive) statements.

3.2 Data Dependence

The theory of data dependence emerged in the 1970s, with the pioneering work of Muraoka [59], Banerjee [4], Towle [5], Kuck [60, 61] and a few others. Following extensive research over the last twenty years, and the appearance of comprehensive texts on the subject [8, 12], the data dependence theory is now approaching its maturity.

Due to the broad extent of the topic, this section mentions only results which are directly related to the material in the book. These results were originally introduced by Muraoka [59], Banerjee [4], Kuck [61] and Wolfe [6], being further refined and extended in [7, 8, 12, 28, 29].

$$\begin{array}{ll} & \textbf{for } i_1 = 1, n_1 - 1 \textbf{ do} \\ & \quad \textbf{for } i_2 = 0, n_2 - 2 \textbf{ do} \\ S_1: & \quad\quad a[i_1, i_2] = \ldots \\ S_2: & \quad\quad \cdots = f(a[i_1 - 1, i_2 + 1]) \end{array}$$

(a) flow dependence: the value of $a[x_1,x_2]$ modified by the instance of S_1 for $(i_1,i_2) = (x_1,x_2)$ is later used by the instance of S_2 for $(i_1,i_2) = (x_1+1,x_2-1)$; this is a loop-carried data dependence.

$$\begin{array}{ll} & \textbf{for } i = 0, n-2 \textbf{ do} \\ S_1: & \quad a[i] = f(a[i+1]) \end{array}$$

(b) antidependence: the value of $a[x+1]$ read by the instance of S_1 for $i = x$ is later written by the instance of S_1 for $i = x+1$; this loop-carried data dependence occurs between two instances of the same statement.

$$\begin{array}{ll} & \textbf{for } i_1 = 0, n_1 - 1 \textbf{ do} \\ & \quad \textbf{for } i_2 = 1, n_2 - 1 \textbf{ do} \\ S_1: & \quad\quad a[i_1, i_2] = \ldots \\ S_2: & \quad\quad a[i_1, i_2] = \ldots \end{array}$$

(c) output dependence: the variable $a[x_1,x_2]$ is first written by the instance of S_1 for $(i_1,i_2) = (x_1,x_2)$, then by the instance of S_2 for the same iteration point; this is a loop-independent data dependence.

Figure 3.1: Types of data dependence.

3.2.1 Definition

Given two statements S_1 and S_2 executed in this order, statement S_2 is *data dependent* on statement S_1 if both S_1 and S_2 use the same variable, and at least one of them modifies the value of this variable. There are three types of data dependence:

- *flow dependence* or *true dependence* (denoted $S_1 \delta S_2$), when statement S_1 modifies the value of the commonly referenced variable, and then S_2 uses this value;
- *antidependence* (denoted $S_1 \bar{\delta} S_2$), when statement S_1 reads the value of a variable later modified by statement S_2;
- *output dependence* (denoted $S_1 \delta^o S_2$), when both statements (first S_1, and then S_2) modify the variable.

A generic data dependence between the two statements is denoted $S_1 \delta^* S_2$.

When a statement is part of a loop body, data dependences are analysed in terms of *statement instances* (Figure 3.1). A statement instance represents the execution of a statement for a fixed value of the surrounding loop indices (i.e. for a fixed *iteration point*). Depending on whether the statement instances involved in a dependence occur in the same iteration of the surrounding loops or not, data dependences are further classified into *loop-independent* dependences and *loop-carried* dependences, respectively. Since distinct instances of a statement may use the same variable, the statements involved in a loop-carried data dependence do not need to be different.

3.2.2 Data Dependence Representation

As the straightforward enumeration of all pairs of statement instances involved in a particular data dependence would be extremely tedious, various representations are employed to describe them in a compact way. In this book, we use the *distance vector* [59] and the *direction vector* [21] representations of data dependences.

Consider a data dependence $S_1\delta^* S_2$ between two statements surrounded by $K \geq 1$ common loops indexed by $i_1, i_2, \ldots, i_K$. Also, assume that two of the statement instances generating the dependence are the instance of S_1 corresponding to $(i_1,i_2,\ldots,i_K)=(x_1,x_2,\ldots,x_K)$ and the instance of S_2 corresponding to $(i_1,i_2,\ldots,i_K) = (y_1,y_2,\ldots,y_K)$. The distance vector associated with this pair of interdependent statement instances is $\mathbf{d} = [d_1,d_2,\ldots,d_K]^{\mathrm{T}}$, where $d_k = y_k - x_k$ for all $1 \leq k \leq K$.

When the dependence has the property that an instance of S_2 is data dependent on an instance of S_1 if and only if the associated distance vector is a fixed vector $\mathbf{d} = [d_1,d_2,\ldots,d_K]^{\mathrm{T}}$, this distance vector can be used to fully characterise the entire data dependence, which is denoted $S_1\delta^*_{[d_1,d_2,\ldots,d_K]^{\mathrm{T}}}S_2$. This is for example the case for the three dependences in Figure 3.1, whose associated distance vectors are $[1,-1]^{\mathrm{T}}$, $[1]$ and $[0,0]^{\mathrm{T}}$, respectively.

Direction vectors are defined in a similar way. With the above notation, the direction vector corresponding to the two instances of statements S_1, S_2 is $\mathbf{v} = [v_1,v_2,\ldots, v_K]^{\mathrm{T}}$, where

$$\forall k \in 1..K \bullet v_k = \begin{cases} `<' & \text{if } x_k < y_k \\ `=' & \text{if } x_k = y_k \\ `>' & \text{if } x_k > y_k \end{cases}$$

Again, the notation $S_1\delta^*_{[v_1,v_2,\ldots,v_K]^{\mathrm{T}}}S_2$ is used to describe the dependence in a condensed way. For instance, the three data dependences in Figure 3.1 are (a)$S_1\delta_{[<,>]^{\mathrm{T}}}S_2$, (b)$S_1\bar{\delta}_{[<]}S_1$ and (c)$S_1\delta^{o}_{[=,=]^{\mathrm{T}}}S_2$.

As direction vectors retain only the relationship between the coordinates of the interdependent iteration points, they convey less information than distance vectors. Nevertheless, direction vectors have the advantage of being able to compactly describe dependences that cannot be encoded by a single distance vector, while preserving enough information for the validation of many code transformations.

In any data dependence $S_1\delta^* S_2$, an instance of S_2 can only depend on a previously executed instance of S_1. As the statement instances are performed in the lexicographical order of the associated loop-index vectors, it follows that the first non-zero component of a distance vector is positive, and the first non-'=' component of a direction vector is '<'. Furthermore, the distance and direction vectors of a loop-independent data dependence have only null and '=' components, respectively.

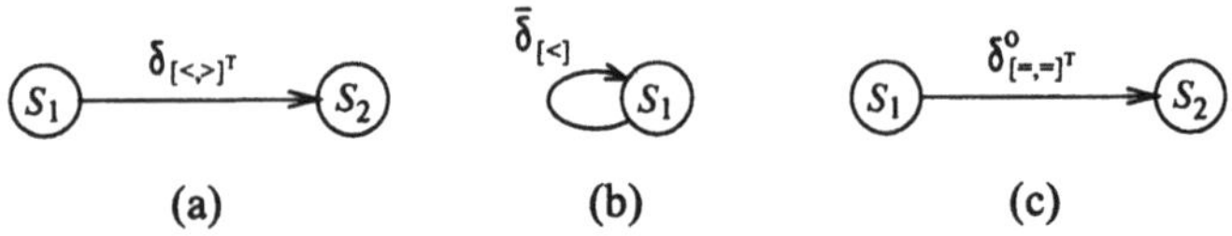

Figure 3.2: The dependence graphs of the loop nests in Figure 3.1.

3.2.3 Dependence Tests

A broad collection of dependence analysis methods has been devised over the last two decades or so. Most of these methods are dependence tests that, given a loop nest, verify if two array references address the same array element across the iteration space of their surrounding loops. Typically, these tests require that the subscripts of the analysed array references are linear combinations of the surrounding loop indices, and compute the direction or distance vector representation of the dependences they identify.

The first developed dependence tests [8, 21, 28] were approximate tests, i.e. tests which attempt to recognise independence, and can succeed only in certain conditions. Whenever such a test is unable to prove independence, dependence is unconditionally assumed. In recent years, exact dependence tests [9, 10] have also been proposed, but due to their complexity they are seldom used in practice.

In this book, we introduce no new dependence tests. Instead, our parallelisation techniques rely on the existing collection of dependence tests for the gathering of the dependence information they use. As for the BSP parallelisation tool devised in Chapter 7, its dependence analysis module implements a subset of the dependence tests in this collection.

3.2.4 Dependence Graphs

In Section 3.2.2, we saw how distance vectors and direction vectors can be used to represent individual data dependences in a compact and convenient way. Dependence graphs [12] serve a similar purpose for an entire loop nest or program: they are used to represent all the data dependences in a block of code.

Given a block of code, its dependence graph $\mathcal{G}$ is a directed graph comprising a vertex for each statement in the block, and an edge between each pair of vertices that stand for interdependent statements. Each edge is labelled with the type and direction vector(s) of the associated data dependence(s). Assuming that $S_1\delta_{[<,>]^T}S_2$, $S_1\bar{\delta}_{[<]}S_1$ and $S_1\delta^o_{[=,=]^T}S_2$ are the only data dependences of the three loop nests in Figure 3.1, the dependence graphs of these loop nests are depicted in Figure 3.2.

3.2.5 Directed Acyclic Graphs

When addressing the parallelisation of perfect loop nests, it is often convenient to represent them as directed acyclic graphs (or *dags*) comprising a vertex for each iteration point, and an edge between each pair of interdependent iteration points. In this representation, a parallel schedule of the loop nest corresponds to the partitioning of the dag into blocks whose execution is assigned to the processors of the parallel machine using some well-defined policy.

Assuming that each block is assigned to a unique processor, any edge which stands for a flow dependence and links vertices belonging to blocks assigned to different processors has to be satisfied through inter-processor communication. In particular, when no such *communication edge* exists, the schedule takes one superstep, and is communication free. Otherwise, the communication overhead of the schedule can be assessed by counting, for each superstep, the maximum number of communication edges leaving or pointing to vertices executed by any single processor.

3.3 Code Transformation Techniques

3.3.1 Generalities

The notion of code transformation appeared with the first sequential compiler tackling the optimisation of the code it generated. Since then, the code transformation paradigm has developed into an extensive theory whose results are relevant to areas ranging from sequential compiler design and systolic arrays to vector and parallel computing.

Of particular importance for automatic parallelisation are the code transformations for high-performance computing, a research topic which has received much attention over the past two decades. Based on the dependence information obtained through data dependence analysis, these transformations aim at exposing and increasing the parallelism available in a block of sequential code or in a sequential program. In the following sections, we briefly describe a set of high-performance computing transformations which are used by the parallelisation techniques developed in the book.

3.3.2 Loop Parallelisation

Loop parallelisation [6, 11] represents the most simple and effective loop transformation: given a sequential loop, it replaces the control of the loop with a parallel loop control. This indicates that all the iterations of the parallelised loop can be executed concurrently, without any synchronisation or communication.

Consider, for instance, the nested loop in Figure 3.3a. According to its dag representation (Figure 3.3b), the only data dependence of this loop is $S_1\delta_{[1,0]^\mathrm{T}}S_1$. As this dependence occurs between instances of S_1 that correspond to the same iteration of the loop indexed by i_2, different iterations of this loop can be executed in parallel. Hence, the inner loop can be parallelised:

for $i_1 = 1, n_1 - 1$ **do**
  forall $i_2 = 0, n_2 - 1$ **do in parallel**
S_1: $a[i_1, i_2] = f(a[i_1 - 1, i_2])$

$$\begin{array}{ll} & \textbf{for } i_1 = 1, n_1 - 1 \textbf{ do} \\ & \quad \textbf{for } i_2 = 0, n_2 - 1 \textbf{ do} \\ S_1: & \quad\quad a[i_1, i_2] = f(a[i_1 - 1, i_2]) \end{array}$$

(a)

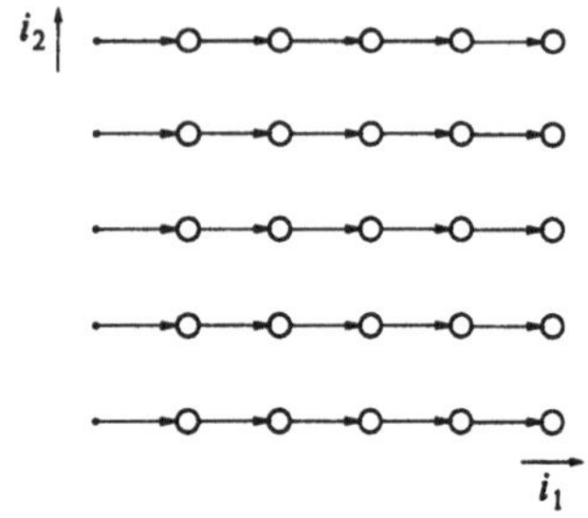

(b)

Figure 3.3: Loop parallelisation: a two-level loop nest comprising a parallel inner loop (a), and its dag representation (b).

In this case, we say that the inner loop does not *carry* the data dependence. Generally, whenever a loop belonging to a loop nest carries no data dependence, the loop can be parallelised. A loop can also be parallelised when it carries a data dependence, if an outer loop which carries the same data dependence is kept sequential [17].

It can be seen immediately that a loop carries a data dependence if and only if it corresponds to a non-null component in the distance vector of the data dependence. Furthermore, when direction vectors are used to represent data dependences, the loops which carry a data dependence correspond to non-'=' elements in the associated direction vector.

3.3.3 Loop Interchange and Loop Permutation

Loop interchange [21, 28] is a code transformation technique which swaps the controls of two perfectly nested loops in a loop nest. We shall use this transformation either to enable the parallelisation of the loop brought into the inner position, or to increase the granularity of the available parallelism by moving a parallelised loop into an outer position.

To illustrate the first case, consider the loop nest in Figure 3.4a. In this example, the data dependence $S_1 \delta_{[2,1]^T} S_1$ is carried by both loops (Figure 3.4b). However, the iterations of the inner loop corresponding to a fixed iteration of the outer loop are independent. Therefore, as long as the outer loop is kept sequential, the inner loop can be parallelised. Nevertheless, the parallelisation of a loop comprising three iterations is of little use in the development of scalable parallel code. Fortunately, loop interchange can be legally applied to bring the loop indexed by i_1 into the inner position, where it can be parallelised:

$$\begin{array}{ll} & \textbf{for } i_2 = 1, 3 \textbf{ do} \\ & \quad \textbf{forall } i_1 = 2, 999 \textbf{ do in parallel} \\ S_1: & \quad\quad a[i_1, i_2] = f(a[i_1 - 2, i_2 - 1]) \end{array}$$

for $i_1 = 2,999$ **do**
  for $i_2 = 1,3$ **do**
S_1: $a[i_1, i_2] = f(a[i_1 - 2, i_2 - 1])$

(a)

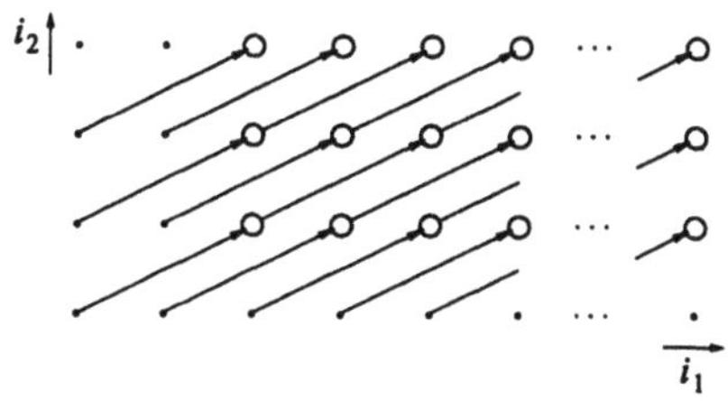

(b)

Figure 3.4: Loop interchange: a tightly nested loop comprising two interchangeable loops (a), and its dag representation (b).

For the second case, consider again the loop nest presented in the previous section. The parallelism revealed by loop parallelisation can be readily mapped on a BSP computer, yielding an $(n_1 - 1)$-superstep schedule. However, the barrier synchronisation of the p processors after each iteration of the outer loop is not necessary. In fact, loop interchange can be employed to swap the two loops, bringing the parallel loop into the outermost position and permitting the derivation of an optimal, one-superstep schedule.

By legally interchanging two loops in a nested loop, the associated components in the distance and direction vectors of any data dependence are also swapped. To understand the conditions under which loop interchange is possible, remember that distance vectors are always lexicographically positive, and the first non-'=' element of any direction vector is always '<'. Therefore, the interchange of two loops is legal only if by swapping the corresponding components in the distance (or direction) vectors of any data dependence in the loop nest the modified distance (or direction) vectors maintain this property. This condition is also sufficient to guarantee the correctness of loop interchange.

Loop permutation [15] is the generalisation of loop interchange, and can be regarded as a sequence of loop interchanges. A legal loop permutation produces an identical permutation of the components of the distance and direction vectors describing the data dependences in the nested loop. Hence, a loop permutation is legal if and only if the identical permutation of the distance (or direction) vectors defining the dependences of the loop nest yields valid distance (or direction) vectors. In particular, when the data dependences of a tightly nested loop are described by a set of distance vectors comprising only non-negative elements, any permutation of its loops is legal. Such a nested loop is called a *fully permutable loop nest* [16].

3.3.4 Loop Distribution

Loop distribution (or loop fission) [20, 28, 60, 61] is a transformation which duplicates a loop control and distributes it over the statements in the loop body. Loop distribution is typically used to break a loop-carried data dependence that prevents the

for $i = 1, n-1$ **do**
S_1: $a[i] = f_1(a[i], b[i-1])$
S_2: $b[i] = f_2(i)$

(a)

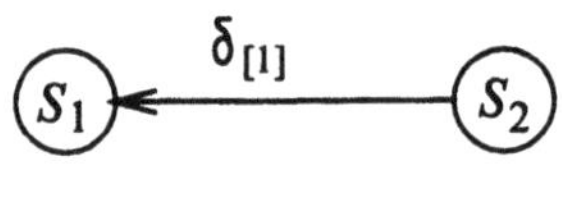

(b)

Figure 3.5: Loop distribution: a loop (a) whose dependence graph (b) comprises no cycles.

parallelisation of some loop. We shall illustrate its application with an example.

Consider the loop in Figure 3.5a. As indicated by its dependence graph in Figure 3.5b, this loop carries the data dependence $S_2\delta_{[1]}S_1$, so it cannot be parallelised in this form. However, since the corresponding edge in the dependence graph of the loop is not part of a cycle, the loop can be distributed over the two statements [28, 61], yielding a sequence of two loops which can be parallelised:

forall $i = 1, n-1$ **do in parallel**
S_2: $b[i] = f_2(i)$
forall $i = 1, n-1$ **do in parallel**
S_1: $a[i] = f_1(a[i], b[i-1])$

3.3.5 Loop Skewing, Wavefront Scheduling, and Iteration Space Tiling

Loop skewing [17, 21, 25, 62, 63] represents one of the most useful loop transformation techniques. This technique works by applying an affine transformation to the iteration space of a perfect loop nest so as to align independent points in it [24].

For the two-level loop nest in Figure 3.6a for instance, the data dependence pattern prevents the parallelisation of either loop. Consider now the affine transformation given by the matrix

$$\mathsf{S} = \begin{bmatrix} 1 & 1 \\ 0 & 1 \end{bmatrix}.$$

If i'_1 and i'_2 denote the loop indices of the transformed iteration space, the old loop indices satisfy

$$\begin{bmatrix} i_1 \\ i_2 \end{bmatrix} = \mathsf{S}^{-1} \begin{bmatrix} i'_1 \\ i'_2 \end{bmatrix} = \begin{bmatrix} 1 & -1 \\ 0 & 1 \end{bmatrix} \begin{bmatrix} i'_1 \\ i'_2 \end{bmatrix} = \begin{bmatrix} i'_1 - i'_2 \\ i'_2 \end{bmatrix}.$$

By replacing each occurrence of i_1 and i_2 in the loop body with $i'_1 - i'_2$ and i'_2, respectively, we obtain the skewed loop nest in Figure 3.6b; the new loop bounds are computed from the original loop bounds by solving the inequalities $1 \le i_1 = i'_1 - i'_2 \le n_1 - 1$ and $1 \le i_2 = i'_2 \le n_2 - 1$.

Furthermore, if D is the matrix whose columns are the distance vectors of the two data dependences (i.e. $[1,0]^{\mathrm{T}}$ and $[0,1]^{\mathrm{T}}$), the distance vectors of the skewed loop nest

```
    for i1 = 1, n1 - 1 do
      for i2 = 1, n2 - 1 do
S1:     a[i1, i2] = f(a[i1 - 1, i2], a[i1, i2 - 1])
```

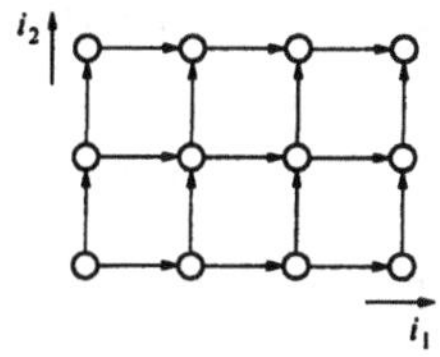

(a) a two-level loop nest and its dag representation; due to the data dependence pattern, neither of the two loops can be parallelised.

```
    for i'1 = 2, n1 + n2 - 2 do
      for i'2 = max{1, i'1 - n1 + 1},
                min{n2 - 1, i'1 - 1} do
S1:     a[i'1 - i'2, i'2] = f(a[i'1 - i'2 - 1, i'2],
                              a[i'1 - i'2, i'2 - 1])
```

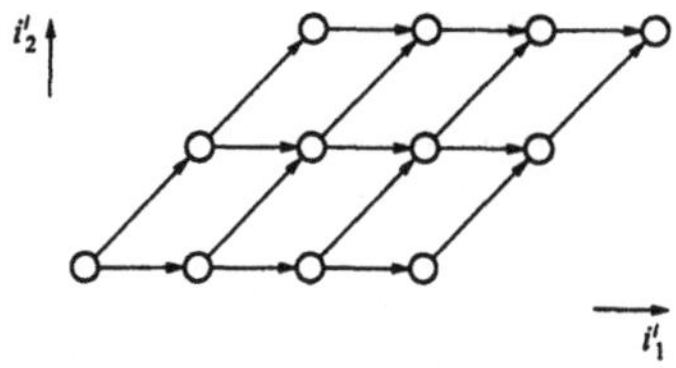

(b) in the skewed version of the loop nest, the iterations of the inner loop can be executed in parallel.

Figure 3.6: Loop skewing.

are the columns of the matrix

$$\mathsf{D}' = \mathsf{SD} = \begin{bmatrix} 1 & 1 \\ 0 & 1 \end{bmatrix} \begin{bmatrix} 1 & 0 \\ 0 & 1 \end{bmatrix} = \begin{bmatrix} 1 & 1 \\ 0 & 1 \end{bmatrix}.$$

As the first row of D' comprises no null elements (i.e. the distance vectors of both dependences have a non-zero first component), all the data dependences are carried by the outer loop and the inner loop can now be parallelised [17, 21] (Figure 3.6b).

This extremely useful parallelisation method is called the *hyperplane method* in the seminal paper of Lamport [62]. This name accounts for the way in which the method parallelises a K-level perfect loop nest. Indeed, the iteration points assigned to the same steps of the resulting schedule are in this case given by the intersections of the original iteration space with a family of $(K-1)$-dimensional parallel and equidistant hyperplanes. Because the computation of the resulting parallel schedule swaps as a wavefront through the iteration space of the loop, the method is also called *wavefront scheduling* [21].

In order to reveal the coarse-grained parallelism required to hide the communication and synchronisation overheads specific to distributed-memory parallel computers, wavefront scheduling is often associated with *iteration space tiling* [22–24, 42, 64, 65]. In iteration space tiling (or *blocking*), the iteration space of the nested loop is partitioned into blocks, and instead of applying the wavefront scheduling technique to individual iteration points, it is applied to such blocks viewed as indivisible entities.

3.3.6 Other Transformations for High-Performance Computing

Many other code transformations for high-performance computing have been proposed. Among them, there are many more loop transformation techniques, including:

- loop fusion—the joining of two loops (i.e. the opposite of loop distribution) [66];
- loop reversal—the execution of a loop in reversed iteration order [67];
- loop coalescing—the reduction of a perfect loop nest to a single loop whose index takes one value for each point in the original iteration space [14, 68];
- loop unrolling—the replication of the loop body and shrinking of the iteration space [69].

Some other transformations are related to the elimination of data dependences by modifying the structure of the underlying data (e.g. *scalar expansion*—the replacement of a scalar involved in a data dependence with an array comprising an element for each iteration point of the surrounding loop nest [21, 25]). Comprehensive surveys of the subject can be found in [13, 17, 21, 25, 70].

4. Communication Overheads in Loop Nest Scheduling

For which of you, intending to build a tower, sitteth not down first, and counteth the cost, whether he have sufficient to finish it?

St. Luke xiv. 28

4.1 Introduction

One of the most important tasks in the analysis of a BSP schedule is the accurate assessment of its communication cost. Indeed, the communication cost will be repeatedly used throughout the book, either to choose the best parallelisation strategy for a given problem or to establish the parameters of a certain scheduling technique.

In this chapter we develop a theoretical framework for the analysis of the communication overheads associated with the architecture-independent parallelisation of nested loops. This framework considers the parallelisation of a generic K-level tightly nested loop $\mathcal{L}$, $K \geq 1$. For ease of exposition, we shall assume that the k-th loop of $\mathcal{L}$, $1 \leq k \leq K$, is indexed by i_k, and iterates from 0 to $n_k - 1$ (Figure 4.1). The K-dimensional iteration space $I = 0..(n_1 - 1) \times 0..(n_2 - 1) \times \cdots \times 0..(n_K - 1)$ is partitioned into tiles spanned by a set of K linearly independent K-dimensional vectors $\mathbf{t}_1$, $\mathbf{t}_2, \ldots, \mathbf{t}_K$ with integer components. The set of iteration points included in a generic tile T is given by

$$\left\{ \mathbf{i} \in I \;\middle|\; \mathbf{i} = \sum_{k=1}^{K} c_k \mathbf{t}_k + \sum_{k=1}^{K} \alpha_k \mathbf{t}_k, 0 \leq \alpha_k < 1 \text{ for all } 1 \leq k \leq K \right\} \tag{4.1}$$

where the integers $c_1, c_2, \ldots, c_K$ represent the coordinates of T in the *tile space*. This partition of the iteration space I is fully characterised by the *tiling matrix*

$$\mathsf{T} = [\mathbf{t}_1, \mathbf{t}_2, \ldots, \mathbf{t}_K], \tag{4.2}$$

i.e. by the matrix whose columns are the K vectors that span its tiles.

In most practical situations, the tiles are rectangular blocks of size $x_1 \times x_2 \times \ldots \times x_K$. When this is the case, each tile T comprises the iteration points satisfying

$$\forall k \in 1..K \bullet c_k x_k \leq i_k \leq (c_k + 1)x_k - 1, \tag{4.3}$$

for $i_1 = 0, n_1 - 1$ **do**
  for $i_2 = 0, n_2 - 1$ **do**
  ...
    for $i_K = 0, n_K - 1$ **do**
      loop_body

Figure 4.1: A K-level perfect loop nest.

where $(c_1, c_2, \ldots, c_K)$, the coordinates of the tile, satisfy $0 \le c_k < \lceil n_k/x_k \rceil$ for all $1 \le k \le K$. Some of the boundary tiles may be incomplete. The tiling matrix of a rectangular partition is a diagonal matrix with the elements $x_1, x_2, \ldots, x_K$ on the main diagonal.

Our communication cost analysis framework assumes that the parallel schedule of the loop nest is built by assigning each tile computation to a superstep of the schedule and to one of the p processors of the target parallel computer.[1] This must be done in a manner which is consistent with the data dependences of the loop nest, with typically more than one tile computation per superstep.

According to this model, the execution of a parallel schedule involves two types of communication cost. Firstly, there is an *input communication* cost corresponding to the preliminary step in which loop-external (or *input*) data are brought into the local memories of the processors. These input data represent data that are used within the loop body, but are either computed outside the loop nest, or provided as input to the program. Secondly, there is an *inter-tile communication* cost related to the communication steps that take place between successive tile computations. These communication steps bring into the local memories data required for the computation of a tile and which are generated during previous tile computations. Hence, they solve the flow data dependences between iteration points computed by different processors. Our communication cost analysis framework comprises new techniques for the assessment of both types of communication overheads.

We shall begin by introducing techniques that assess the communication cost due to input data. Given an array referenced within the loop body of $\mathcal{L}$, these techniques compute the number of array elements used for the computation of a tile of its iteration space I, both for single and for multiple references. The techniques work for array references whose subscripts are affine functions of the surrounding loop indices i_1, i_2, $\ldots$, i_K. The generic form of such a reference to an m-dimensional array, $m \ge 1$, is

$$a[s_1, s_2, \ldots, s_m], \; \mathbf{s} = [s_1, s_2, \ldots, s_m]^{\mathrm{T}} = \mathsf{G}\mathbf{i} + \mathbf{v}, \qquad (4.4)$$

where $\mathsf{G} = [g_{j,k}]$ is an $m \times K$ matrix with integer elements, $\mathbf{i} = [i_1, i_2, \ldots, i_K]^{\mathrm{T}}$ is the loop index vector, and $\mathbf{v} = [v_1, v_2, \ldots, v_m]^{\mathrm{T}}$ is an m-dimensional vector with integer elements. For the sake of brevity, we shall sometimes use the notation $a[\mathsf{G}\mathbf{i} + \mathbf{v}]$ for the generic array reference in (4.4).

Next, in the second part of the chapter, we shall assess the inter-tile communication cost due to uniform flow dependences, i.e. to flow dependences described by distance vectors. Again, this will be done for a tile of the considered iteration space.

[1] While the partial duplication of computation on several processors has sometimes been considered as a means to reduce communication overheads, this represents by far the most common scheduling approach.

4.2 Related Work

Our analysis of input communication costs is based on the concept of *data footprint*. A similar notion, called a *program footprint*, was introduced by Thiebaut and Stone [71] in the context of cache-reload transient analysis. The footprint paradigm was then extended to array references belonging to a loop nest by Agarwal et al. [72, 73], who provided the definition of a data footprint used in this chapter. According to this definition, given a loop nest $\mathcal{L}$, a tile T of its iteration space, and an array a referenced within the body of $\mathcal{L}$, the footprint of a across T represents the set of array elements used during the computation of the iteration points in T.

In their work [72, 73], Agarwal et al. also propose a framework for computing the size of data footprints, and use it to optimise cache coherency traffic on shared-memory parallel computers. This framework assumes that array references have the form in (4.4), and computes the size of a data footprint by case analysis on the matrix G. The authors identify no less than four cases requiring a different approach, namely when G is square and unimodular (i.e. $|\det \mathrm{G}| = 1$), when G is invertible, when the rows of G are dependent and its columns are independent, and when the columns of G are dependent. Their framework is then able to provide solutions to the first three cases. These solutions are exact for single references and close approximations for multiple references.

Our footprint size computation framework extends and significantly simplifies the one proposed by Agarwal et al. To achieve this, we design a simple two-step algorithm for the computation of the footprint size for single references. Following a normalisation of the G matrix in its first step, this algorithm distinguishes only two cases demanding different treatment. In the first case, which corresponds to all situations in which the method in [72, 73] is able to solve the problem, we provide an exact answer at very low cost. In the second case, which corresponds to the situation when the columns of G are dependent and the method of Agarwal et al. offers no solution, we use a set of rules that generates an exact answer or a useful, non-trivial upper bound for most instances of the problem. As for the case of multiple references, we extend the framework in [72, 73] with an algorithm that gives the exact value of the footprint size of a multiply referenced array across a rectangular tile when the matrix G satisfies certain constraints.

The data footprint paradigm is also used by Ding and Stefanescu [43] as a means to compute the communication cost and to find the optimal parallel schedule of a particular class of perfect loop nests in the BSP model of computation. Ding and Stefanescu extend the results in [72, 73] with techniques for the computation of a footprint size for the case when the $m \times K$ matrix G is a non-square unimodular matrix (i.e. the determinant of any $m \times m$ submatrix of G is 0 or ± 1) and $m < K$. Our footprint size computation algorithm uses these valuable techniques, but is more general since it also solves the problem when the above constraints are not satisfied. Moreover, our theoretical framework provides an exact value for the footprint size of an important class of multiple references, whereas the techniques in [43] can only approximate this value.

The analysis of the inter-tile communication overheads associated with uniform flow data dependences has been addressed in the context of loop nest tiling, a subject extensively studied in recent years. Irigoin and Triolet [64], the first to formally introduce the theory of tiling, also emphasise the importance of communication cost analysis in choosing an appropriate tiling. However, they provide no means for the estimation of these costs. Later, Schreiber and Dongarra [23] restate the significance of communication cost assessment in the automatic *blocking* of loop nests, and propose the tile surface area as a crude measure of the communication overheads associated with the computation of a tile. Based on this measure, the authors develop a heuristic which aims at finding legal tiles whose volume to surface area ratio is maximised.

Ramanujam and Sadayappan [24, 74] describe a framework for the derivation of communication-optimal tiles which are generated by a unimodular lower triangular tiling matrix. Although their framework takes into account the individual distance vectors that describe the dependences which need to be satisfied through interprocessor communication, it still uses an approximation of the real communication cost. The same approximation of the communication volume is employed by Boulet et al. [42], who propose a method for generating the tiling that, for a fixed amount of computation, minimises this approximation of the communication cost. More recently, Xue [19] extends the results in [42] with a new strategy for the derivation of communication-minimal tiles for a perfect loop nest. Nevertheless, the optimisation problem solved in [19] is again defined in terms of the approximation of the communication cost originally introduced by Ramanujam and Sadayappan in [24, 74].

In comparison with the above mentioned approaches, our communication cost analysis framework is able to compute the exact volume of communication required for the computation of a rectangular tile of the iteration space. Furthermore, our analysis of the inter-tile communication overheads takes into consideration the fact that tiles along certain directions of the iteration space are mapped on the same processor. This feature—which is unique among the existing techniques for the assessment of communication costs—is then used by many scheduling strategies developed in the book to choose a communication-minimal mapping of tiles to processors.

Finally, Andonov and Rajopadhye [75] devise a technique for the optimal orthogonal tiling of nested loops. While this technique accurately models the execution time of the resulting parallel schedules (and, therefore, the associated communication cost), it is restricted to two-dimensional iteration spaces and to a particular class of parallel architectures (i.e. linear arrays or rings of processors). Unlike this technique, our framework succeeds in modelling the communication cost of the considered parallel schedules for K-dimensional iteration spaces, $K \geq 1$, and for any parallel architecture.

4.3 Communication Overheads Due to Input Data

In this section, we use the loop nest scheduling model described in the introductory section to develop a method for the analysis of input communication overheads. We begin by formally defining the notion of input data.

Definition 4.1 Let $\mathcal{L}$ be a perfect loop nest, and a an array referenced within the loop body of $\mathcal{L}$. If during the execution of $\mathcal{L}$ the value of at least one element from a is read without being previously written, a is said to be an *input array* of $\mathcal{L}$. Furthermore, if no element of a is written as a result of executing $\mathcal{L}$, a is called a *pure-input array*; otherwise, a is an *input/output array*.

The computation of a generic tile T of the iteration space of $\mathcal{L}$ involves input communication overheads due to both types of input array. As the associated interprocessor communication takes place in a preliminary superstep of the parallel schedule, we are interested in the magnitude of the h-relation implemented in this superstep. The maximum amount of data sent by any processor in this superstep depends on the initial data distribution, and is very difficult to compute. Nevertheless, for the dense computations whose automatic parallelisation is addressed in this book, the initial data are typically distributed uniformly across the processors of the parallel machine. Furthermore, the execution of the parallel schedules we consider always leaves the data uniformly distributed. Hence, the amount of data received by a processor during the preliminary superstep is also a good measure for the amount of data sent by a processor, and we shall use it to quantify the size of the h-relation.

For a pure-input array, the array elements required for the computation of the iteration points in a generic tile T are exactly those in the footprint of the array across the tile. The situation is more complex for an input/output array, since some of the array values used within the loop body are not loop-external, but are obtained while computing a previous tile, or even the current tile. Both cases are thoroughly examined in the following sections.

4.3.1 The Footprint Size of a Pure-Input Array

The Footprint Size of a Single Array Reference

With the notation in the introductory section of this chapter, the footprint of the array reference (4.4) across a tile T is the set

$$\text{footprint}(a) = \{a[\mathsf{Gi}+\mathbf{v}] \mid \mathbf{i} \in T\}.$$

Since the presence of $\mathbf{v}$ merely introduces a shift in the subscript space of a, the size of this footprint depends only on the underlying tiling matrix T and on the matrix G:

$$\#\{a[\mathsf{Gi}+\mathbf{v}] \mid \mathbf{i} \in T\} = F(\mathsf{T},\mathsf{G}). \tag{4.5}$$

In order to compute $F(\mathsf{T},\mathsf{G})$, the footprint size of a single array reference, we use a two-step algorithm. In its first step, the result introduced by the following theorem is employed to *normalise* the G matrix.

Theorem 4.1 *Let* G *be a generic* $m \times K$ *matrix with integer elements, and* G' *the* $m' \times K$ *matrix obtained by retaining a maximum number of linearly independent rows from* G, $m' \leq m$. *Then for any* $K \times K$ *tiling matrix* T, $F(\mathsf{T},\mathsf{G}) = F(\mathsf{T},\mathsf{G}')$.

Proof Assume that the j-th row of G is either zero or a linear combination of the other rows, and let $s_1, s_2, \ldots, s_m$ be the subscripts of the considered array reference.

Then s_j is a constant in the first case, and, up to a constant, a linear combination of the other subscripts in the second. In both situations,

$$s_j = \alpha_0 + \sum_{j' \in 1..m \setminus \{j\}} \alpha_{j'} s_{j'},$$

where $\alpha_{j'}$, $j' \in 0..m \setminus \{j\}$ is a constant. Consider now the $(m-1)$-dimensional array reference defined by

$$a'[s_1, s_2, \ldots, s_{j-1}, s_{j+1}, \ldots, s_m] = a[s_1, s_2, \ldots, s_{j-1}, \alpha_0 + \sum_{j' \in 1..m \setminus \{j\}} \alpha_{j'} s_{j'}, s_{j+1}, \ldots, s_m].$$

The footprint sizes of the two array references are identical for any tile. Hence, by eliminating the j-th row of G, we obtain a reference whose footprint size is equal to $F(\mathsf{T}, \mathsf{G})$. This property can be applied repeatedly to reduce the rows of G to a set of linearly independent rows, and the proof is complete. □

According to Theorem 4.1, the first step of our algorithm reduces the computation of a generic footprint size to the computation of a footprint size $F(\mathsf{T}, \mathsf{G})$ in which the matrix G is composed of m linearly independent rows of K elements. Due to this property of the G matrix, we necessarily have $m \leq K$. The following theorem provides an upper bound for the footprint size in the generic case, and an exact solution for the case when $m = K$. Notice that the latter case corresponds to the situation when the G matrix is non-singular.

Theorem 4.2 *The footprint size of a single array reference satisfies*

$$F(\mathsf{T}, \mathsf{G}) \leq |\det \mathsf{T}|. \tag{4.6}$$

This upper bound is attained when G *is non-singular.*

Proof In the worst case, the footprint comprises a distinct element for each iteration point in T. Since $|\det \mathsf{T}|$, the volume of T, gives the number of iteration points in the tile, it also represents an upper bound for $F(\mathsf{T}, \mathsf{G})$. When G is a non-singular $K \times K$ matrix, the only solution of $\mathsf{G}\mathbf{i} = \mathsf{G}\mathbf{i}'$ is $\mathbf{i} = \mathbf{i}'$, i.e. the mapping from the iteration space to the data space induced by G is an injection. Therefore, the footprint size is given in this case by $|\det \mathsf{T}|$, the number of iteration points in the tile. □

The upper bound introduced in Theorem 4.2 holds irrespective of the fact that the array subscripts are linear combinations of the surrounding loop indices. Therefore, this upper bound can also be used when the array subscripts are not affine functions of the K loop indices and the other results in this section do not apply.

Example 4.1 To illustrate the usage of the theoretical results introduced so far, consider a 3-level perfect loop nest $\mathcal{L}$ (i.e. $K = 3$) whose iteration space is partitioned into rectangular tiles generated by the tiling matrix $\mathsf{T} = \mathsf{I}_3[x_1, x_2, x_3]^{\mathsf{T}}$. Let a be a pure-input array of $\mathcal{L}$, and $a[i_1 + i_2 - i_3, i_3 - 1, 2i_1 + 2i_2 + 1]$ be the only reference to array

a within the loop body of $\mathcal{L}$. This reference can be written as $a[\mathsf{G}\mathbf{i}+\mathbf{v}]$, where

$$\mathsf{G}=\begin{bmatrix} 1 & 1 & -1 \\ 0 & 0 & 1 \\ 2 & 2 & 0 \end{bmatrix}, \quad \mathbf{i}=[i_1,i_2,i_3]^{\mathsf{T}}, \quad \text{and} \quad \mathbf{v}=[0,-1,1]^{\mathsf{T}}.$$

As the rows of G are linearly dependent, it follows from Theorem 4.1 that $F(\mathsf{T},\mathsf{G})$, the footprint size of the array reference across a tile generated by the tiling matrix T satisfies

$$F(\mathsf{T},\mathsf{G})=F(\mathsf{T},\mathsf{G}'),$$

where

$$\mathsf{G}'=\begin{bmatrix} 0 & 0 & 1 \\ 2 & 2 & 0 \end{bmatrix}.$$

As the G matrix is singular, we can only use the first part of Theorem 4.2, obtaining an upper bound for the footprint size:

$$\#\text{footprint}(a[\mathsf{G}\mathbf{i}+\mathbf{v}])=F(\mathsf{T},\mathsf{G}')\leq|\det\mathsf{T}|=x_1x_2x_3.$$

We shall see in the remainder of this section how to better this result and to compute the exact value of $F(\mathsf{T},\mathsf{G}')$.

When the normalised G matrix has more columns than rows (i.e. when $m<K$), the exact computation of the footprint size is not always possible. The following theorem introduces a set of rules for the computation of the footprint size of a single array reference across a rectangular tile or of a good approximation of it in many practical situations when $m<K$.

Theorem 4.3 *Let* $\mathsf{G}=[\mathbf{g}_1,\mathbf{g}_2,\ldots,\mathbf{g}_K]$ *be an* $m\times K$ *matrix with integer elements, and* $\mathbf{x}=[x_1,x_2,\ldots,x_K]^{\mathsf{T}}$ *a K-dimensional vector with positive integer elements. Assume that* $m<K$*, and that the m rows of* G *are linearly independent. Then the following rules hold:*

Rule 1 (Ding and Stefanescu [43]): If G *is unimodular in the sense that the determinant of any* $m\times m$ *submatrix of* G *is* 0 *or* ±1,

$$F(\mathsf{I}_K\mathbf{x},\mathsf{G})=\sum_{\substack{\{k_1,k_2,\ldots,k_m\}\in\mathbf{P}1..K\\ \det[\mathbf{g}_{k_1},\mathbf{g}_{k_2},\ldots,\mathbf{g}_{k_m}]\neq0}} x_{k_1}x_{k_2}\ldots x_{k_m} \tag{4.7}$$

Rule 2: If the k-th column of G, $1\leq k\leq K$, *is zero,*

$$F(\mathsf{I}_K\mathbf{x},\mathsf{G})=F(\mathsf{I}_{K-1}[x_1,x_2,\ldots,x_{k-1},x_{k+1},\ldots,x_K]^{\mathsf{T}},\\ [\mathbf{g}_1,\mathbf{g}_2,\ldots,\mathbf{g}_{k-1},\mathbf{g}_{k+1},\ldots,\mathbf{g}_K]) \tag{4.8}$$

Rule 3: *If $g_{j,k}$, $1 \le j \le m$, $1 \le k \le K$, is the only non-zero element in the j-th row of* G,

$$F(\mathsf{I}_K\mathbf{x},\mathsf{G}) = x_k F(\mathsf{I}_{K-1}[x_1,x_2,\dots,x_{k-1},x_{k+1},\dots,x_K]^{\mathsf{T}}, [\mathbf{g}_1,\mathbf{g}_2,\dots,\mathbf{g}_{k-1},\mathbf{g}_{k+1},\dots,\mathbf{g}_K]) \quad (4.9)$$

Rule 4: *Let $g_{j,1}$, $g_{j,2}$, …, $g_{j,K}$ be the elements of the j-th row of* G, $1 \le j \le m$, *and $\alpha = \gcd(g_{j,1}, g_{j,2}, \dots, g_{j,K})$. Then for any tiling matrix* T, $F(\mathsf{T},\mathsf{G}) = F(\mathsf{T},\mathsf{G}')$, *where* G′ *is the $m \times K$ matrix whose j-th row has the elements $g_{j,1}/\alpha$, $g_{j,2}/\alpha$, …, $g_{j,K}/\alpha$, and whose other rows are copied from* G.

Rule 5: *Let g_{j,k_1}, g_{j,k_2}, …, g_{j,k_r}, $r \ge 1$, $1 \le k_1 < k_2 < \dots < k_r \le K$ be the only non-null elements in the j-th row of* G, $1 \le j \le m$. *Then,*

$$F(\mathsf{I}_K\mathbf{x},\mathsf{G}) \le \left(|g_{j,k_1}|x_{k_1} + |g_{j,k_2}|x_{k_2} + \dots + |g_{j,k_r}|x_{k_r}\right) F(\mathsf{I}_K\mathbf{x},\mathsf{G}'), \quad (4.10)$$

where G′ *is the $(m-1) \times K$ matrix obtained by eliminating the j-th row from* G. *Furthermore, if $|g_{j,k_1}| = |g_{j,k_2}| = \dots = |g_{j,k_r}| = 1$ and for any row $j' \ne j$ $g_{j',k_1} = g_{j',k_2} = \dots = g_{j',k_r} = 0$,*

$$F(\mathsf{I}_K\mathbf{x},\mathsf{G}) = (x_{k_1} + x_{k_2} + \dots + x_{k_r} - r + 1) F(\mathsf{I}_{K-r}\mathbf{x}',\mathsf{G}'), \quad (4.11)$$

where $\mathbf{x}' = [x_1,\dots,x_{k_1}-1,x_{k_1}+1,\dots,x_{k_2}-1,x_{k_2}+1,\dots,x_{k_r}-1,x_{k_r}+1,\dots,x_K]^{\mathsf{T}}$ and G′ *is the $(m-1) \times (K-r)$ matrix obtained by eliminating the columns $\mathbf{g}_{k_1}$, $\mathbf{g}_{k_2}$, …, $\mathbf{g}_{k_r}$ and the j-th row from* G.

The proof of this theorem is provided in Appendix A.

Example 4.2 In order to demonstrate the usage of the rules in Theorem 4.3, we shall consider again the single array reference $a[i_1+i_2-i_3, i_3-1, 2i_1+2i_2+1]$ from Example 4.1. We have already shown that, for any tiling matrix $\mathsf{T} = \mathsf{I}_3[x_1,x_2,x_3]^{\mathsf{T}}$, the footprint size of this array reference is $F(\mathsf{T},\mathsf{G}')$, where

$$\mathsf{G}' = \begin{bmatrix} 0 & 0 & 1 \\ 2 & 2 & 0 \end{bmatrix}.$$

By applying Rule 4 to the second row of G′, we get $F(\mathsf{T},\mathsf{G}') = F(\mathsf{T},\mathsf{G}'')$, where

$$\mathsf{G}'' = \begin{bmatrix} 0 & 0 & 1 \\ 1 & 1 & 0 \end{bmatrix}.$$

We can now employ either Rule 1, or Rule 5 twice to obtain the exact value of the footprint size of array a:

$$\#\text{footprint}(a[i_1+i_2-i_3, i_3-1, 2i_1+2i_2+1]) = (x_1+x_2)x_3.$$

```
FOOTPRINT_SIZE(T, G)
    Step 1. Normalisation of the G matrix
1     Discard zero rows and rows that are linear combinations of other rows from G,
      until the matrix is left with m linearly independent rows of K elements
    Step 2. Computation of the footprint size F(T,G)
2     if m = K then                       /* G is a square, non-singular matrix */
3       return | det T |
4     if T = I_K x then                   /* m < K and T is a diagonal matrix */
5       for j = 1,m do
6         α = gcd(g_j1, g_j2, ..., g_jK)
7         (g_j1, g_j2, ..., g_jK) = (g_j1/α, g_j2/α, ..., g_jK/α)
8       if G is unimodular then
9         return F(I_K x, G) given by eq. (4.7)
10      if the k-th column of G is zero then
11        G' = [g_1, g_2, ..., g_{k-1}, g_{k+1}, ..., g_K]
12        return FOOTPRINT_SIZE(I_{K-1}[x_1, ..., x_2, ..., x_{k-1}, x_{k+1}, ..., x_K]^T, G')
13      if the only non-null element in the j-th row of G is g_{j,k} then
14        G' = [g_1, g_2, ..., g_{k-1}, g_{k+1}, ..., g_K]
15        return x_k FOOTPRINT_SIZE(I_{K-1}[x_1, ..., x_2, ..., x_{k-1}, x_{k+1}, ..., x_K]^T, G')
16      if the only non-zero elements in the j-th row of G are g_{jk_l} ∈ {-1,1}, 1 ≤ l ≤ r
        and for any row j' ≠ j, g_{j'k_l} = 0 for 1 ≤ l ≤ r then
17        x' = [x_1, ..., x_{k_1-1}, x_{k_1+1}, ..., x_{k_2-1}, x_{k_2+1}, ..., x_{k_r-1}, x_{k_r+1}, ..., x_K]^T
18        G' = the matrix obtained by eliminating the columns k_1, k_2, ... k_r and
          the j-th row from G
19        return (x_{k_1} + x_{k_2} + ... + x_{k_r} - r + 1) FOOTPRINT_SIZE(I_{K-r} x', G')
20    return | det T |
```

Figure 4.2: The algorithm for the computation of the footprint size of a single array reference.

The footprint size computation algorithm described so far is shown in Figure 4.2. This algorithm takes two arguments: a tiling matrix T, and the G matrix describing the analysed array reference. Following the normalisation step of the algorithm (line 1), the G matrix is left with a maximum number of linearly independent rows.

The second step of the algorithm performs the actual computation of the footprint size. First, if G is non-singular, the second result of Theorem 4.2 is used to generate the answer (lines 2–3). Otherwise, the algorithm checks whether the tiling matrix T is a diagonal matrix (line 4). If it is, the rules of Theorem 4.3 are applied. Firstly, Rule 4—an "enabling rule"—is used in lines 5–7 to further simplify the G matrix. Next, Rules 1 (lines 8–9), 2 (lines 10–12), 3 (lines 13–15), and 5 (lines 16–19) are employed to compute the footprint size. For the application of the last three rules, function FOOTPRINT_SIZE is recursively called to compute the footprint size of a simpler array reference. Finally, when none of these rules can be used or the tiling matrix is not a diagonal matrix, the algorithm returns the upper bound provided by the first part of Theorem 4.2 (line 20).

The most expensive step of the algorithm is the assessment of the unimodularity of matrix G, which requires exponential time in K; the other steps can be completed in polynomial time in m and K. Notice, however, that the dimensionality of the arrays and the depth of the nested loops occurring in typical imperative programs is seldom larger than 3 or 4. Therefore, the cost of computing the footprint size of a single array reference using the algorithm in Figure 4.2 is negligible for all practical instances of the problem.

The Footprint Size of a Multiple Array Reference

When a pure-input array is referenced more than once within the loop body, the accurate computation of its overall footprint size can be very difficult. Therefore, in many situations one has to conservatively assume that footprints corresponding to different references are disjoint, and compute the overall footprint size as the sum of the individual footprint sizes. Since even for very simple examples of multiple references such as $a[i_1]$ and $a[2i_1]$, or $a[2i_1]$ and $a[2i_1+1]$ the overall footprint size is indeed equal to the sum of the individual footprint sizes, this approximation is appropriate in most cases.

Nevertheless, there is a particular case which occurs very often in practice, and therefore deserves a special consideration. This is the case when:

a. all the subscripts are linear combinations of the loop nest indices;
b. the corresponding subscripts from different references differ only in their constant terms;
c. the iteration space is partitioned into rectangular tiles (i.e. the tiling matrix used to partition the iteration space is a diagonal matrix $\mathsf{T} = \mathsf{I}_K\mathbf{x}$);
d. the individual footprints of the input array occupy contiguous rectangular blocks in the array.

Indeed, in this case the overlaps of individual footprints can be identified, and their size subtracted from the above mentioned approximation of the overall footprint size.

According to the first two requirements, the $R > 1$ multiple references whose overall footprint size we intend to compute have the generic form:

$$a[\mathsf{G}\mathbf{i}+\mathbf{v}^r],\ 1 \le r \le R, \tag{4.12}$$

where $\mathsf{G} = [g_{j,k}]$ represents an $m \times K$ matrix with integer elements, $\mathbf{i}$ denotes the K-dimensional loop index vector, and $\mathbf{v}^r$, $1 \le r \le R$, are m-dimensional vectors with integer components. Let us now identify in which circumstances the footprint of a single array reference is a contiguous rectangular block.

As shown in the proof of Theorem 4.3, the values taken by a generic array subscript $s_j^r = g_{j,1}i_1 + g_{j,2}i_2 + \cdots + g_{j,K}i_K + v_j^r$ across a tile with coordinates $(c_1, c_2, \ldots, c_K)$ belong to the set

$$\sum_{\substack{k=1\\ g_{j,k}>0}}^{K} |g_{j,k}|\, c_k x_k - \sum_{\substack{k=1\\ g_{j,k}<0}}^{K} |g_{j,k}|\, ((c_k+1)x_k - 1) + v_j^r \;..$$

$$\sum_{\substack{k=1\\ g_{j,k}>0}}^{K} |g_{j,k}|\, ((c_k+1)x_k - 1) - \sum_{\substack{k=1\\ g_{j,k}<0}}^{K} |g_{j,k}|\, c_k x_k + v_j^r.$$

Moreover, a sufficient condition to have the subscript taking each value in this set is $|g_{j,k}| \leq 1$ for any $1 \leq k \leq K$. When all possible rectangular tiles are considered, this is also a necessary condition as suggested by the values taken by the subscripts in the array references $a[2i_1]$ and $a[3i_1+i_2]$ across tiles generated by $\mathsf{T} = [x_1]$ and $\mathsf{T} = \mathsf{I}_2[x_1, 2]^{\mathrm{T}}$, respectively.

Clearly, having all the subscripts taking a contiguous set of values is not enough to ensure that an individual footprint is a contiguous rectangular block, as illustrated for instance by the footprint of $a[i_1, i_1+i_2]$. However, if in addition to the above condition any loop index appears in at most one subscript, the subscripts vary independently across the tile, and the resulting individual footprints satisfy the last requirement. Again, this is a necessary constraint when the generic case is taken into account.

When all four requirements are fulfilled, the intersection of several individual footprints can be assessed exactly, and the overall footprint size computed as:

$$F_{multiple}(\mathsf{I}_K\mathbf{x}, \mathsf{G}, \mathbf{v}^1, \mathbf{v}^2, \ldots, \mathbf{v}^R) = \#\text{footprint}(a) = \#\bigcup_{r=1}^{R} \text{footprint}^r(a) =$$

$$= \sum_{r=1}^{R} \#\text{footprint}^r(a) - \sum_{\{r_1,r_2\}\subset 1..R} \#(\text{footprint}^{r_1}(a) \cap \text{footprint}^{r_2}(a)) +$$

$$+ \cdots + (-1)^{R-1}\#\bigcap_{r=1}^{R} \text{footprint}^r(a), \quad (4.13)$$

where $\text{footprint}^r(a)$ represents the individual footprint for the r-th array reference, $1 \leq r \leq R$. The following theorem introduces a method for the computation of the various terms in relation (4.13).

Theorem 4.4 *Consider the $R > 1$ array references given by (4.12), and assume that $g_{j,k} \in \{-1, 0, 1\}$ for all $1 \leq j \leq m$ and $1 \leq k \leq K$, and that for any $1 \leq k \leq K$, $\sum_{j=1}^{m} |g_{j,k}| \leq 1$. Then for any tile generated by the tiling matrix $\mathsf{I}_K\mathbf{x}$, and for any $\{r_1, r_2, \ldots, r_Q\} \subseteq 1..R$, $Q \geq 1$,*

$$\#\bigcap_{q=1}^{Q} \text{footprint}^{r_q}(a) = \begin{cases} \prod_{j=1}^{m} \alpha_j & \mathit{if} \ \forall j \in 1..m \bullet \alpha_j \geq 1 \\ 0, & \mathit{otherwise} \end{cases} \quad (4.14)$$

where

$$\alpha_j = \sum_{\substack{k=1 \\ g_{j,k}\neq 0}}^{K} (x_k - 1) + \min_{1\leq q\leq Q} v_j^{r_q} - \max_{1\leq q\leq Q} v_j^{r_q} + 1,$$

for any $1 \leq j \leq m$.

Proof According to the analysis of the circumstances in which an individual footprint is a contiguous rectangular block, the individual footprints of the R references we are analysing correspond to such blocks. Moreover, for a generic tile with coordinates $(c_1, c_2, \ldots, c_K)$ generated by the tiling matrix $\mathsf{I}_K\mathbf{x}$, s^r_j, the j-th subscript from the r-th array reference, takes all the integer values defined by $L^r_j \leq s^r_j \leq U^r_j$, where

$$L^r_j = v^r_j + \sum_{\substack{k=1 \\ g_{j,k}=1}}^{K} c_k x_k - \sum_{\substack{k=1 \\ g_{j,k}=-1}}^{K} ((c_k+1)x_k - 1)$$

and

$$U^r_j = v^r_j + \sum_{\substack{k=1 \\ g_{j,k}=1}}^{K} ((c_k+1)x_k - 1) - \sum_{\substack{k=1 \\ g_{j,k}=-1}}^{K} c_k x_k.$$

Consequently, the r-th individual footprint of a, $1 \leq r \leq R$ is the rectangular block of a defined by

$$\text{footprint}^r(a) = \{a[s^r_1, s^r_2, \ldots, s^r_m] \mid (s^r_1, s^r_2, \ldots, s^r_m) \in L^r_1..U^r_1 \times L^r_2..U^r_2 \times \cdots \times L^r_m..U^r_m\}.$$

The intersection of Q, $1 \leq Q \leq R$, arbitrary blocks footprint$^{r_1}(a)$, footprint$^{r_2}(a)$, $\ldots$, footprint$^{r_Q}(a)$, $\{r_1, r_2, \ldots, r_Q\} \subseteq 1..R$ is obviously the block

$$\Big\{a[s_1, s_2, \ldots, s_m] \;\Big|\; (s_1, s_2, \ldots, s_m) \in \max_{1\leq q\leq Q} L^{r_q}_1 .. \min_{1\leq q\leq Q} U^{r_q}_1 \times \\ \times \max_{1\leq q\leq Q} L^{r_q}_2 .. \min_{1\leq q\leq Q} U^{r_q}_2 \times \cdots \times \max_{1\leq q\leq Q} L^{r_q}_m .. \min_{1\leq q\leq Q} U^{r_q}_m \Big\}$$

if $\forall j \in 1..m \bullet \min_{1\leq q\leq Q} U^{r_q}_j \geq \max_{1\leq q\leq Q} L^{r_q}_j$, and the empty set otherwise. Since for any j, $1 \leq j \leq m$,

$$\min_{1\leq q\leq Q} U^{r_q}_j - \max_{1\leq q\leq Q} L^{r_q}_j + 1 = \alpha_j,$$

equation (4.14) gives the size of this intersection, and the proof is complete. □

Example 4.3 Consider for instance a 3-level loop nest $\mathcal{L}$, and a pure-input array a of $\mathcal{L}$ whose references within the loop body are $a[i_1+3, i_2-i_3-1]$ and $a[i_1, i_2-i_3+4]$. The two references to array a can be written as $a[\mathsf{G}\mathbf{i}+\mathbf{v}^r]$, $1 \leq r \leq 2$, where

$$\mathsf{G} = \begin{bmatrix} 1 & 0 & 0 \\ 0 & 1 & -1 \end{bmatrix}, \quad \mathbf{i} = [i_1, i_2, i_3]^{\mathrm{T}}, \quad \mathbf{v}^1 = [3, -1]^{\mathrm{T}}, \quad \text{and} \quad \mathbf{v}^2 = [0, 4]^{\mathrm{T}}.$$

The overall footprint size of a is

$$\#\text{footprint}(a) = \#\text{footprint}^1(a) + \#\text{footprint}^2(a) - \#(\text{footprint}^1(a) \cap \text{footprint}^2(a)),$$

where footprint$^1(a)$ and footprint$^2(a)$ are the footprints of a corresponding to the two references. As the assumptions in the hypothesis of Theorem 4.4 are satisfied, the terms on the right-hand side of the above equality can be computed for any rectangular tile generated by the generic tiling matrix $\mathsf{T} = \mathsf{I}_3[x_1, x_2, x_3]^{\mathrm{T}}$ using relation (4.14):

- $\#\text{footprint}^1(a) = \alpha_1\alpha_2$, with

$$\alpha_1 = \sum_{\substack{k=1\\ g_{1,k}\neq 0}}^{3} (x_k - 1) + \min\{v_1^1\} - \max\{v_1^1\} + 1 = (x_1 - 1) + 3 - 3 + 1 = x_1,$$

$$\alpha_2 = \sum_{\substack{k=1\\ g_{2,k}\neq 0}}^{3} (x_k - 1) + \min\{v_2^1\} - \max\{v_2^1\} + 1 =$$

$$(x_2 - 1) + (x_3 - 1) - 1 + 1 + 1 = x_2 + x_3 - 1.$$

- $\#\text{footprint}^2(a) = \alpha_1\alpha_2$, with

$$\alpha_1 = \sum_{\substack{k=1\\ g_{1,k}\neq 0}}^{3} (x_k - 1) + \min\{v_1^2\} - \max\{v_1^2\} + 1 = (x_1 - 1) + 0 - 0 + 1 = x_1,$$

$$\alpha_2 = \sum_{\substack{k=1\\ g_{2,k}\neq 0}}^{3} (x_k - 1) + \min\{v_2^2\} - \max\{v_2^2\} + 1 =$$

$$(x_2 - 1) + (x_3 - 1) + 4 - 4 + 1 = x_2 + x_3 - 1.$$

- $\#\text{footprint}^2(a) \cap \#\text{footprint}^2(a) = \alpha_1\alpha_2$, with

$$\alpha_1 = \sum_{\substack{k=1\\ g_{1,k}\neq 0}}^{3} (x_k - 1) + \min\{v_1^1, v_1^2\} - \max\{v_1^1, v_1^2\} + 1 =$$

$$(x_1 - 1) + 0 - 3 + 1 = x_1 - 3,$$

$$\alpha_2 = \sum_{\substack{k=1\\ g_{2,k}\neq 0}}^{3} (x_k - 1) + \min\{v_2^1, v_2^2\} - \max\{v_2^1, v_2^2\} + 1 =$$

$$(x_2 - 1) + (x_3 - 1) - 1 - 4 + 1 = x_2 + x_3 - 6.$$

As a result, the overall footprint size of a is

$$\#\text{footprint}(a) = 2x_1(x_2 + x_3 - 1) - (x_1 - 3)(x_2 + x_3 - 6) = (x_1 + 3)(x_2 + x_3 + 4) - 30.$$

4.3.2 Input Communication Overheads Due to Input/Output Arrays

So far we have only analysed the input communication overheads induced by pure-input arrays. In this section, we shall concentrate on the other class of loop-external communication costs, namely the input communication costs due to input/output arrays.

One can distinguish several cases of input/output references to an array. Firstly, as an extreme case, the input and output references to the input/output array can be totally independent, as illustrated by the following example of a loop body:

$$a[2i_1, i_2, i_3] = f_1(\ldots)$$
$$b[i_1, i_2, i_3] = f_2(a[2i_1 + 1, i_2, i_3])$$

Clearly, the contribution of array a to the input communication cost must be computed in this case as though the array were a pure-input array, taking into account only the array reference that appears on the right-hand side of an assignment statement.

Secondly, the input and output references to the same array can be related through a loop-independent data dependence. Two subcases can be identified here: when the data dependence between the statements containing the two references is a flow dependence—as in the following example of a loop body

$$a[i_1, i_2, i_3] = \ldots$$
$$b[i_1, i_2, i_3] = f(a[i_1, i_2, i_3])$$

and when this dependence is an antidependence:

$$b[i_1, i_2, i_3] = f(a[i_1, i_2, i_3])$$
$$a[i_1, i_2, i_3] = \ldots$$

In the first subcase, all read references to an array element use values computed by a previous statement in the loop body, whereas in the second subcase all read references address values from outside the loop nest. Consequently, the input/output array adds no contribution to the input communication cost in the former subcase, and a contribution equivalent to that corresponding to a pure-input array in the latter subcase.

Finally, the input and output references to the same array can be related through a loop-carried dependence. Again, one can distinguish two subcases, namely when the loop-carried dependence is a flow dependence—as in the following example

$$a[i_1, i_2, i_3] = f(a[i_1, i_2 - 1, i_3], \ldots)$$

and when the loop-carried dependence is an antidependence:

$$a[i_1, i_2, i_3] = f(a[i_1, i_2 + 1, i_3], \ldots)$$

For the antidependence subcase, any usage of an element of the input/output array refers to a value not previously modified within the loop nest. Therefore, the contribution of such a reference to the amount of input communication is identical to the contribution of a similar reference to a pure-input array.

As for the subcase of a flow dependence, the contribution of the associated input/output array to the input communication overheads is given by the following theorem. This theorem addresses the case when the loop nest is partitioned into rectangular tiles, and the flow dependence is described by a distance vector.

Theorem 4.5 *Let $\mathcal{L}$ be a K-level perfect loop nest partitioned into rectangular tiles generated by the tiling matrix $\mathsf{T} = \mathsf{I}_K\mathbf{x}$. Also, let a be an m-dimensional array referenced in two statements S_1 and S_2 belonging to the loop body of $\mathcal{L}$. Assume that all array subscripts are affine functions of the surrounding loop indices, and that a flow data dependence $S_1\delta S_2$ of distance vector $\mathbf{d} = [d_1, d_2, \ldots, d_K]^{\mathrm{T}}$ exists due to the use of array a by the two statements. Then, if $x_k \geq |d_k|$ for all $1 \leq k \leq K$, the number of array elements required for the computation of any tile and which are not previously modified within the loop body of $\mathcal{L}$ is bounded above by*

$$\prod_{k=1}^{K} x_k - \prod_{k=1}^{K} (x_k - |d_k|), \tag{4.15}$$

and there is a tile for which this upper bound is attained.

Proof Let $a[\mathsf{G}^1\mathbf{i}+\mathbf{v}^1]$, $a[\mathsf{G}^2\mathbf{i}+\mathbf{v}^2]$ be the generic forms of the two array references in statements S_1 and S_2, respectively. According to the hypothesis of the theorem,

$$\mathsf{G}^1\mathbf{i}+\mathbf{v}^1 = \mathsf{G}^2\mathbf{i}'+\mathbf{v}^2 \Leftrightarrow \mathbf{i}' = \mathbf{i}+\mathbf{d}$$

for any iteration points $\mathbf{i}$ and $\mathbf{i}'$. Hence, for any iteration point $\mathbf{i}$, $(\mathsf{G}^1 - \mathsf{G}^2)\mathbf{i} = \mathsf{G}^2\mathbf{d} + \mathbf{v}^2 - \mathbf{v}^1$. Since the right-hand side of this equality is a constant, we necessarily have $\mathsf{G}^1 = \mathsf{G}^2 = \mathsf{G}$, and $\mathsf{G}\mathbf{d} + \mathbf{v}^2 - \mathbf{v}^1 = \mathbf{0}$. Furthermore, the only solution of $\mathsf{G}\mathbf{i} + \mathbf{v}^1 = \mathsf{G}(\mathbf{i}+\mathbf{y}) + \mathbf{v}^2$ (or $\mathsf{G}\mathbf{y} = \mathbf{v}^1 - \mathbf{v}^2$) is $\mathbf{y} = \mathbf{d}$, so $\mathrm{rank}(\mathsf{G}) = K$ and $m \geq K$. It follows from Theorems 4.1 and 4.2 that the two array references address a different array element for each iteration point.

We shall now consider a generic tile T with coordinates $(c_1, c_2, \ldots, c_K)$, and compute the number of iteration points $\mathbf{i} \in T$ for which $a[\mathsf{G}\mathbf{i} + \mathbf{v}^2]$ refers an array element not previously modified in T. In the worst case, all these (different) array elements are not modified within the loop body of $\mathcal{L}$. Consequently, this quantity represents an upper bound for the number of array elements used by T and that must be fetched into the local memory in the preliminary communication superstep of the parallel schedule.

Consider a generic iteration point $\mathbf{i} \in T$. It follows from the definition of a distance vector that $a[\mathsf{G}\mathbf{i}+\mathbf{v}^2]$ is computed in a previous iteration from T if and only if $\mathbf{i}-\mathbf{d} \in T$. Hence, the desired upper bound is

$$\#\{\mathbf{i} \in T \mid \mathbf{i}-\mathbf{d} \notin T\} = \#(T \setminus \{\mathbf{i} \in T \mid \mathbf{i}-\mathbf{d} \in T\}).$$

Since the second set is a subset of the first, the upper bound is

$$\begin{aligned}
&\#T - \#\{\mathbf{i} \in T \mid \mathbf{i}-\mathbf{d} \in T\} = \\
&= \#\{(i_1, i_2, \ldots, i_K) \in \mathbf{N}^K \mid \forall 1 \leq k \leq K \bullet c_k x_k \leq i_k \leq (c_k+1)x_k - 1\} - \\
&- \#\{(i_1, i_2, \ldots, i_K) \in \mathbf{N}^K \mid \forall 1 \leq k \leq K \bullet c_k x_k \leq i_k,\ i_k - d_k \leq (c_k+1)x_k - 1\} = \\
&\qquad = \textstyle\prod_{k=1}^{K} x_k - \prod_{k=1}^{K} (x_k - |d_k|).
\end{aligned}$$

It can be seen immediately that this upper bound is actually attained for the tile whose coordinates are given by

$$c_k = \begin{cases} 0, & \text{if } d_k \geq 0 \\ \lceil n_k/x_k \rceil - 1, & \text{otherwise} \end{cases}, \quad 1 \leq k \leq K.$$

Since in the BSP model the communication cost of a superstep depends on the maximum amount of data received or sent by any processor in that superstep, this last result indicates that relation (4.15) can be used to compute the actual cost of communication and not only an upper bound for it. □

Example 4.4 To illustrate the application of the result in Theorem 4.5, consider the following loop nest:

$$\begin{array}{ll} & \textbf{for } i_1 = 0, n_1 - 1 \textbf{ do} \\ & \quad \textbf{for } i_2 = 1, n_2 - 1 \textbf{ do} \\ & \quad\quad \textbf{for } i_3 = 0, n_3 - 3 \textbf{ do} \\ S_1: & \quad\quad\quad a[i_1, i_2, i_3] = \ldots \\ S_2: & \quad\quad\quad \cdots = \ldots a[i_1, i_2 - 1, i_3 + 2] \ldots \end{array}$$

This loop nest comprises a flow dependence $S_1 \delta S_2$ of distance vector $\mathbf{d} = [0, 1, -2]^T$ due to the definition of array a in statement S_1 and its use in statement S_2. According to Theorem 4.5, for any rectangular tile of size $x_1 \times x_2 \times x_3$, the number of loop-external array elements required for the computation of the tile is bounded above by

$$\prod_{k=1}^{3} x_k - \prod_{k=1}^{3} (x_k - \mid d_k \mid) = x_1x_2x_3 - (x_1 - 0)(x_2 - 1)(x_3 - 2) = x_1(2x_2 + x_3 - 2).$$

This upper bound is attained for the (boundary) tile with coordinates $(0, 0, \lceil n_3/x_3 \rceil - 1)$.

4.4 Inter-Tile Communication Overheads

As emphasised in the introductory section of this chapter, the computation of a tile may require two kinds of *tile-external* data: data initialised outside the loop nest, and data whose values are assigned by preceding tile computations. In the previous sections, we examined the communication costs incurred by the first type of tile-external data. As for the communication due to inter-tile dependences, its cost is assessed in this section.

We shall first show that non-flow data dependences incur no inter-tile communication. There are two types of non-flow data dependences, namely antidependences and output dependences. The former type is associated with dependences in which the value of a variable is first used, and then modified by a subsequent statement instance. Hence, the value that is used comes from outside the loop nest, and the antidependence itself involves no data "movement" from one iteration to another.

As for output dependences, they correspond to the modification of the same variable by two statement instances. Again, no data need to be passed from one iteration to another, so no inter-tile communication cost is involved. However, it is worth mentioning that both types of non-flow data dependences make possible the existence of non-coherent copies of the same variable in different local memories. Of course, this is not a problem as long as the out-of-date copies are known to be so.

Following the above discussion, the remainder of this section concentrates on the analysis of the inter-tile communication overheads due to loop-carried flow dependences. Once more, it is impossible to compute the exact value of the communication cost (or a non-trivial upper bound for it) in the general case. Therefore, taking into account the fact that our communication cost analysis framework is used in the parallelisation of regular computations, we shall only consider the case when all the dependences of the loop nest can be represented by distance vectors. Under these circumstances, the amount of remote data to be received by any processor before the computation of an inner tile and for a single flow data dependence is given by the following theorem and its corollary.

Theorem 4.6 *Let $\mathcal{L}$ be a K-level tightly nested loop, T a non-boundary rectangular tile generated by the tiling matrix $\mathsf{I}_K\mathbf{x}$, and* **d** *the distance vector of a flow data dependence of $\mathcal{L}$. Then, if $|d_k| \leq x_k$ for all $1 \leq k \leq K$, the amount of data required for the computation of T due to the dependences encoded by* **d**, *and which is computed in other tiles is exactly*

$$\prod_{k=1}^{K} x_k - \prod_{k=1}^{K} (x_k - |d_k|) . \tag{4.16}$$

Proof This theorem is merely an extension of the result in Theorem 4.5 to the case of inter-tile communication. In the proof of Theorem 4.5, we demonstrated that the quantity in (4.16) gives the amount of tile-external data required for the computation of T due to the data dependences encoded by the distance vector **d**. To see that all these data come from previous tile computations, it is enough to recall that T is not a boundary tile and that for all $1 \leq k \leq K, x_k \geq |d_k|$. □

In many loop nest schedules generated through automatic parallelisation, each processor is assigned the computation of a set of tiles during the supersteps of the schedule. Hence, some of the tile-external data referred to in the above theorem are actually computed by the same processor that computes tile T, and the volume of data in (4.16) represents only an upper bound for the communication that takes place due to the considered distance vector. The exact amount of communication for the case when all the tiles along some direction(s) of the iteration space are computed by the same processor is evaluated in the following corollary to Theorem 4.6.

Corollary 4.7 *With the notation in Theorem 4.6, consider that the computation of all tiles along the direction(s) corresponding to the loops indexed by $i_{k_1}, i_{k_2}, \ldots, i_{k_r}, r \geq 0$ is assigned to the same processor. Then the amount of remote data to be received by any processor before the computation of a non-boundary tile T due to the dependences encoded by the distance vector* **d** *is*

$$\prod_{k=1}^{K} x_k - \prod_{k=1}^{K} (x_k - |d'_k|) , \tag{4.17}$$

where, for any $1 \le k \le K$,

$$d'_k = \begin{cases} d_k & \text{if } k \notin \{k_1, k_2, \ldots, k_r\} \\ 0 & \text{otherwise} \end{cases}$$

Proof According to Theorems 4.5 and 4.6, the amount of tile-external data required for the computation of T due to the distance vector $\mathbf{d}$ is the number of iteration points in the set $\{\mathbf{i} \in T \mid \mathbf{i} - \mathbf{d} \notin T\}$. In an entirely similar manner, one can prove that the amount of remote data we want to compute is given by the number of iteration points in the set $\{\mathbf{i} \in T \mid \mathbf{i} - \mathbf{d} \notin S(T)\}$, where $S(T)$ represents the union of all tiles computed by the processor which is assigned the computation of T. If the coordinates of T in the tile space are $(c_1, c_2, \ldots, c_K)$, it follows from the hypothesis of the corollary that

$$S(T) = \{\mathbf{i} \in I \mid \forall k \in 1..K \bullet k \notin \{k_1, k_2, \ldots, k_r\} \Rightarrow c_k x_k \le i_k \le (c_k + 1)x_k - 1\}.$$

Hence, we are looking for the value of

$$\begin{aligned} \#\{\mathbf{i} \in T \mid \mathbf{i} - \mathbf{d} \notin S(T)\} &= \#T - \#\{\mathbf{i} \in T \mid \mathbf{i} - \mathbf{d} \in S(T)\} = \\ &= \prod_{k=1}^{K} x_k - \#\{\mathbf{i} \in I \mid \forall k \in 1..K \bullet (c_k x_k \le i_k \le (c_k+1)x_k - 1) \wedge \\ &\qquad (k \notin \{k_1, k_2, \ldots, k_r\} \Rightarrow c_k x_k \le i_k - d_k \le (c_k+1)x_k - 1)\}. \end{aligned}$$

The remaining set in the above expression is a rectangular block comprising the iteration points $\mathbf{i} \in I$ that satisfy:

$$\begin{array}{rl} c_k x_k \le i_k \le (c_k+1)x_k - 1 & \text{if } k \in \{k_1, k_2, \ldots, k_r\} \\ c_k x_k + d_k \le i_k \le (c_k+1)x_k - 1 & \text{if } k \notin \{k_1, k_2, \ldots, k_r\} \wedge d_k \ge 0 \\ c_k x_k \le i_k \le (c_k+1)x_k + d_k - 1 & \text{if } k \notin \{k_1, k_2, \ldots, k_r\} \wedge d_k < 0 \end{array}$$

Since the size of this block is exactly $\prod_{k=1}^{K} (x_k - \mid d'_k \mid)$, the proof is complete. □

Many scheduling techniques, including several techniques developed in this book, partition the iteration space of a nested loop into rectangular tiles, and assign each processor the computation of all tiles along some arbitrarily chosen direction(s) of the iteration space. Corollary 4.7 provides the means for choosing these directions so as to minimise the communication cost of the resulting parallel schedule.

When the considered loop nest comprises several uniform flow dependences, an estimate of the inter-tile communication cost due to all these dependences can be built by summing the communication overheads corresponding to each individual dependence. Nevertheless, this value represents an overestimate in many cases.

Example 4.5 Consider for instance the following example of a perfect loop nest

for $i_1 = 1, n-1$ **do**
  for $i_2 = 3, n-1$ **do**
S_1: $a[i_1, i_2] = f_1(a[i_1 - 1, i_2 - 2], a[i_1 - 1, i_2 - 3])$

and assume that its iteration space is partitioned into rectangular tiles of size $x_1 \times x_2$. This loop nest has two flow dependences whose distance vectors are $\mathbf{d}^1 = [1,2]^T$ and $\mathbf{d}^2 = [1,3]^T$. Hence, if all the tiles along the direction corresponding to the loop indexed by i_1 are assigned to the same processor, the estimate of the amount of inter-tile communication per tile is

$$\sum_{\mathbf{d}\in\{\mathbf{d}^1,\mathbf{d}^2\}} \left(\prod_{k=1}^{2} x_k - \prod_{k=1}^{2}(x_k - |d_k^l|)\right) = [x_1x_2 - (x_1-0)(x_2-2)] + [x_1x_2 - (x_1-0)(x_2-3)] = 5x_1.$$

It is however straightforward to see that the exact amount of inter-tile communication is in this case $3x_1$. This accurate expression of the communication cost can be obtained using the result provided by the following theorem.

Theorem 4.8 *Let $\mathcal{L}$ be a K-level tightly nested loop, and a an array whose elements are defined once (i.e. an array that appears on the left-hand side of a single assignment statement) and are subsequently read $R \geq 1$ times within the loop body of $\mathcal{L}$. Assume that the R flow dependences in which array a is involved are described by the distance vectors $\mathbf{d}^1$, $\mathbf{d}^2$, ..., $\mathbf{d}^R$. Then the overall amount of inter-tile communication is equal to the amount of inter-tile communication corresponding to the single data dependence of distance vector $\mathbf{d} = [d_1, d_2, \ldots, d_K]^T$, where, for any $1 \leq k \leq K$,*

$$d_k = \max\{d_k^r \mid 1 \leq r \leq R \wedge d_k^r \geq 0\} + \max\{-d_k^r \mid 1 \leq r \leq R \wedge d_k^r < 0\}.$$

(For the scope of this theorem, we define $\max\{\} = 0$.*)*

Proof Consider a generic rectangular tiling matrix $\mathsf{T} = \mathsf{I}_K\mathbf{x}$, and the inner tile T with coordinates $(c_1, c_2, \ldots, c_K)$ generated by T. For simplicity, the proof will use the notation $\max\{d_k^r \mid 1 \leq r \leq R \wedge d_k^r \geq 0\} = \alpha_k$, $\max\{-d_k^r \mid 1 \leq r \leq R \wedge d_k^r < 0\} = \beta_k$ (i.e. $d_k = \alpha_k + \beta_k$) for all $1 \leq k \leq K$. With this notation, we shall prove that the set of iteration points belonging to T and using no tile-external element of a is given by

$$S = \{\mathbf{i} \in \mathbf{N}^K \mid \forall k \in 1..K \bullet c_kx_k + \alpha_k \leq i_k \leq (c_k+1)x_k - 1 - \beta_k\}.$$

As the number of iteration points in S is equal to the number of iteration points satisfying

$$c_kx_k \leq i_k, i_k - d_k \leq (c_k+1)x_k - 1, \qquad 1 \leq k \leq K,$$

i.e. to the number of iteration points in T that would incur no inter-tile communication due to a data dependence of distance vector $\mathbf{d}$, this will also prove the theorem. We shall demonstrate our claim by equivalence:

$$
\begin{aligned}
&\mathbf{i} \in S \\
&\iff \text{(definition of } S) \\
&\forall k \in 1..K \bullet c_k x_k + \alpha_k \leq i_k \leq (c_k+1)x_k - 1 - \beta_k \\
&\iff \text{(for any } 1 \leq k \leq K,\ \alpha_k \geq 0,\ \beta_k \geq 0, \text{ and } \forall r \in 1..R \bullet (d_k^r \geq 0 \land d_k^r \leq \alpha_k) \lor \\
&\qquad (d_k^r < 0 \land -d_k^r \leq \beta_k)) \\
&\forall r \in 1..R \bullet \forall k \in 1..K \bullet c_k x_k \leq i_k, i_k - d_k^r \leq (c_k+1)x_k - 1 \\
&\iff \text{(definition of a rectangular tile—relation (4.3))} \\
&\mathbf{i} \in T \land \forall r \in 1..R \bullet \mathbf{i} - \mathbf{d}^r \in T.
\end{aligned}
$$

Hence, S represents the set of iteration points in T that do not use tile-external data due to the considered set of R data dependences, and the proof is complete. □

4.5 Summary

This chapter has introduced a framework capable of assessing all the communication costs associated with the parallelisation of tightly nested loops in a unitary manner. This framework distinguishes two types of communication, and employs powerful theoretical results to accurately analyse the overheads induced by each of them.

For the communication due to data read within a loop nest but initialised before its computation, we have provided techniques that analyse the footprint size of single and multiple array references across an iteration space tile. Additionally, our framework addresses the computation of the input communication costs associated with the presence of input/output arrays—arrays whose elements are both read and modified by the loop nest.

The framework also comprises novel techniques for the analysis of the communication costs due to the computation of inter-dependent iteration points on different processors. These techniques are applicable to tightly nested loops whose dependences can be represented by distance vectors, and take into account the fact that tiles along certain directions of the iteration space are typically mapped on the same processor. The latter feature—unique to our framework—is extremely useful when deciding on the assignment of tiles to processors. Moreover, we identify the case when several distance vectors stand for dependences involving the same array. Hence, we accurately compute the communication overheads even when some of the arrays in the loop nest are involved in more than one data dependence.

The communication cost analysis framework devised in this chapter will be used in assessing the performance and establishing the parameters of parallel schedules throughout the remainder of the book. At the same time, the usefulness of the new framework extends to other research areas, such as optimisation of cache usage in shared-memory multiprocessors, or analysis of the space complexity of parallel programs.

5. Template-Matching Parallelisation

If you want to succeed, limit yourself.

Charles Augustin Sainte-Beuve

5.1 Introduction

In this chapter, we introduce a collection of techniques for the architecture-independent parallelisation of nested loops that match certain computation patterns. As each of these computation patterns describes a class of loop nests frequently appearing in sequential programs, the derivation of dedicated techniques for their scheduling represents an important part of our novel approach to automatic parallelisation.

The chapter begins with an overview of previous work on architecture-independent template-matching scheduling. In Section 5.3, we present a technique for the *communication-free parallelisation* of uniform-dependence loop nests whose iteration space can be partitioned into fully independent tiles. Section 5.4 is entirely dedicated to *wavefront block scheduling*, a BSP extension of the wavefront parallelisation technique described in Section 3.3.5. Next, an alternative parallelisation strategy called *iterative scheduling* is introduced in Section 5.5. We then continue with the *scheduling of reductions* and *recurrences* in Sections 5.6 and 5.7, respectively. Finally, Section 5.8 addresses the automatic parallelisation of a loop structure comprising non-uniform data dependences, and called a *broadcast loop nest*. The instances of this loop structure include important linear algebra computations such as Gaussian elimination and the algebraic path problem.

5.2 Related Work

The overwhelming part of the template-matching parallelisation techniques developed so far merely aim at identifying the potential parallelism of the nested loops they parallelise [14–16, 26, 27, 45, 46, 62, 63] . Furthermore, in the few cases when the extraction of this potential parallelism is followed by its mapping on a real parallel computer, the current scheduling techniques are typically targeted at a specific parallel architecture (e.g. [75, 76]). Consequently, the parallel code they produce lacks portability.

At the same time, most of these scheduling approaches have adopted an asynchronous parallel programming model, i.e. they assume that the processors operate asynchronously and synchronise pairwise when communicating. The drawback of using such a programming model is that the performance of the resulting parallel programs cannot be assessed analytically. The best one can do is to rate their effectiveness through experiments.

In comparison to the above mentioned approaches, the parallelisation techniques devised in this chapter succeed in generating real parallel code that is architecture-independent, scalable, and whose performance is predictable analytically. All these features are achieved by using the BSP model of parallel computation as a target platform for the mapping of the potential parallelism identified in a nested loop. Only two other parallelisation techniques that generate code with these properties have been reported so far. These techniques, both of which also use the BSP programming model, are briefly described in the remainder of this section.

The first technique is due to McColl [35] and tackles the scheduling of regular-structure two- and three-dimensional dags of computations in the context of triangular linear system solving and LU decomposition, respectively. This technique proposes a tiling of the two regular-structure dags into subdags isomorphic with the initial dags, followed by the distribution of the subdag computations among the p processors of a BSP computer. Both patterns of computation can be represented as uniform-dependence loop nests, and parallelised using our wavefront block scheduling technique, which is a generalisation of the scheduling strategy proposed in [35]. A preliminary version of this generalisation is presented in [65]. In addition to extending the scheduling strategy in [35] to generic uniform-dependence perfect loop nests, in Section 5.4 we address the improvement of the load balancing of the resulting parallel schedules.

The second technique belongs to Ding and Stefanescu [43]. This technique addresses the BSP scheduling of a particular case of loop nest, namely of a K-level perfect loop nest consisting of K' outermost parallel loops and $K-K'$ innermost sequential loops, and having a reduction operation as the loop body. Two possible decompositions of the iteration space (i.e. two schedules) are proposed in [43], block$^{K'}$-serial$^{K-K'}$ decomposition, and block^{K} decomposition (the terminology is from [17]), and the one yielding the lowest cost is eventually preferred. Since both decompositions are chosen to be computationally optimal, the selection of the best schedule is actually done by taking into account the associated communication overheads. Ding and Stefanescu tested their scheduling technique against a couple of manually coded BSP programs on matrix multiplication, obtaining identical schedules. Due to the importance of matrix multiplication, the novel parallelisation strategy introduced in Chapter 7 will use this technique together with the scheduling techniques developed in this chapter.

5.3 Communication-Free Scheduling

In this section, we address the parallelisation of uniform-dependence perfect loop nests whose iteration space can be partitioned into fully independent tiles. The conditions under which this partitioning is possible are given by the following theorem.

Theorem 5.1 *Consider a generic K-level perfect loop nest $\mathcal{L}$ which comprises $R \geq 0$ data dependences described by the distance vectors $\mathbf{d}^1$, $\mathbf{d}^2$, ..., $\mathbf{d}^R$. Then, the iteration space of $\mathcal{L}$ can be partitioned into fully independent tiles if and only if*

$$\text{rank}[\mathbf{d}^1, \mathbf{d}^2, \ldots, \mathbf{d}^R] < K. \tag{5.1}$$

Proof A generic tiling of the iteration space of $\mathcal{L}$ produces independent tiles if and only if no data dependence exists between iteration points belonging to different tiles. Clearly, this is possible if and only if the $(K-1)$-dimensional hyperplanes that define the tile boundaries in the K-dimensional iteration space are parallel to all the R distance vectors. As such hyperplanes can be built if and only if the R distance vectors do not form a basis in the K-dimensional space, the result in (5.1) is immediate. □

5.3.1 Scheduling Loop Nests Comprising Fully Parallel Loops

In many practical situations when the dependences of a tightly nested loop $\mathcal{L}$ satisfy (5.1), the matrix $\mathsf{D} = [\mathbf{d}^1, \mathbf{d}^2, \ldots, \mathbf{d}^R]$ comprises K' zero rows, $0 < K' \leq K$. When this is the case, the same K' elements of each distance vector are null. Furthermore, as shown in Section 3.3, the K' loops corresponding to these elements are *fully parallel*, i.e. they can be brought into the outermost positions using loop interchange, and parallelised.

Example 5.1 Consider for instance the following example of a perfect loop nest:

for $i_1 = 1, n_1 - 1$ **do**
  for $i_2 = 0, n_2 - 1$ **do**
    for $i_3 = 0, n_3 - 1$ **do**
S_1: $a[i_1, i_2, i_3] = f(b[i_1, i_2 + i_3], c[i_1, i_2], a[i_1 - 1, i_2, i_3])$

The only data dependence of this loop nest is the flow dependence $S_1 \delta_{[1,0,0]^\mathrm{T}} S_1$. Accordingly, the loops indexed by i_2 and i_3 are fully parallel loops, and the following loop nest is equivalent to the original one:

forall $i_2 = 0, n_2 - 1$ **do in parallel**
  forall $i_3 = 0, n_3 - 1$ **do in parallel**
    for $i_1 = 1, n_1 - 1$ **do**
S_1: $a[i_1, i_2, i_3] = f(b[i_1, i_2 + i_3], c[i_1, i_2], a[i_1 - 1, i_2, i_3])$

Without restricting the generality, we shall assume that the K' fully parallel loops of $\mathcal{L}$ are those indexed by i_1, i_2, ..., $i_{K'}$, and that $\mathcal{L}$ has a rectangular iteration space of size $n_1 \times n_2 \times \cdots \times n_K$. As a result, any tiling matrix $\mathsf{T} = \mathsf{I}_K [x_1, x_2, \ldots, x_{K'}, n_{K'+1}, \ldots, n_K]^\mathrm{T}$ with $\prod_{k=1}^{K'} x_k = (\prod_{k=1}^{K'} n_k)/p$ partitions the iteration space of $\mathcal{L}$ into p equally sized independent tiles. Following a preliminary communication superstep in which loop-external data required for the tile computations are fetched from the appropriate remote locations, these tiles can be executed in a single computation superstep on the p processors of a BSP computer. The cost of the resulting parallel schedule is

$$2L + \frac{(\prod_{k=1}^{K} n_k)c}{p} + g\, Comm(x_1, x_2, \ldots, x_{K'}), \tag{5.2}$$

where c represents the cost of computing the loop body for a single iteration point, and $Comm(x_1,x_2,\ldots,x_{K'})$ is the maximum amount of data sent or received by any processor during the preliminary communication superstep.

As the schedule is one-optimal in computation, and the synchronisation cost is also optimal, the tiling matrix T must be chosen so as to minimise $Comm(x_1,x_2,\ldots,x_{K'})$. Once the value of $Comm(x_1,x_2,\ldots,x_{K'})$ is computed using the techniques introduced in Section 4.3, the optimal schedule corresponds to the instances of $x_1, x_2, \ldots, x_{K'}$ that minimise this value subject to the *load balancing constraint* $\prod_{k=1}^{K'} x_k = (\prod_{k=1}^{K'} n_k)/p$.

One method to find the minimum of the scalar field $Comm{=}Comm(x_1,x_2,\ldots,x_{K'})$, under the (load balancing) constraint $h(x_1,x_2,\ldots,x_{K'}) = \prod_{k=1}^{K'} x_k - (\prod_{k=1}^{K'} n_k)/p = 0$, $1 \le x_k \le n_k$, $1 \le k \le K'$, is to apply the Lagrange multiplier rule [77]. According to this rule, the constrained minima must be among the solutions of

$$\nabla Comm(x_1,x_2,\ldots,x_{K'}) = \lambda \nabla h(x_1,x_2,\ldots,x_{K'})$$

with $\lambda \in \mathbf{R}$. The relation between the arithmetic, geometric, and harmonic means of $x_1, x_2, \ldots, x_{K'}$ has also proved to be useful in many of our tests.

Example 5.2 For the parallel version of the 3-level loop nest in Example 5.1, a schedule which is optimal in computation and synchronisation is obtained by partitioning its iteration space into tiles of size $x_2 \times x_3 \times n_1$, with $x_2x_3 = n_2n_3/p$. The p processors are viewed as being arranged into a logical 2-dimensional array of size $p_1 \times p_2$, where $p_1 = \lceil n_2/x_2 \rceil$ and $p_2 = \lceil n_3/x_3 \rceil$. The processor with coordinates (me_1,me_2), $0 \le me_1 < p_1$, $0 \le me_2 < p_2$, in this array executes the following BSP pseudocode:

```
      /* preliminary communication superstep */
      get input data for the tile with coordinates (me1,me2,0)
      bsp_sync
      /* computation superstep */
      for i2 = me1x2, min{(me1+1)x2 - 1, n2 - 1} do
        for i3 = me2x3, min{(me2+1)x3 - 1, n3 - 1} do
          for i1 = 1, n1 - 1 do
S1:         a[i1,i2,i3] = f(b[i1,i2+i3], c[i1,i2], a[i1-1,i2,i3])
      bsp_sync
```

The cost of this BSP schedule is

$$2L + \frac{n_1n_2n_3cost(f)}{p} + g\,Comm(x_2,x_3),$$

where $cost(f)$ represents the cost of a single call to function f, and $Comm(x_2,x_3)$ represents the input communication cost for a rectangular tile of size $n_1 \times x_2 \times x_3$. The latter can be computed using the techniques described in Section 4.3. If A denotes the set of loop-external elements from a required for the computation of such a tile, then

$$\begin{aligned} Comm(x_2,x_3) &= \#\text{footprint}(b[i_1,i_2+i_3]) + \#\text{footprint}(c[i_1,i_2]) + \#A = \\ &[n_1(x_2+x_3)] + [n_1x_2] + [n_1x_2x_3 - (n_1-1)x_2x_3] = x_2x_3 + 2n_1x_2 + n_1x_3. \end{aligned}$$

The application of the Lagrange multiplier rule yields the system

$$\begin{cases} x_3 + 2n_1 = \lambda x_3 \\ x_2 + n_1 = \lambda x_2 \\ x_2 x_3 = n_2 n_3 / p \end{cases},$$

with the immediate solution

$$x_2 = \sqrt{\frac{n_2 n_3}{2p}}, \quad x_3 = \sqrt{\frac{2 n_2 n_3}{p}}.$$

Hence, the best BSP schedule corresponds to $x_2 = \left\lceil \sqrt{n_2 n_3/(2p)} \right\rceil, x_3 = \left\lceil \sqrt{2 n_2 n_3 / p} \right\rceil$. This schedule achieves optimality in the sense defined in Section 2.5 if $L \leq n_1 n_2 n_3 / p$, $g \leq n_1 n_2 n_3 / (n_2 n_3 + 2n_1 \sqrt{2pn_2 n_3})$.

5.3.2 Scheduling Loop Nests with no Fully Parallel Loop

So far, we have addressed the communication-free scheduling of loop nests comprising fully parallel loops. Nevertheless, it is possible that a K-level loop nest $\mathcal{L}$ whose data dependences satisfy the communication-free scheduling constraint (5.1) comprises no such loop. When this is the case, loop skewing (see Section 3.3) can be employed in order to obtain a loop nest equivalent to $\mathcal{L}$ and which contains $K' = K - \operatorname{rank} \mathsf{D}$ fully parallel loops. This loop nest can then be scheduled using the technique presented in the previous section.

Here, we provide a method for computing the $K \times K$ matrix S of the above mentioned loop skewing. This method comprises two steps:

Step 1: We identify $B = \{\mathbf{v}^1, \mathbf{v}^2, \ldots, \mathbf{v}^{\operatorname{rank}\mathsf{D}}\}$, a basis for the vector space spanned by the distance vectors $\mathbf{d}^1, \mathbf{d}^2, \ldots, \mathbf{d}^R$, such that

$$\forall j \in 1..\operatorname{rank}\mathsf{D} \bullet \mathbf{v}^j = [0, 0, \ldots, 0, v^j_{k_j}, v^j_{k_j+1}, \ldots, v^j_K]^{\mathrm{T}} \wedge v^j_{k_j} \neq 0 \tag{5.3}$$

with $1 = k_1 < k_2 < \cdots < k_{\operatorname{rank} D} \leq K$, and

$$\forall r \in 1..R \bullet \mathbf{d}^r = \sum_{j=1}^{\operatorname{rank}\mathsf{D}} \alpha_{r,j} \mathbf{v}^j \wedge [\alpha_{r,1}, \alpha_{r,2}, \ldots, \alpha_{r,\operatorname{rank}\mathsf{D}}]^{\mathrm{T}} > \mathbf{0}. \tag{5.4}$$

Any basis of $\operatorname{span}\{\mathbf{d}^1, \mathbf{d}^2, \ldots, \mathbf{d}^R\}$ which satisfies (5.4) is called a *positive basis*.

Step 2: We take

$$\mathsf{S} = [\mathbf{v}^1, \mathbf{e}^2, \ldots, \mathbf{e}^{k_2 - 1}, \mathbf{v}^2, \mathbf{e}^{k_2+1}, \ldots, \mathbf{e}^{k_{\operatorname{rank}\mathsf{D}} - 1}, \mathbf{v}^{\operatorname{rank}\mathsf{D}}, \mathbf{e}^{k_{\operatorname{rank}\mathsf{D}}+1}, \ldots, \mathbf{e}^K]^{-1}, \tag{5.5}$$

where, for any $1 \leq k \leq K$, $\mathbf{e}^k$ represents the k-th column of the identity matrix I_K. Notice that the $K \times K$ matrix whose inverse appears on the right-hand side of relation (5.5) is lower triangular with non-zero elements on the main diagonal, so it is non-singular.

BUILD_POSITIVE_BASIS $(\mathbf{x}^1, \mathbf{x}^2, \ldots, \mathbf{x}^R)$

1 $k = 1, J = \text{rank}[\mathbf{x}^1, \mathbf{x}^2, \ldots, \mathbf{x}^R], X = \{\mathbf{x}^1, \mathbf{x}^2, \ldots, \mathbf{x}^R\}$
2 **for** $j = 1, J$ **do**
3   **while** $\forall \mathbf{x} \in X \bullet x_k = 0$ **do**
4     $k = k + 1$
5   $\mathbf{v}^j = \mathbf{x}$, with $\mathbf{x} \in X$ and $x_k > 0 \vee (x_k < 0 \wedge \forall \mathbf{x} \in X \bullet x_k \leq 0)$
6   **for** $r = 1, R$ **do**
7     $\alpha_{r,j} = x^r_k / v^j_k$
8     $\mathbf{x}^r = \mathbf{x}^r - \alpha_{r,j} \mathbf{v}^j$
9 **return** $\{\mathbf{v}^1, \mathbf{v}^2, \ldots, \mathbf{v}^J\}$

Figure 5.1: The positive basis computation algorithm.

Before introducing an algorithm for the first step of the method, we shall prove that the matrix S from (5.5) induces a loop skewing with the desired properties.

Theorem 5.2 *The $K \times K$ matrix* S *obtained through the previously described method induces a loop skewing that yields a loop nest equivalent to $\mathcal{L}$ and which comprises $K' = K - \text{rank}\,\mathsf{D}$ fully parallel loops.*

Proof The loop skewing induced by S produces a loop nest equivalent to $\mathcal{L}$ iff for any distance vector $\mathbf{d}^r$, $1 \leq r \leq R$, the corresponding distance vector of the transformed loop nest is lexicographically positive (i.e. $\mathbf{d}'^r = \mathsf{S}\mathbf{d}^r > \mathbf{0}$). Moreover, the transformed loop nest $\mathcal{L}'$ has K' fully parallel loops iff the matrix $\mathsf{D}' = [\mathbf{d}'^1, \mathbf{d}'^2, \ldots, \mathbf{d}'^R] = \mathsf{SD}$ contains K' zero rows. We shall prove that S satisfies both these requirements.

Consider a generic distance vector $\mathbf{d}^r$, $1 \leq r \leq R$. According to (5.4), the corresponding distance vector in the skewed iteration space is:

$$\mathbf{d}'^r = \mathsf{S}\mathbf{d}^r = \sum_{j=1}^{\text{rank}\,\mathsf{D}} \alpha_{r,j} \mathsf{S}\mathbf{v}^j.$$

It follows from the definition of S in (5.5) that, for any $1 \leq j \leq \text{rank}\,\mathsf{D}$, $\mathsf{S}\mathbf{v}^j = \mathbf{e}^{k_j}$, so

$$\mathbf{d}'^r = \sum_{j=1}^{\text{rank}\,\mathsf{D}} \alpha_{r,j} \mathbf{e}^{k_j} = [0, \ldots, 0, \alpha_{r,1}, 0, \ldots, 0, \alpha_{r,2}, 0, \ldots, 0, \alpha_{r,\text{rank}\,\mathsf{D}}, 0, \ldots, 0]^{\mathrm{T}},$$

where the element $\alpha_{r,j}$, $1 \leq j \leq \text{rank}\,\mathsf{D}$ appears in position k_j. Since according to equation (5.4) the vector $[\alpha_{r,1}, \alpha_{r,2}, \ldots, \alpha_{r,\text{rank}\,\mathsf{D}}]^{\mathrm{T}}$ is lexicographically positive, so is $\mathbf{d}'^r$. Furthermore, each distance vector of the skewed loop nest has at most rank D non-zero elements, appearing in positions k_1, k_2, ..., $k_{\text{rank}\,\mathsf{D}}$. Thus, any row k, $k \notin \{k_1, k_2, \ldots, k_{\text{rank}\,\mathsf{D}}\}$ of the matrix D' is a zero row, and the proof is complete. □

An algorithm that builds a positive basis for the vector space spanned by $R \geq 1$ distance vectors $\mathbf{x}^1$, $\mathbf{x}^2$, ..., $\mathbf{x}^R$ is depicted in Figure 5.1. This algorithm computes the $J = \text{rank}[\mathbf{x}^1, \mathbf{x}^2, \ldots, \mathbf{x}^R]$ components of the positive basis in the J iterations of the for loop in lines 2–8, and returns this basis in line 9. The correctness of the algorithm is demonstrated by the following theorem, whose proof is provided in Appendix A.

Theorem 5.3 *The function* BUILD_POSITIVE_BASIS *in Figure 5.1 computes a positive basis of a set of $R \geq 1$ K-dimensional distance vectors $\mathbf{x}^1, \mathbf{x}^2, \ldots, \mathbf{x}^R$ in $O(K^2R)$ time.*

Once a positive basis for the vector space spanned by the distance vectors of the loop nest is obtained in $O(K^2R)$ time, the affine transformation S in (5.5) can be computed in $O(K^3)$ time. Hence, the overall cost of obtaining the matrix of the required loop skewing is $O(K^2(K+R))$. Since the loop nests appearing in imperative programs have a nesting level K which is rarely larger than 3, and R is always a small constant, the entire method is inexpensive.

Example 5.3 To illustrate the application of loop skewing in the communication-free parallelisation of loop nests, consider the following example of a tightly nested loop:

for $i_1 = 1, n_1 - 1$ **do**
  for $i_2 = 1, n_2 - 2$ **do**
    for $i_3 = 1, n_3 - 2$ **do**
S_1: $a[i_1,i_2,i_3] = f(a[i_1-1,i_2-1,i_3+1], a[i_1-1,i_2,i_3],$
          $a[i_1,i_2-1,i_3+1], a[i_1-1,i_2+1,i_3-1])$

The distance vectors of the four flow dependences in this loop nest are the columns of the matrix

$$\mathsf{D} = \begin{bmatrix} 1 & 1 & 0 & 1 \\ 1 & 0 & 1 & -1 \\ -1 & 0 & -1 & 1 \end{bmatrix},$$

and $\operatorname{rank} \mathsf{D} = 2$. Let us use the algorithm in Figure 5.1 to compute a positive basis for $\operatorname{span}\{\mathbf{d}^1, \mathbf{d}^2, \mathbf{d}^3, \mathbf{d}^4\}$. In the first iteration of the while loop, we have to choose $\mathbf{v}^1$ among the distance vectors whose first element is non-zero. In order to obtain as simple an affine transformation as possible, we select $\mathbf{v}^1 = [1,0,0]^{\mathrm{T}} = \mathbf{e}^1$. After the first iteration of the algorithm, we have

$$[\mathbf{x}^1, \mathbf{x}^2, \mathbf{x}^3, \mathbf{x}^4] = \begin{bmatrix} 0 & 0 & 0 & 0 \\ 1 & 0 & 1 & -1 \\ -1 & 0 & -1 & 1 \end{bmatrix},$$

and the only choice for the second vector of the positive basis is $\mathbf{v}^2 = [0,1,-1]^{\mathrm{T}}$. Accordingly, the matrix of the affine transformation inducing the required loop skewing is

$$\mathsf{S} = [\mathbf{v}^1, \mathbf{v}^2, \mathbf{e}^3]^{-1} = \begin{bmatrix} 1 & 0 & 0 \\ 0 & 1 & 0 \\ 0 & -1 & 1 \end{bmatrix}^{-1} = \begin{bmatrix} 1 & 0 & 0 \\ 0 & 1 & 0 \\ 0 & 1 & 1 \end{bmatrix}.$$

The index vector of the transformed loop nest is

$$\mathbf{i}' = \begin{bmatrix} i_1' \\ i_2' \\ i_3' \end{bmatrix} = \mathsf{S}\,\mathbf{i} = \begin{bmatrix} 1 & 0 & 0 \\ 0 & 1 & 0 \\ 0 & 1 & 1 \end{bmatrix} \begin{bmatrix} i_1 \\ i_2 \\ i_3 \end{bmatrix} = \begin{bmatrix} i_1 \\ i_2 \\ i_2 + i_3 \end{bmatrix},$$

so the skewed loop nest has the form

$$
\begin{array}{ll}
 & \textbf{for } i'_1 = 1, n_1 - 1 \textbf{ do} \\
 & \quad \textbf{for } i'_2 = 1, n_2 - 2 \textbf{ do} \\
 & \quad\quad \textbf{for } i'_3 = i'_2 + 1, i'_2 + n_3 - 2 \textbf{ do} \\
S_1: & \quad\quad\quad a[i'_1, i'_2, i'_3 - i'_2] = f(a[i'_1 - 1, i'_2 - 1, i'_3 - i'_2 + 1], a[i'_1 - 1, i'_2, i'_3 - i'_2], \\
 & \quad\quad\quad\quad a[i'_1, i'_2 - 1, i'_3 - i'_2 + 1], a[i'_1 - 1, i'_2 + 1, i'_3 - i'_2 - 1])
\end{array}
$$

The distance vectors of the data dependences in this equivalent loop nest are the columns of the matrix

$$
\mathsf{D}' = \mathsf{S}\,\mathsf{D} = \begin{bmatrix} 1 & 0 & 0 \\ 0 & 1 & 0 \\ 0 & 1 & 1 \end{bmatrix} \begin{bmatrix} 1 & 1 & 0 & 1 \\ 1 & 0 & 1 & -1 \\ -1 & 0 & -1 & 1 \end{bmatrix} = \begin{bmatrix} 1 & 1 & 0 & 1 \\ 1 & 0 & 1 & -1 \\ 0 & 0 & 0 & 0 \end{bmatrix}.
$$

The last row of this matrix is zero, so, following adequate loop bound adjustments, the loop indexed by i'_3 can be parallelised in the outermost position of the loop nest:

$$
\begin{array}{ll}
 & \textbf{forall } i'_3 = 2, n_2 + n_3 - 4 \textbf{ do in parallel} \\
 & \quad \textbf{for } i'_1 = 1, n_1 - 1 \textbf{ do} \\
 & \quad\quad \textbf{for } i'_2 = \max\{1, i'_3 - n_3 + 2\}, \min\{n_2 - 2, i'_3 - 1\} \textbf{ do} \\
S_1: & \quad\quad\quad a[i'_1, i'_2, i'_3 - i'_2] = f(a[i'_1 - 1, i'_2 - 1, i'_3 - i'_2 + 1], a[i'_1 - 1, i'_2, i'_3 - i'_2], \\
 & \quad\quad\quad\quad a[i'_1, i'_2 - 1, i'_3 - i'_2 + 1], a[i'_1 - 1, i'_2 + 1, i'_3 - i'_2 - 1])
\end{array}
$$

The scheduling technique presented in the previous section can now be used to generate a communication-free BSP schedule of this loop nest.

5.3.3 Improving the Load Balancing of Communication-Free Scheduling

In the preceding sections, we have devised communication-free parallel schedules of K-level loop nests comprising K' fully parallel loops by applying block$^{K'}$-serial$^{K-K'}$ decomposition to their iteration spaces. As we saw in Section 5.3.1, this approach leads to an optimal BSP schedule whenever the iteration space of the parallelised loop nest is rectangular. However, when used to schedule a non-rectangular iteration space, the method assigns different amounts of work to different processors, generating schedules that may be highly imbalanced. Since non-rectangular iteration spaces appear frequently in imperative programs (or are introduced by loop skewing and other parallelisation-enabling code transformations), this section discusses the usage of block-cyclic partitioning for the reduction of load imbalance in communication-free scheduling.

In block-cyclic partitioning, the iteration space of the target loop nest is partitioned into a number of tiles larger than p, the number of processors. Each processor is then assigned the computation of several of these tiles, many of which are incomplete when the iteration space is non-rectangular.

To describe the technique, consider a generic K-level loop nest $\mathcal{L}$ whose outer K' loops, $1 \le K' \le K$ are fully parallel. As in block$^{K'}$-serial$^{K-K'}$ decomposition, the p processors are arranged into a logical K'-dimensional array of size $p_1 \times p_2 \times \cdots \times p_{K'}$, with $\prod_{k=1}^{K'} p_k = p$. However, while in block partitioning the number of tiles along the

k-th direction of the iteration space, $1 \leq k \leq K'$ is p_k, in block-cyclic partitioning this number is raised to $\alpha_k p_k$, where $\alpha_k \geq 1$ is an integer value called the *block-cyclic decomposition factor* in direction k. This tiling produces $\alpha_1\alpha_2\ldots\alpha_{K'}p$ rectangular tiles of equal size. Notice however that in the general case some of these tiles are incomplete, whereas others may contain no iteration points whatsoever.

The computation of the $\alpha_1\alpha_2\ldots\alpha_{K'}p$ tiles obtained in block-cyclic partitioning is assigned to the p processors in a cyclic fashion. Thus, the tile whose coordinates in the K-dimensional tile space are $(c_1,c_2,\ldots,c_{K'},0,0,\ldots,0)$, $0 \leq c_k < \alpha_k p_k$, $1 \leq k \leq K'$, is computed on the processor with coordinates $(c_1 \bmod p_1, c_2 \bmod p_2, \ldots, c_{K'} \bmod p_{K'})$ in the processor array.

It can be seen immediately that block decomposition is a block-cyclic partitioning with unitary block-cyclic decomposition factor(s). Alternatively, block-cyclic partitioning can be regarded as a block partitioning for an array of $\alpha_1 p_1 \times \alpha_2 p_2 \times \cdots \times \alpha_{K'} p_{K'}$ virtual processors, followed by the cyclic mapping of the virtual processors on the real processors.

When block-cyclic partitioning is used to improve the load balancing of a schedule, supra-unitary block-cyclic decomposition factors need only be used for those directions of the iteration space along which the number of iteration points varies across the computation. We define the load imbalance of a schedule as

$$load\_imbalance = \frac{\max_{0 \leq me < p} \left| W_{me} - \overline{W} \right|}{\overline{W}}, \tag{5.6}$$

where W_{me} represents the amount of computation performed by processor me, $0 \leq me < p$, and $\overline{W} = (\sum_{me=0}^{p-1} W_{me})/p$ is the average processor workload. The use of a block-cyclic decomposition factor α for all directions along which the number of iteration points is non-constant decreases the load imbalance of block decomposition approximately α times.

Example 5.4 The application of block-cyclic decomposition for the scheduling of a triangular loop nest comprising a fully parallel outer loop is illustrated in Figure 5.2. The overall computation cost of this loop nest is $n^2c/2$, where c is the cost of computing the loop body for a single iteration point. Accordingly, the average processor workload is $\overline{W} = n^2c/(2p)$. As processor me, $0 \leq me < p$, computes all the iteration points corresponding to

$$i_1 \in \bigcup_{i=0}^{\alpha-1} (me+ip)\frac{n}{\alpha p} \,..\, (me+ip+1)\frac{n}{\alpha p} - 1,$$

its workload is

$$W_{me} = \sum_{i=0}^{\alpha-1} \left[\frac{n}{\alpha p} \cdot \frac{1}{2} \left((me+ip)\frac{n}{\alpha p} + (me+1+ip)\frac{n}{\alpha p} \right) \right] c =$$

$$\frac{(2me+1+(\alpha-1)p)n^2c}{2\alpha p^2}.$$

forall $i_1 = 0, n-1$ **do in parallel**
  for $i_2 = 0, i_1$ **do**
    loop-body

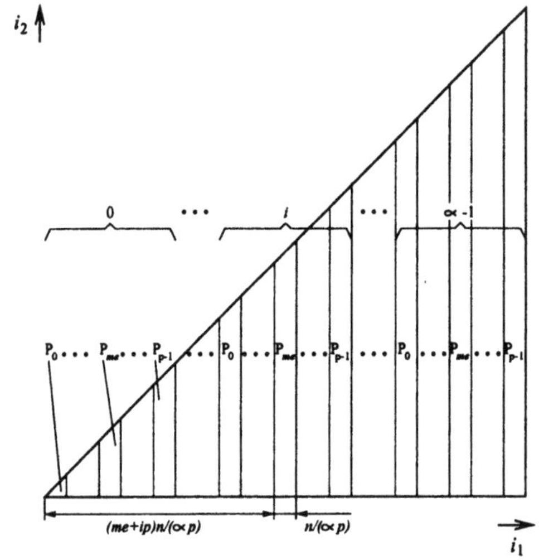

Figure 5.2: A triangular loop nest and the block-cyclic partitioning of its iteration space.

As a result, the load imbalance of this schedule is

$$load\_imbalance = \frac{\overline{W} - W_0}{\overline{W}} = \frac{W_{p-1} - \overline{W}}{\overline{W}} = \frac{p-1}{\alpha p} < \frac{1}{\alpha},$$

i.e. it is at least α times smaller than that of the schedule induced by block partitioning. For instance, a block-cyclic decomposition factor of $\alpha = 10$ is sufficient to obtain a schedule whose load imbalance is less than 0.1 (i.e. for any $0 \le me < p$, $0.9\overline{W} < W_{me} < 1.1\overline{W}$).

5.4 Wavefront Block Scheduling

This section addresses the architecture-independent scheduling of tightly nested loops whose dependences are described by distance vectors that span the entire iteration space. As proved in Theorem 5.1, the use of communication-free scheduling is no longer possible in this case. Consequently, the scheduling technique introduced in this section will first partition the iteration space of a sequential loop nest into interdependent tiles or blocks. It will then use wavefront scheduling to execute these blocks in more than one computation superstep, and in an order that preserves the data dependences among different blocks.

We shall start with the parallelisation of nested loops whose distance dependence vectors comprise only non-negative elements. Since their constituent loops can be legally permuted in any way, these nested loops have been termed *fully permutable loop nests* [16]. Next, we shall describe the extension of the technique to generic

```
for t = 0, Σ_{k=1}^{K} n_k/x_k − K do
  c_1 = t − Σ_{k=1}^{K−1} me_k
  if 0 ≤ c_1 < n_1/x_1 then
    get boundary data computed in previous supersteps and required for
    the computation of the tile with coordinates (c_1, me_1, me_2, ..., me_{K−1})
  bsp_sync
  if 0 ≤ c_1 < n_1/x_1 then
    for i_1 = c_1 x_1, (c_1 + 1)x_1 − 1 do
      for i_2 = me_1 x_2, (me_1 + 1)x_2 − 1 do
      ...
          for i_K = me_{K−1} x_K, (me_{K−1} + 1)x_K − 1 do
            loop_body
```

Figure 5.3: The wavefront block schedule of a fully permutable loop nest.

uniform-dependence loop nests. Given that wavefront block scheduling produces imbalanced schedules even when applied to rectangular iteration spaces, we shall conclude the section by proposing a means of overcoming this serious limitation.

5.4.1 Scheduling Fully Permutable Loop Nests

Consider a generic K-level fully permutable loop nest $\mathcal{L}$, $K \geq 2$, and let $D = \{\mathbf{d}^1, \mathbf{d}^2, \ldots, \mathbf{d}^R\}$ be its set of distance dependence vectors. For ease of exposition, assume that the k-th loop of $\mathcal{L}$, $1 \leq k \leq K$, is indexed by i_k, and iterates from 0 to $n_k - 1$. A nested loop with an identical structure was used in Chapter 4 (Figure 4.1).

In order to schedule the execution of $\mathcal{L}$ on a p-processor parallel computer, its iteration space is first partitioned using the tiling matrix $\mathsf{T} = \mathrm{diag}(x_1, x_2, \ldots, x_K)$, where $x_k \in 1..n_k$, $1 \leq k \leq K$, represent the parameters of the schedule. The last $K-1$ of these parameters must also satisfy the load balancing constraint $\prod_{k=2}^{K} x_k = (\prod_{k=2}^{K} n_k)/p$. For simplicity, we shall additionally assume that, for any $1 \leq k \leq K$, n_k is a multiple of x_k.

The p processors are organised into a logical $(K-1)$-dimensional array of size $p_1 \times p_2 \times \cdots \times p_{K-1}$, where $p_k = n_{k+1}/x_{k+1}$ for all $1 \leq k \leq K-1$. The coordinates of a generic processor in this array are $(me_1, me_2, \ldots, me_{K-1})$, $0 \leq me_k < p_k$ for all $1 \leq k \leq K-1$. With this notation, the computation of the rectangular tiles generated by T is scheduled such that, for all $0 \leq c_1 < n_1/x_1$, processor $(me_1, me_2, \ldots, me_{K-1})$ computes the tile with coordinates $(c_1, me_1, me_2, \ldots, me_{K-1})$ in superstep $c_1 + \sum_{k=1}^{K-1} me_k$. As shown in Figure 5.3, which depicts the pseudocode executed by processor $(me_1, me_2, \ldots, me_{K-1})$, each tile computation is preceded by boundary data transfers between processors that hold neighbouring blocks.

This schedule comprises exactly $\sum_{k=1}^{K} n_k/x_k - K + 1$ supersteps, and any processor is assigned the computation of at most one tile per superstep. The following theorem proves the correctness of the schedule.

Theorem 5.4 *The schedule in Figure 5.3 is correct.*

Proof To prove the theorem it is sufficient to demonstrate that the schedule executes any interdependent iteration points of the parallelised loop nest in the correct order. Consider two such iteration points $\mathbf{i}^1 < \mathbf{i}^2$. As $\mathbf{i}^1$ and $\mathbf{i}^2$ are interdependent, $\mathbf{i}^2 = \mathbf{i}^1 + \mathbf{d}$ for some $\mathbf{d} \in D$. Moreover, $\mathbf{d}$ has only non-negative elements, so $i_k^1 \leq i_k^2$ for any $1 \leq k \leq K$. Thus, if $(c_1^1, c_2^1, \ldots, c_K^1)$ and $(c_1^2, c_2^2, \ldots, c_K^2)$ represent the coordinates of the tiles that contain the two iteration points, we have:

$$\forall k \in 1..K \bullet c_k^1 = \lfloor i_k^1 / x_k \rfloor \leq \lfloor i_k^2 / x_k \rfloor = c_k^2.$$

Hence, t_1 and t_2, the supersteps in which $\mathbf{i}^1$ and $\mathbf{i}^2$ are executed, satisfy:

$$t_1 = \sum_{k=1}^{K} c_k^1 \leq \sum_{k=1}^{K} c_k^2 = t_2,$$

with the equality holding only if $c_k^1 = c_k^2$ for any $1 \leq k \leq K$, i.e. only if $\mathbf{i}^1$ and $\mathbf{i}^2$ belong to the same tile. Or, in other words, either $\mathbf{i}^1$ is computed in a superstep which precedes the superstep when $\mathbf{i}^2$ is computed, or both iteration points belong to the same tile. In the first case, $\mathbf{i}^1$ is clearly computed before $\mathbf{i}^2$. This also holds in the second case because the execution order of iteration points belonging to the same tile is not changed by the schedule. Thus, the two iteration points are executed in the correct order under any circumstances. □

Let us analyse the cost of the schedule in Figure 5.3. As each processor computes at most one tile per superstep, the computation cost of any superstep is given by the product between $\prod_{k=1}^{K} x_k$, the volume of a tile, and c, the cost of computing the loop body for a single iteration point:

$$Comp = \prod_{k=1}^{K} x_k \, c = x_1 \frac{\prod_{k=2}^{K} n_k}{p} c = \frac{x_1}{n_1} \frac{\prod_{k=1}^{K} n_k \, c}{p}.$$

Assuming that the R data dependences of $\mathcal{L}$ are flow dependences requiring the inter-processor communication of disjoint data, and using the result in Corollary 4.7, we obtain the value of the communication cost per superstep:

$$\begin{aligned}
Comm &= g \sum_{\mathbf{d} \in D} \left(\prod_{k=1}^{K} x_k - x_1 \prod_{k=2}^{K} (x_k - |d_k|) \right) = \\
&= g \sum_{\mathbf{d} \in D} (x_1 d_2 x_3 \ldots x_K + x_1 x_2 d_3 \ldots x_K + \cdots + x_1 x_2 x_3 \ldots d_K)(1 + \mathrm{o}(1)) = \\
&= g \prod_{k=1}^{K} x_k \sum_{\mathbf{d} \in D} \left(\frac{d_2}{x_2} + \frac{d_3}{x_3} + \cdots + \frac{d_K}{x_K} \right) (1 + \mathrm{o}(1)) = \\
&= g x_1 \frac{\prod_{k=2}^{K} n_k}{p} \sum_{k=2}^{K} \frac{\sum_{\mathbf{d} \in D} d_k}{x_k} (1 + \mathrm{o}(1)).
\end{aligned}$$

Notice that the data dependences along the first direction of the iteration space do not contribute to the communication overhead because the tiles along this direction are scheduled on the same processor. Furthermore, since the loop nest is fully permutable, this direction can be arbitrarily chosen. As a result, whenever the sizes of the iteration space in the K dimensions are comparable, the communication cost can be decreased by generating the schedule after a preliminary stage in which a loop $k_0 \in 1..K$ that satisfies

$$\sum_{\mathbf{d} \in D} d_{k_0} = \max_{1 \le k \le K} \sum_{\mathbf{d} \in D} d_k$$

is brought into the outermost position of the loop nest.

Next, the values of the parameters $x_2, x_3, \ldots, x_k$ are fixed so as to minimise the communication cost per tile, subject to the constraint $\prod_{k=2}^{K} x_k = (\prod_{k=2}^{K} n_k)/p$. To determine these values, we take into account the fact that $\sum_{\mathbf{d} \in D} d_k \neq 0$ for all $1 \le k \le K$ (otherwise, $\mathcal{L}$ can be parallelised using communication-free scheduling), and we apply the Lagrange multiplier rule in the manner described in Section 5.3.1. Consequently, the sought parameter values are found to form the solution of the system

$$\begin{cases} \frac{\sum_{\mathbf{d} \in D} d_2}{x_2} = \frac{\sum_{\mathbf{d} \in D} d_3}{x_3} = \cdots = \frac{\sum_{\mathbf{d} \in D} d_K}{x_K} \\ \prod_{k=2}^{K} x_k = \frac{\prod_{k=2}^{K} n_k}{p} \end{cases}.$$

The solution of this system is

$$x_k = \sum_{\mathbf{d} \in D} d_k \sqrt[K-1]{\frac{\prod_{k'=2}^{K} n_{k'}}{p \prod_{k'=2}^{K} \sum_{\mathbf{d} \in D} d_{k'}}}, \qquad \text{for all } 2 \le k \le K,$$

and the associated communication cost is

$$Comm = (K-1) g x_1 \frac{\prod_{k=2}^{K} n_k}{p} \sqrt[K-1]{\frac{p \prod_{k=2}^{K} \sum_{\mathbf{d} \in D} d_k}{\prod_{k=2}^{K} n_k}} (1 + o(1)) = \frac{g x_1 \alpha_{comm} (1 + o(1))}{n_1 p^{(K-2)/(K-1)}},$$

where $\alpha_{comm} = (K-1) \prod_{k=1}^{K} n_k (\prod_{k=2}^{K} \sum_{\mathbf{d} \in D} d_k / \prod_{k=2}^{K} n_k)^{1/(K-1)}$ represents a constant that depends on the structure of $\mathcal{L}$. In particular, when the iteration space to be parallelised is a K-dimensional hypercube (i.e. when $n_1 = n_2 = \cdots = n_K = n$), and $\sum_{\mathbf{d} \in D} d_k = 1$ for all $1 \le k \le K$, we obtain $x_2 = x_3 = \cdots = x_K = n/p^{1/(K-1)}$ and $Comm = (K-1) g x_1 n^{K-2} (1 + o(1))/p^{(K-2)/(K-1)}$.

According to the results obtained so far, the cost of each superstep of the BSP schedule in Figure 5.3 is

$$L + \frac{x_1}{n_1} \frac{\prod_{k=1}^{K} n_k c}{p} + \frac{g x_1 \alpha_{comm} (1 + o(1))}{n_1 p^{(K-2)/(K-1)}}.$$

Before assessing the overall cost of the schedule, we notice that $\sum_{k=1}^{K} n_k / x_k - K + 1$, its number of supersteps, is bounded above by $n_1/x_1 + p - 1$. To prove this, consider the function $h : [1, \infty)^m \to \mathbf{R}, m > 0, h(y_1, y_2, \ldots, y_m) = y_1 + y_2 + \cdots + y_m - y_1 y_2 \ldots y_m$. Since $\nabla h(1, 1, \ldots, 1) = \mathbf{0}$ and $\nabla h(y_1, y_2, \ldots, y_m)$ has only non-positive components if $(y_1, y_2, \ldots, y_m) \in [1, \infty)^m \setminus \{(1, 1, \ldots, 1)\}$, we necessarily have $h(y_1, y_2, \ldots, y_m) \le$

$h(1,1,\ldots,1) = m-1$ for all $(y_1,y_2,\ldots,y_m) \in [1,\infty)^m$. By taking $m = K-1$ and $y_1 = n_2/x_2, y_2 = n_3/x_3, \ldots, y_{K-1} = n_K/x_K$ in this inequality, we obtain:

$$\sum_{k=2}^{K} \frac{n_k}{x_k} - \prod_{k=2}^{K} \frac{n_k}{x_k} \le K-2,$$

or, using the fact that $\prod_{k=2}^{K} n_k/x_k = p$, $\sum_{k=2}^{K} n_k/x_k \le p+K-2$. Hence, the number of schedule supersteps satisfies $\sum_{k=1}^{K} n_k/x_k - K + 1 \le n_1/x_1 + p - 1$, and the overall cost of the schedule is bounded above by

$$\left(\frac{n_1}{x_1} + p - 1\right)L + \left(1 + \frac{(p-1)x_1}{n_1}\right)\frac{\prod_{k=1}^{K} n_k\, c}{p} + \left(1 + \frac{(p-1)x_1}{n_1}\right)\frac{g\alpha_{\text{comm}}(1+o(1))}{p^{(K-2)/(K-1)}}. \quad (5.7)$$

The three terms of the above cost stand for the synchronisation overheads, computation cost, and communication overheads, respectively. It can be immediately seen that the communication overheads decrease and the computation cost approaches one-optimality when x_1 decreases. On the other hand, any decrease in the value of x_1 increases the number of supersteps and therefore the synchronisation overheads.

In order to perceive the efficiency of the schedule before finding the value of x_1 that minimises the above upper bound, consider for instance that $x_1 = n_1/(p-1)$. In this case, the cost of the schedule will be bounded above by

$$2(p-1)L + 2\frac{\prod_{k=1}^{K} n_k\, c}{p} + 2g(K-1)\prod_{k=1}^{K} n_k \left(\frac{\prod_{k=2}^{K}\sum_{\mathbf{d}\in D} d_k}{p^{K-2}\prod_{k=2}^{K} n_k}\right)^{1/(K-1)}.$$

This instance of the schedule is two-optimal in computation, and has a number of supersteps which is independent on the problem size. The entire schedule achieves optimal $O(\prod_{k=1}^{K} n_k\, c/p)$ cost if the synchronisation and communication overheads are dominated by the cost of computation, i.e. if

$$L \le \frac{\prod_{k=1}^{K} n_k}{p^2} \quad \text{and} \quad g \le \left(\frac{\prod_{k=2}^{K} n_k}{p\prod_{k=2}^{K}\sum_{\mathbf{d}\in D} d_k}\right)^{1/(K-1)}.$$

These requirements can be easily fulfilled for average problem sizes.

Having emphasised the effectiveness of the wavefront block scheduling technique, we can now concentrate on determining the value of x_1 that minimises expression (5.7).[1] Since this value corresponds to the zero of the derivative of this expression with respect to x_1, it can be obtained by solving the equation:

$$-\frac{n_1 L}{x_1^2} + \frac{p-1}{n_1}\frac{\prod_{k=1}^{K} n_k\, c}{p} + \frac{p-1}{n_1}\frac{g\alpha_{\text{comm}}}{p^{(K-2)/(K-1)}} = 0.$$

[1] Clearly, the schedule corresponding to this value will better the one obtained for $x_1 = n_1/(p-1)$.

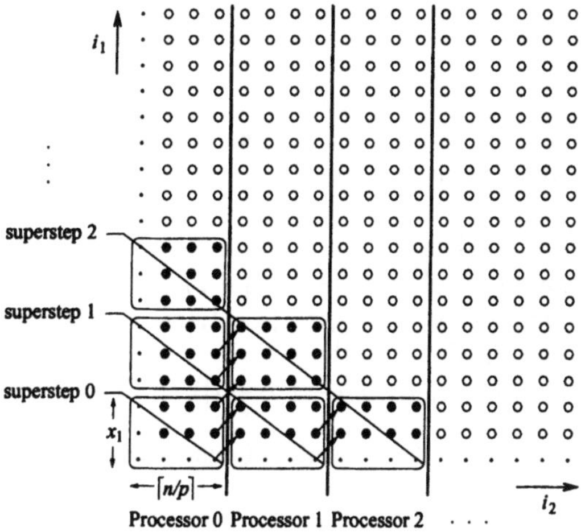

Figure 5.4: The wavefront block scheduling of the loop nest in Example 5.5.

As a result, the value of x_1 which induces the optimal schedule is

$$x_1 = \left\lceil n_1 \sqrt{\frac{pL}{(p-1)\left(\prod_{k=1}^{K} n_k\, c + g\alpha_{\text{comm}} p^{1/(K-1)}\right)}} \right\rceil . \tag{5.8}$$

This value depends both on the problem structure and on the parameters of the parallel computer on which the schedule is executed, and can be obtained at run time.

Example 5.5 In order to illustrate the usage of wavefront block scheduling, we shall apply it to the following 2-level fully permutable loop nest:

for $i_1 = 1, n-1$ **do**
  for $i_2 = 1, n-1$ **do**
    $a[i_1, i_2] = f_1(a[i_1 - 1, i_2])$
    $b[i_1, i_2] = f_2(a[i_1, i_2], b[i_1 - 1, i_2 - 1])$

The three data dependences of this loop nest are encoded by the distance vectors in the set $D = \{[1,0]^{\mathrm{T}}, [0,0]^{\mathrm{T}}, [1,1]^{\mathrm{T}}\}$. As all the elements of these distance vectors are non-negative, the loop nest is fully permutable and can be scheduled using the technique described in this section. Thus, the iteration space is partitioned into rectangular blocks using the tiling matrix $\mathsf{T} = \mathrm{diag}(x_1, x_2)$. Since $\sum_{\mathbf{d} \in D} d_1 = 2$ and $\sum_{\mathbf{d} \in D} d_2 = 1$, the tiles along the direction corresponding to the loop indexed by i_1 are assigned to the same processor. It follows immediately that $x_2 = \lceil n/p \rceil$.

The iteration space partitioning, the tile assignment to processors and supersteps, and the dependences that need to be satisfied through inter-processor communication are depicted in Figure 5.4. Each processor *me*, $0 \le me < p$, executes the following code:

for $t = 0, \lceil n/x_1 \rceil + p - 2$ **do**
  $c_1 = t - me$
  if $0 \leq c_1 < \lceil n/x_1 \rceil$ **and** $me > 0$ **then**
    bsp_get $b[\max\{0, c_1x_1 - 1\}..\min\{n-2, (c_1+1)x_1 - 2\}, me\lceil n/p \rceil - 1]$
        from processor $me - 1$
  bsp_sync
  if $0 \leq c_1 < \lceil n/x_1 \rceil$ **then**
    for $i_1 = \max\{1, c_1x_1\}, \min\{n-1, (c_1+1)x_1 - 1\}$ **do**
      for $i_2 = \max\{1, me\lceil n/p \rceil\}, \min\{n-1, (me+1)\lceil n/p \rceil - 1\}$ **do**
        $a[i_1, i_2] = f_1(a[i_1 - 1, i_2])$
        $b[i_1, i_2] = f_2(a[i_1, i_2], b[i_1 - 1, i_2 - 1])$

According to (5.7), the cost of the schedule is bounded above by

$$\left(\frac{n}{x_1} + p - 1\right)L + \left(1 + \frac{(p-1)x_1}{n}\right)\frac{n^2 c}{p} + \left(1 + \frac{(p-1)x_1}{n}\right)gn(1 + o(1)),$$

where $c = cost(f_1) + cost(f_2)$. Notice that for this particular example the number of supersteps is exactly $\lceil n/x_1 \rceil + p - 1$, so the schedule cost actually attains this upper bound. (In fact, the upper bound given by (5.7) is tight for most practical values of K and p.) As a result, the best schedule is obtained for

$$x_1 = \left\lceil \sqrt{\frac{pL}{(p-1)(c + gp/n)}} \right\rceil .$$

This schedule achieves $O(n^2/p)$ optimal cost if $L \leq n/p$, $g \leq n/p$. Furthermore, with the notation introduced in equation (2.2), the synchronisation and communication overheads $N(n,p)L + gH(n,p)$ satisfy

$$N(n,p)L + gH(n,p) = \left(1 + \frac{(p-1)x_1}{n}\right)\left(\frac{n}{x_1}L + gn\right) \leq$$
$$\leq \left(1 + \frac{(p-1)x_1}{n}\right)n(L+g) = \frac{p(L+g)}{cn}W(n,p).$$

It follows that n_ε, the minimum value of n for which $N(n,p)L + gH(n,p) \leq \varepsilon W(n,p)$, satisfies $n_\varepsilon \leq p(L+g)/(c\varepsilon)$.

5.4.2 Extension to Generic Uniform-Dependence Loop Nests

Before parallelising a generic uniform-dependence loop nest by means of wavefront block scheduling, it has to be converted into a fully permutable loop nest. This conversion is achieved by applying an appropriate affine transformation to its iteration space. As fully permutable loop nests are very convenient to manipulate, they are regarded as the normalised form of uniform-dependence loop nests [16], and the identification of such affine transformations has been extensively studied [16, 23, 24, 42, 74].

It is worth noticing that the affine transformation of a loop nest followed by its partitioning into rectangular tiles is entirely equivalent to the tiling of the original iteration space with hyperplanes normal to the rows of the affine transformation matrix. Therefore, strategies for finding an appropriate affine transformation of the loop nest are often introduced as tiling techniques; no real difference exists between the two ways of modelling the problem.

This section presents a brief overview of the techniques for the conversion of generic loop nests into fully permutable loop nests reported so far; no new result is provided. A formal description of the problem follows.

Let $\mathcal{L}$ be a K-level uniform-dependence loop nest, $K \geq 2$, and $D = \{\mathbf{d}^1, \mathbf{d}^2, \ldots, \mathbf{d}^R\}$, $R > 0$, its set of distance dependence vectors, some of which have negative elements. The $K \times K$ matrix S of an affine transformation is sought such that for all $\mathbf{d} \in D$, $\mathbf{d}^+ = \mathbf{Sd}$, the distance vector corresponding to $\mathbf{d}$ in the transformed iteration space, comprises only non-negative elements. If we let D, D^+ be the $K \times R$ matrices whose columns are the R distance vectors in the original and in the transformed iteration space, respectively, this requirement may be rewritten [24] as

$$\mathsf{D}^+ = \mathsf{S} \cdot \mathsf{D} \geq 0, \tag{5.9}$$

where 0 stands for the $K \times R$ matrix with all elements 0, and '$\geq$' is applied to all corresponding pairs of elements from its two matrix operands.

Since distance vectors are lexicographically positive, an affine transformation S satisfying (5.9) always exists. Moreover, the solution of (5.9) is not unique, and a carefully chosen criterion must be used to select a suitable transformation. Two different criteria have been advocated so far: the simplicity of the solution, and the minimisation of an estimated communication to computation ratio for the tiles of the transformed iteration space.

Wolf and Lam [16] for instance, propose an $O(K^2R)$ algorithm which computes a lower triangular transformation S satisfying (5.9). As the authors do not consider the scheduling of the transformed iteration space onto a distributed-memory parallel computer, the criterion they use is the simplicity of the resulting transformation.

A different strategy has been adopted in [23], where a heuristic is employed to search the solution space for a *blocking* (i.e. tiling) that minimises the ratio between the surface area and the volume of the resulting tiles.[2] The affine transformation corresponding to the blocking selected by this heuristic can be used to convert a generic uniform-dependence loop nest into a fully permutable loop nest.

Another approach is due to Ramanujam and Sadayappan [24, 74], who, based on results introduced in [64], formulate the following linear programming problem whose solution is a unimodular lower-triangular transformation S:

Find $S = [s_{k,j}]$, $s_{k,j} = 0$ for all $1 \leq k < j \leq K$, $s_{k,k} = 1$ for all $1 \leq k \leq K$, that minimises

$$Comm = \sum_{\mathbf{d}^+ \in \{\mathsf{Sd}^1, \mathsf{Sd}^2, \ldots, \mathsf{Sd}^R\}} \sum_{k=1}^{K} d_k^+ = \sum_{\mathbf{d} \in D} \sum_{k=1}^{K} \left(\sum_{j=1}^{k-1} s_{k,j} d_j + d_k \right)$$

[2]As explained in Section 4.2, this is a crude approximation of the communication to computation ratio.

subject to

$$\sum_{j=1}^{k-1} s_{k,j}d_j + d_k = d_k^+ \geq 0 \text{ for all } \mathbf{d} \in D,\ 2 \leq k \leq K.$$

Clearly, $x^{K-1}Comm$ approximates the amount of communication required for the computation of a K-dimensional hypercubic tile of size $x \times x \times \cdots \times x$ of the transformed iteration space. An optimal lower-triangular transformation S satisfying (5.9) can be obtained by solving the above linear programming problem for the exact communication cost, computed as indicated in Chapter 4.

Finally, in [42], Boulet et al. argue that minimising the total communication overheads or the communication to computation ratio per tile is very difficult. Hence, they devise a method that yields, for any fixed amount of computation per tile, a legal tiling which minimises *Comm*, the approximation of the communication overheads proposed by Ramanujam and Sadayappan [24, 74]. In particular, when the dependence matrix D is a square matrix, the matrix of the affine transformation generated by this method is $\mathsf{S} = \mathsf{D}^{-1}$ (recall that D is non-singular), which is optimal under all circumstances.

5.4.3 Improving the Load Balancing of Wavefront Block Scheduling

Due to the existence of idle processors in the supersteps at the beginning and end of the schedules it generates, wavefront block scheduling produces workload-imbalanced parallel code even when applied to rectangular iteration spaces. As in the case of communication-free scheduling, this serious limitation can be overcome by adding block-cyclic decomposition to the basic wavefront block scheduling technique. Block-cyclic decomposition works by decreasing the granularity of the parallelism exploited in each superstep of the parallel schedule in order to improve the distribution of computation among processors. A formal description of the method follows.

Let $\mathcal{L}$ be a K-level fully permutable loop nest, and $I = 0..n_1 - 1 \times 0..n_2 - 1 \times \cdots \times 0..n_K - 1$ the smallest rectangular iteration space that contains all the iteration points of $\mathcal{L}$. With the notation introduced in Section 5.4.1, assume that the application of the basic technique to the iteration space I requires the use of the tiling matrix $\mathsf{T} = \mathrm{diag}(x_1, x_2, \ldots, x_K)$. Given the block-cyclic decomposition factors $\alpha_k \geq 1, 2 \leq k \leq K$, the enhanced technique partitions the iteration space of $\mathcal{L}$ by means of the tiling matrix $\mathsf{T}' = \mathrm{diag}(x_1, x_2/\alpha_2, \ldots, x_K/\alpha_K)$.

The processor organisation is identical with that used by the basic schedule: the p processors are arranged into a logical $(K-1)$-dimensional array of size $p_1 \times p_2 \times \cdots \times p_{K-1}$, where for all $1 \leq k \leq K-1$, $p_k = n_{k+1}/x_{k+1}$. However, the tiling employed by the enhanced technique generates $\alpha_k p_k$ tiles in the $(k+1)$-th direction of the iteration space, $1 \leq k \leq K-1$, instead of only the p_k tiles generated by the basic technique. These tiles are assigned to the p_k processors available in the $(k+1)$-th direction of the iteration space in a cyclic fashion. Thus, a generic tile with coordinates $(c_1, c_2, \ldots, c_K)$, $0 \leq c_k < n_k/p_k$, is executed in superstep $\sum_{k=1}^{K} c_k$, on the processor whose coordinates in the processor array are $(c_2 \mod p_1, c_3 \mod p_2, \ldots, c_K \mod p_{K-1})$.

Being mostly designed for the parallelisation of non-rectangular loop nests, the scheduling technique introduced in this section yields schedules whose cost has to be individually analysed for each case in point. As a general remark, by suitably choosing the block-cyclic decomposition factors (i.e. by using supra-unitary factors for the directions in which the number of iteration points varies across the iteration space), one-optimality in computation can be approached in most practical cases. Since this improvement in the workload distribution is achieved at the expense of an increase in the synchronisation and communication overheads, block-cyclic decomposition should always be applied to wavefront block scheduling with some degree of caution.

5.5 Iterative Scheduling

Iterative scheduling represents an alternative to the wavefront block scheduling of uniform-dependence loop nests. It is itself a variant of wavefront parallelisation, and works by performing the iterations of the outermost loop of a loop nest in different, consecutive supersteps (hence the name of the technique). The main advantage of this scheduling technique is its extreme simplicity. Thus, when non-fully permutable nested loops are to be parallelised and iterative scheduling is applicable, it does not require a preliminary affine transformation of the iteration space as in the case when wavefront block scheduling is used. As we shall see in this section, the price that must be paid for this straightforwardness is an increased synchronisation cost.

5.5.1 Description of the Technique

Consider a K-level uniform-dependence loop nest $\mathcal{L}$, $K \geq 2$, and let $D = \{\mathbf{d}^1, \mathbf{d}^2, \ldots, \mathbf{d}^R\}$ be its set of distance dependence vectors. Also assume that $\text{rank}[\mathbf{d}^1, \mathbf{d}^2, \ldots, \mathbf{d}^R] = K$: in all other cases, the usage of communication-free scheduling is possible and preferable. If for some $k_0 \in 1..K$ we have

$$\forall \mathbf{d} \in D \bullet d_{k_0} > 0 \tag{5.10}$$

(i.e. if there is a loop which carries all the data dependences), $\mathcal{L}$ can be parallelised using iterative scheduling as follows.

Firstly, the k_0-th loop of $\mathcal{L}$ is brought into the outermost position. This is a legal transformation because any data dependence of $\mathcal{L}$ relates two iteration points whose k_0-th coordinates are different, and the execution order of such pairs of iteration points is preserved by the transformation. For the same reason, all the iterations of the inner loops can be performed concurrently provided that the k_0-th loop is kept sequential in the outermost position.

For ease of exposition, assume that for any $1 \leq k \leq K$ the k-th loop of the transformed loop nest is indexed by i_k and iterates from 0 to $n_k - 1$. In this case, the iteration space is partitioned using the tiling matrix $\mathsf{T} = \text{diag}(n_1, x_2, x_3, \ldots, x_K)$, with $x_2, x_3, \ldots, x_K$ chosen so as to minimise the communication overheads of the resulting schedule, under the load balancing constraint $\prod_{k=2}^{K} x_k = (\prod_{k=2}^{K} n_k)/p$.

```
for i_1 = 0, n_1 - 1 do
  get halo data required for the current iteration of the schedule
  bsp_sync
  for i_2 = me_1 x_2, (me_1 + 1)x_2 - 1 do
    ...
      for i_K = me_{K-1} x_K, (me_{K-1} + 1)x_K - 1 do
        loop_body
```

Figure 5.5: The iterative schedule of a K-level uniform-dependence loop nest.

The p processors are viewed as arranged into a logical $(K-1)$-dimensional array of size $n_2/x_2 \times n_3/x_3 \times \cdots \times n_K/x_K$, with a generic processor having the coordinates $(me_1, me_2, \ldots, me_{K-1})$, $0 \le me_k < n_{k+1}/x_{k+1}$, $1 \le k \le K-1$, in this array. The iterative schedule comprises n_1 supersteps, one for each iteration of the outermost loop of $\mathcal{L}$. During these supersteps, the processor $(me_1, me_2, \ldots, me_{K-1})$ computes the tile with coordinates $(0, me_1, me_2, \ldots, me_{K-1})$.

As shown by the code assigned to processor $(me_1, me_2, \ldots, me_{K-1})$ (Figure 5.5), this is done such that in the iteration i_1 of the outermost loop each processor executes the iteration points that belong to its tile and whose first coordinate is i_1. Before the actual computation of these iteration points, however, the processors get the remote data obtained in previous iterations of the outermost loop and required for this computation. Given the dependence pattern of the loop nest, these remote data are available from neighbour processors, and are therefore termed *halo data*.

In order to analyse the performance of the n_1-superstep iterative schedule described so far, we need to assess its computation and communication costs. For the computation cost, it is enough to notice that the $\prod_{k=2}^{K} n_k$ iteration points computed in each superstep are equally distributed among the p processors. Therefore, the schedule is one-optimal in computation, and the overall computation cost is exactly

$$\frac{\prod_{k=1}^{K} n_k \, c}{p},$$

where c represents the cost of computing the loop body of $\mathcal{L}$ for a single iteration point.

As concerns the communication cost of a superstep, we are interested in finding *Comm*, the amount of tile-external data required for the computation of a rectangular tile of size $1 \times x_2 \times x_3 \times \cdots \times x_K$ of $\mathcal{L}$. Indeed, it is such a tile that the processors compute in each superstep. For the case when the R data dependences of $\mathcal{L}$ are flow dependences and require the inter-processor communication of disjoint data, it follows from Corollary 4.7 that

$$Comm = \sum_{\mathbf{d} \in D} \left(\prod_{k=2}^{K} x_k - \prod_{k=2}^{K} (x_k - |d_k|) \right) = \frac{\prod_{k=2}^{K} n_k}{p} \sum_{\mathbf{d} \in D} \sum_{k=2}^{K} \frac{|d_k|}{x_k} (1 + o(1)).$$

Hence, the cost of the entire iterative schedule is given by

$$n_1 L + \frac{\prod_{k=1}^{K} n_k}{p} c + g \frac{\prod_{k=1}^{K} n_k}{p} \sum_{\mathbf{d} \in D} \sum_{k=2}^{K} \frac{|d_k|}{x_k}. \tag{5.11}$$

The BSP schedule is one-optimal in computation, and has optimal $O((\prod_{k=1}^{K} n_k)/p)$ cost if $L \leq (\prod_{k=2}^{K} n_k)/p$, $g \leq \left(\sum_{\mathbf{d} \in D} \sum_{k=2}^{K} \frac{|d_k|}{x_k}\right)^{-1}$.

Example 5.6 Consider the following 3-level uniform-dependence loop nest:

$$\begin{array}{l} \textbf{for } i_1 = 1, n-1 \textbf{ do} \\ \quad \textbf{for } i_2 = 1, n-2 \textbf{ do} \\ \quad\quad \textbf{for } i_3 = 1, n-2 \textbf{ do} \\ \quad\quad\quad a[i_1,i_2,i_3] = f(a[i_1-1,i_2-1,i_3], a[i_1-1,i_2+1,i_3], \\ \quad\quad\quad\quad\quad\quad\quad a[i_1-1,i_2,i_3-1], a[i_1-1,i_2,i_3+1]) \end{array}$$

As its set of distance dependence vectors is $D = \{[1,1,0]^{\mathrm{T}}, [1,-1,0]^{\mathrm{T}}, [1,0,1]^{\mathrm{T}}, [1,0,-1]^{\mathrm{T}}\}$, this loop nest can be parallelised using iterative scheduling, with the loop indexed by i_1 in the outermost position. The iteration space is partitioned using the tiling matrix $\mathsf{T} = \mathrm{diag}(n, x_2, x_3)$, $x_2 x_3 = n^2/p$. According to (5.11), the communication cost of the resulting schedule is

$$g\frac{n^3}{p} \sum_{\mathbf{d} \in D} \left(\frac{|d_2|}{x_2} + \frac{|d_3|}{x_3}\right) = g\frac{n^3}{p}\left(\frac{2}{x_2} + \frac{2}{x_3}\right).$$

It follows from the relation between the arithmetic and geometric means of x_2 and x_3 that this cost is minimised when $x_2 = x_3 = n/\sqrt{p}$.

Assuming that $\sqrt{p}$ is an integer value, the processors are regarded as organised into a logical $\sqrt{p} \times \sqrt{p}$ array, and the processor with coordinates (me_1, me_2), $0 \leq me_1, me_2 < \sqrt{p}$, in this array executes the code presented in Figure 5.6. The tiles computed by a generic, non-boundary processor (me_1, me_2) in two successive supersteps of the schedule are depicted in Figure 5.7. The cost of this iterative schedule is

$$nL + \frac{n^3 cost(f)}{p} + \frac{4gn^2}{\sqrt{p}},$$

so the schedule is one-optimal in computation and achieves optimal $O(n^3/p)$ execution time if $L \leq n^2/p$, $g \leq n/\sqrt{p}$. Furthermore, a practical implementation of this BSP schedule is expected to yield a speedup of at least $p/(1+\varepsilon)$, $\varepsilon > 0$, if the problem size satisfies

$$n \geq n_\varepsilon = \frac{2g\sqrt{p} + \sqrt{4pg^2 + \varepsilon pL\, cost(f)}}{\varepsilon\, cost(f)}.$$

For a typical parallel computer with $p = 8$, $g = 6$ and $L = 600$, and for $cost(f) = 5$, we obtain $n_{0.2} \approx 110$. This result shows that close to optimal speedups can be obtained starting from average problem sizes.

for $i_1 = 1, n-1$ **do**
  if $me_1 > 0$ **then**
    bsp_get $a[i_1{-}1, me_1\lceil n/\sqrt{p}\rceil{-}1, \max\{1, me_2\lceil n/\sqrt{p}\rceil\}..\min\{n{-}2, (me_2{+}1)\lceil n/\sqrt{p}\rceil{-}1\}]$
        from processor (me_1-1, me_2)
  if $me_1 < \sqrt{p}-1$ **then**
    bsp_get $a[i_1{-}1, (me_1{+}1)\lceil n/\sqrt{p}\rceil, \max\{1, me_2\lceil n/\sqrt{p}\rceil\}..\min\{n{-}2, (me_2{+}1)\lceil n/\sqrt{p}\rceil{-}1\}]$
        from processor (me_1+1, me_2)
  if $me_2 > 0$ **then**
    bsp_get $a[i_1{-}1, \max\{1, me_1\lceil n/\sqrt{p}\rceil\}..\min\{n{-}2, (me_1{+}1)\lceil n/\sqrt{p}\rceil{-}1\}, me_2\lceil n/\sqrt{p}\rceil{-}1]$
        from processor (me_1, me_2-1)
  if $me_2 < \sqrt{p}-1$ **then**
    bsp_get $a[i_1{-}1, \max\{1, me_1\lceil n/\sqrt{p}\rceil\}..\min\{n{-}2, (me_1{+}1)\lceil n/\sqrt{p}\rceil{-}1\}, (me_2{+}1)\lceil n/\sqrt{p}\rceil]$
        from processor (me_1, me_2+1)
  bsp_sync
  for $i_2 = \max\{1, me_1\lceil n/\sqrt{p}\rceil\}, \min\{n-2, (me_1+1)\lceil n/\sqrt{p}\rceil - 1\}$ **do**
    for $i_3 = \max\{1, me_2\lceil n/\sqrt{p}\rceil\}, \min\{n-2, (me_2+1)\lceil n/\sqrt{p}\rceil - 1\}$ **do**
      $a[i_1, i_2, i_3] = f(a[i_1{-}1, i_2{-}1, i_3], a[i_1{-}1, i_2{+}1, i_3], a[i_1{-}1, i_2, i_3{-}1], a[i_1{-}1, i_2, i_3{+}1])$

Figure 5.6: Parallel schedule for Example 5.6.

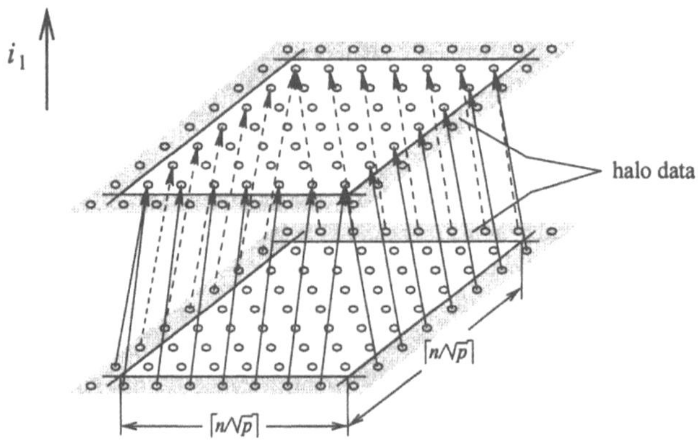

Figure 5.7: The tiles computed by a non-boundary processor in two successive supersteps of the iterative schedule in Example 5.6.

5.5.2 Extension to Generic Loops and Load Balancing

As in the case of other scheduling techniques, we can discuss the extension of iterative scheduling to generic uniform-dependence loop nests, and the load balancing of the iterative schedules of non-rectangular iteration spaces.

In order to apply iterative scheduling to uniform-dependence loop nests comprising no loop that carries all the data dependences, their iteration space must be skewed first using an appropriate affine transformation. For a K-level loop nest $\mathcal{L}$, $K \geq 2$, the

$K \times K$ matrix S of a suitable affine transformation must satisfy

$$\exists k_0 \in 1..K \bullet \forall \mathbf{d} \in D \bullet \mathbf{d}' = \mathsf{S}\mathbf{d} \Rightarrow d'_{k_0} > 0, \tag{5.12}$$

where D denotes the set of distance dependence vectors of $\mathcal{L}$. As the distance vectors in D are lexicographically positive, a transformation S satisfying (5.12) for $k_0 = 1$ and having the form

$$\mathsf{S} = \left[\begin{array}{c|ccc} \beta_1 & \beta_2 & \dots & \beta_K \\ \hline 0 & & & \\ \vdots & & \mathsf{I}_{K-1} & \\ 0 & & & \end{array}\right]$$

always exists, and the skewing factors $\beta_k \geq 0, 1 \leq k \leq K$ can be computed in $O(K\, \#D)$ time along the lines of the techniques described in [17, 21, 62, 78].

As concerns the load balancing of the iterative schedules of non-rectangular loop nests, this can be achieved by employing block-cyclic decomposition in a similar way to that presented in the section on communication-free scheduling. Thus, assume that the iteration space to be parallelised is a subset of $I = 0..n_1 - 1 \times 0..n_2 - 1 \times \cdots \times 0..n_K - 1$, and is not enclosed in any smaller K-dimensional lattice. Under this assumption, it is first tiled using the tiling matrix $\mathsf{T} = \mathrm{diag}(n_1, x_2/\alpha_2, x_3/\alpha_3, \dots, x_K/\alpha_K)$, where $\prod_{k=2}^{K} x_k = (\prod_{k=2}^{K} n_k)/p$, and $\alpha_k \geq 1, 2 \leq k \leq K$, denote the block-cyclic decomposition factors.

With the notation introduced in the previous section, processor $(me_1, me_2, \dots, me_{K-1})$ is assigned the execution of all tiles whose coordinates $(0, c_2, c_3, \dots, c_K)$ satisfy

$$\forall k \in 2..K \bullet c_k \mod (n_k/x_k) = me_{k-1}.$$

As in the case of the basic iterative scheduling technique (which corresponds to $\alpha_2 = \alpha_3 = \cdots = \alpha_K = 1$), the computation takes a superstep for each iteration of the outermost loop. In each of these supersteps, the processors execute all iteration points belonging to one of their tiles, and to the current iteration of the outermost loop.

5.5.3 Comparison with Wavefront Block Scheduling

Both wavefront block scheduling and iterative scheduling can be used to parallelise a uniform-dependence loop nest whose iteration space is entirely spanned by the distance vectors of its data dependences. Two criteria are available for selecting the appropriate type of scheduling for a given loop nest, namely the cost and the simplicity of the resulting schedule. Indeed, the cost of the schedule is a measure of the performance of its actual execution on a parallel computer, while the simplicity of the schedule influences the readability of the parallel code, and the feasibility of generating it both manually and mechanically.

By comparing the costs of the schedules produced by the two techniques for a K-level loop nest (i.e. the costs given by relations (5.7) and (5.11)), we can draw the following remarks. Firstly, the two scheduling techniques induce comparable communication overheads. Secondly, iterative scheduling is computationally optimal, whereas

$$
\begin{array}{l}
\textbf{for } i_1 = 0, n_1 - 1 \textbf{ do} \\
\quad \textbf{for } i_2 = 0, n_2 - 1 \textbf{ do} \\
\qquad \ldots \\
\qquad\quad \textbf{for } i_K = 0, n_K - 1 \textbf{ do} \\
\qquad\qquad s = s \oplus exp
\end{array}
$$

Figure 5.8: A generic reduction loop nest.

the computation cost of wavefront block scheduling merely approaches optimality for large problem sizes. Finally, and possibly most important, iterative schedules have a significantly higher synchronisation cost than those produced through wavefront block scheduling. Nevertheless, it is worth noticing that for iteration spaces whose dimensionality is larger than 2, these overheads are largely dominated by the computation cost even for average-sized problems.

As concerns the last criterion, wavefront block scheduling can only generate simpler schedules when the loop nest to be parallelised is fully permutable, and iterative scheduling is not applicable without a preliminary skewing of the iteration space. In fact, the usage of loop skewing as a parallelisation-enabling transformation seriously complicates the schedules derived through both techniques. The result is not only a less readable parallel schedule, but also a schedule whose computation cost is significantly increased by the intricate index and subscript arithmetic incurred by loop skewing.

Given the remarks so far, we can devise the following general rule for choosing between iterative scheduling and wavefront block scheduling. If the nesting level of the loop nest is larger than 2, and iterative scheduling is applicable without preprocessing its iteration space, it is advisable to use this technique. Otherwise, the usage of wavefront block scheduling should be considered. However, this rule should be applied cautiously, and bearing in mind that whenever the utmost performance is sought, the only way of selecting the best parallelisation technique is to build both schedules and to compare them for the loop nest under consideration.

5.6 Reduction Scheduling

In this section, we study the architecture-independent parallelisation of perfect loop nests whose loop body consists of a reduction operation. The generic form of a K-level *reduction loop nest*, $K \geq 1$, is depicted in Figure 5.8, where *exp* is an arbitrary expression free of s, and $\oplus$ denotes an operator which is associative if $K = 1$, and associative and commutative if $K > 1$. Due to the properties of the $\oplus$ operator, the iterations of the loop nest can be executed in any convenient order without affecting the final result. Moreover, it is possible to partition the iteration space into tiles, to independently compute partial reductions over these tiles, and, finally, to obtain the overall result by combining the partial reductions using the $\oplus$ operator.

Consequently, the p-processor schedule of the generic reduction loop nest in Figure 5.8 comprises two stages. In the first stage, which resembles the communication-free schedule of a K-level loop nest, the iteration space is partitioned into p rectangular tiles using the tiling matrix $\mathsf{T} = \mathrm{diag}(x_1, x_2, \ldots, x_K)$, where $\prod_{k=1}^{K} x_k = (\prod_{k=1}^{K} n_k)/p$. Each processor executes the iteration points in one of these tiles, using a local copy of the variable s.[3] Clearly, this computation superstep must by preceded by a preliminary communication superstep, in which remote data required for the execution of the tiles are brought into the local memories of the processors. As in the case of communication-free scheduling, the values of x_1, x_2, $\ldots$, x_K must be chosen so as to minimise the cost of this communication superstep, subject to the load balancing constraint $\prod_{k=1}^{K} x_k = (\prod_{k=1}^{K} n_k)/p$. The cost of this first stage is

$$2L + \frac{\prod_{k=1}^{K} n_k}{p}(cost(exp) + cost(\oplus)) + g\,Comm(x_1, x_2, \ldots, x_K),$$

where $Comm(x_1, x_2, \ldots, x_K)$ represents the maximum amount of data sent or received by any processor during the preliminary communication superstep, and can be computed using the techniques devised in Chapter 4.

Once the first stage is completed, the resulting partial reductions are combined in the second stage of the schedule using the converse of the standard broadcast algorithm of Valiant [1]. The p processors are organised in a logical d-ary tree, $2 \leq d \leq p-1$, and the second stage takes one superstep for each level of the processor tree. If $H_d(p)$ denotes the height of this tree, in each superstep $t = 0, 1, \ldots, H_d(p) - 1$ the processors at distance t from the leaves (i.e. the nodes of depth $H_d(p) - t$) send their data to the parent, which combines these data in the following superstep. The global result is computed by the root processor in superstep $t = H_d(p)$. The cost of the second stage of the schedule is

$$H_d(p)(L + d\,cost(\oplus) + gd) \approx \log_d p(L + d\,cost(\oplus) + gd).$$

It follows that the cost of the entire schedule is approximately

$$(2 + \log_d p)L + \frac{\prod_{k=1}^{K} n_k\,(cost(exp) + cost(\oplus))}{p} + g\,Comm(x_1, x_2, \ldots, x_K). \quad (5.13)$$

This cost is one-optimal in computation, and the schedule has optimal $\mathrm{O}((\prod_{k=1}^{K} n_k)/p)$ time complexity if $L \leq (\prod_{k=1}^{K} n_k)\,/(p \log p)$, $g \leq (\prod_{k=1}^{K} n_k)\,/(p\,Comm(x_1, x_2, \ldots, x_K))$.

Example 5.7 Let $\mathbf{x}$, $\mathbf{y}$ be two n-dimensional vectors. The following pseudocode computes the inner product of $\mathbf{x}$ and $\mathbf{y}$:

```
for i = 0, n − 1 do
    prod = prod + x[i]y[i]
```

As this pseudocode represents a 1-level reduction loop nest, its BSP version can be obtained using the scheduling technique described in this section. In the following, we shall assume that the p processors are arranged into a logical d-ary tree, $2 \leq d <$

[3] This local copy of s must be initialised with $1_{\oplus}$, the identity element for $\oplus$.

p. Processors $0,1,2,\ldots,p-1$ are assigned successive positions in the tree starting from the root, and $H_d(p)$, $first_d(s)$ and $last_d(s)$ denote the height of the tree, the first processor of depth s and the last processor of depth s, respectively. A straightforward computation gives

$$\begin{aligned} H_d(p) &= \lceil \log_d((d-1)p+1) \rceil - 1, \\ first_d(s) &= (d^s-1)/(d-1), \\ last_d(s) &= \min\{(d^{s+1}-1)/(d-1)-1, p-1\} \end{aligned}$$

for $0 \le s \le H_d(p)$. With this notation, a generic processor me, $0 \le me < p$, performs the following code:

```
/* compute partial reduction */
for i = me⌈n/p⌉, min{n − 1, (me + 1)⌈n/p⌉ − 1} do
  prod[me] = prod[me] + x[i]y[i]
/* combine local results */
for t = 0, H_d(p) − 1 do
  s = H_d(p) − t
  /* nodes of depth s send their local result to parent */
  if first_d(s) ≤ me ≤ last_d(s) then
    bsp_put prod[me] on processor ⌊(me − 1)/d⌋
  bsp_sync
  /* nodes of depth s − 1 combine the local result with those from their children */
  if first_d(s − 1) ≤ me ≤ last_d(s − 1) then
    for child = me d + 1, min{(me + 1)d, p − 1} do
      prod[me] = prod[me] + prod[child]
```

Assuming that the two vectors are initially distributed uniformly across the p processors, with processor me holding elements $x[me\lceil n/p\rceil .. \min\{n-1,(me+1)\lceil n/p\rceil -1\}]$ and $y[me\lceil n/p\rceil .. \min\{n-1,(me+1)\lceil n/p\rceil -1\}]$, the cost of the schedule is

$$H_d(p)L + n/p + H_d(p)gd \approx \log_d p\, L + n/p + \log_d p\, gd.$$

Hence, the schedule is one-optimal in computation and achieves $O(n/p)$ overall time complexity if $g \le n/(p\log p)$, $L \le n/(p\log p)$. A speedup of at least $p/(1+\varepsilon)$ is expected if the problem size satisfies $n \ge n_\varepsilon = p\log_d p(L+gd)/\varepsilon$.

5.7 Recurrence Scheduling

Recurrences represent another simple and very common computation pattern. The generic form of a recurrence is illustrated in Figure 5.9, where $f : \mathbf{R}^k \to \mathbf{R}$ denotes a generic function of k variables, $1 \le k \ll n$.

The recurrence loop can be computed sequentially in linear $n\, cost(f)$ time, where $cost(f)$ is the cost of evaluating f at a single iteration point. Therefore, in order to parallelise the recurrence, one must be able to start the computation concurrently at p

```
for i = k, n − 1 do
    a[i] = f(a[i − 1], a[i − 2], ..., a[i − k])
```

Figure 5.9: The generic form of a k-th-order recurrence loop.

equally distanced points of the iteration space, possibly after some sublinear time preprocessing. In this section, we propose an architecture-independent parallel schedule for a broad class of recurrences for which this requirement is satisfied.

Using a technique similar to that suggested in [79, 80], we first rewrite the definition of the recurrence as

$$\begin{aligned}(a_i, a_{i-1}, \ldots, a_{i-k+1}) &= (f(a_{i-1}, a_{i-2}, \ldots, a_{i-k}), a_{i-1}, \ldots, a_{i-k+1}) = \\ &= \widetilde{f}(a_{i-1}, a_{i-2}, \ldots, a_{i-k}) = \widetilde{f}^{i-k+1}(a_{k-1}, a_{k-2}, \ldots, a_0), \quad (5.14)\end{aligned}$$

where $\widetilde{f} : \mathbf{R}^k \to \mathbf{R}^k$, $\widetilde{f}(x_1, x_2, \ldots, x_k) = (f(x_1, x_2, \ldots, x_k), x_1, x_2, \ldots, x_{k-1})$. Now, we consider the class of recurrences for which $\widetilde{f}^m$, $m > 1$, can be evaluated to a function no more complex than $\widetilde{f}$ in $o(m)$ time. As we shall see from the example at the end of the section, this is the case of k-th-order linear recurrences, for which $\widetilde{f}^m$ can be obtained using $\Theta(\log m)$ operations. Nevertheless, linear recurrences do not represent the only instances of the considered class of computations. Indeed, many other problems (including for instance the first-order recurrence defined by $f(x) = (bx + c)/(dx + e)$) fulfill the above requirement, and thus belong to the class of recurrences whose scheduling is addressed in this section.

The parallel schedule of a recurrence satisfying the above requirement comprises two stages. In the first stage, the initial values a_0, a_1, …, a_{k-1}, and any parameters of f are broadcast to the p processors. Using the standard broadcast technique, this stage can be completed in $O(\log p\ (L + gk))$ time [81]. Next, in the second stage of the schedule, each processor me, $0 \le me < p$, computes the elements a_i, $me\ n/p \le i \le (me + 1)n/p - 1$ of the recurrence as follows.[4] Initially, processor me employs the alternative recurrence definition in (5.14) to compute $a_{me\ n/p}$, $a_{me\ n/p+1}$, …, $a_{me\ n/p+k-1}$ in $o(n)$ time. Once these first k elements in its set are available, the processor uses the original recurrence definition to obtain a_i, $me\ n/p + k \le i < (me + 1)n/p$. This last computation requires $n\ cost(f)/p$ operations. The overall cost of the schedule is given by

$$O(\log p\ (L + gk)) + o(n) + \frac{n\ cost(f)}{p} = \\ O(\log p\ L) + \frac{n\ cost(f)}{p}(1 + o(1)) + O(gk \log p).$$

Accordingly, the schedule is one-optimal in computation and has optimal $O(n/p)$ time complexity when $g \le n/(p \log p)$, $L \le n/(p \log p)$. Additionally, its practical

[4]For simplicity, we assume that the problem size n is a multiple of p throughout this section.

implementation is expected to achieve at least $p/(1+\varepsilon)$ speedup, $\varepsilon > 0$ if $n \geq n_\varepsilon = p \log p(L+gk)/(\varepsilon\, cost(f))$.

Example 5.8 Consider the k-th-order linear recurrence defined by

$$a_i = f(a_{i-1}, a_{i-2}, \ldots, a_{i-k}) = \alpha_{k-1}a_{i-1} + \alpha_{k-2}a_{i-2} + \cdots + \alpha_0 a_{i-k},$$

for all $k \leq i < n$. If we construct the $k \times k$ matrix

$$\mathsf{M} = \left[\begin{array}{ccc|c} \alpha_{k-1} & \alpha_{k-2} & \cdots & \alpha_0 \\ \hline & & & 0 \\ & \mathsf{I}_{k-1} & & \vdots \\ & & & 0 \end{array}\right],$$

the definition of the linear recurrence can be rewritten as

$$[a_i, a_{i-1}, \ldots, a_{i-k+1}]^{\mathrm{T}} = \mathsf{M}\ [a_{i-1}, a_{i-2}, \ldots, a_{i-k}]^{\mathrm{T}} = \mathsf{M}^{i-k+1}\ [a_{k-1}, a_{k-2}, \ldots, a_0]^{\mathrm{T}}.$$

Since M^m, $m > 1$, can be computed as the product of some of the matrices M, $\mathsf{M}^2 = \mathsf{MM}$, ..., $\mathsf{M}^{\lfloor \log m \rfloor} = \mathsf{M}^{\lfloor \log m \rfloor /2}\mathsf{M}^{\lfloor \log m \rfloor /2}$ in $\Theta(k^3 \log m) = o(m)$ time, the linear recurrence can be parallelised by applying the scheduling technique introduced in this section. In the first stage of the resulting schedule, a_0, a_1, ..., a_{k-1} and α_0, α_1, ..., α_{k-1} are broadcast to all processors, whereas in the second stage processor *me*, $0 \leq me < p$, computes a_i, $me\ n/p \leq i < (me+1)n/p$. This computation commences with a preliminary phase in which the alternative definition

$$[a_{me\ n/p+k-1}, a_{me\ n/p+k-2}, \ldots, a_{me\ n/p}]^{\mathrm{T}} = \mathsf{M}^{me\ n/p}\ [a_{k-1}, a_{k-2}, \ldots, a_0]^{\mathrm{T}}$$

is used to obtain the first k of these elements, continuing with the actual execution of the other $n/p - k$ iterations assigned to processor *me*.

5.8 Scheduling Broadcast Loop Nests

5.8.1 Definition of a Broadcast Loop Nest

This section addresses the parallelisation of an important loop structure which, although it stands for a regular pattern of computation, has data dependences that cannot be expressed as distance vectors. This is due to the fact that certain items of loop-computed data are used repeatedly during the computation of the loop body at other iteration points. Since its direct mapping on a distributed-memory parallel computer requires broadcasts of the multiply used items of data, we shall call this loop structure a *broadcast loop nest*.

The standard format of a K-level broadcast loop nest, $K > 1$, is illustrated in Figure 5.10. The body of the outermost loop of the broadcast loop nest comprises a number of so-called *broadcast initialisation loops*, and a main computation loop. Each of the $J > 0$ broadcast initialisation loops represents a $(K-2)$-level loop nest with

```
for i_1 = 0, n-1 do
  broadcast-initialisation-loop-1
  broadcast-initialisation-loop-2
  ...
  broadcast-initialisation-loop-J
  /* main computation loop */
  for i_2 = 0, n-1 do
    for i_3 = 0, n-1 do
      ...
        for i_K = 0, n-1 do
          a[i_2, i_3, ..., i_K] = f(a[i_2, i_3, ..., i_K],
                          b_1[i_2, i_3, ..., i_{k_1 - 1}, f_1(i_1), i_{k_1 + 1}, ..., i_K],
                          b_2[i_2, i_3, ..., i_{k_2 - 1}, f_2(i_1), i_{k_2 + 1}, ..., i_K],
                          ...,
                          b_J[i_2, i_3, ..., i_{k_J - 1}, f_J(i_1), i_{k_J + 1}, ..., i_K],
                          ...)
```

Figure 5.10: A K-level broadcast loop nest, $K \geq 2$.

```
for i_2 = 0, n-1 do
  for i_3 = 0, n-1 do
    ...
      for i_{k_j - 1} = 0, n-1 do
        for i_{k_j + 1} = 0, n-1 do
          ...
            for i_K = 0, n-1 do
              b_j[i_2, i_3, ..., i_{k_j - 1}, f_j(i_1), i_{k_j + 1}, ..., i_K] = ...
```

Figure 5.11: The j-th broadcast initialisation loop in Figure 5.10, $1 \leq j \leq J$.

the structure in Figure 5.11, and computes data that are multiply used during the subsequent execution of the main computation loop. The main computation loop has nesting level $K-1$, and updates the elements of a $(K-1)$-dimensional output array a based on their previous values, on the data provided by the broadcast initialisation loops, and, possibly, on pure-input data.

It is worth emphasising that many practical instances of a broadcast loop nest may differ significantly from the standard format shown in Figure 5.10. Nevertheless, none of these differences invalidates the scheduling techniques devised in this section. Thus, although the standard format assumes that all loops iterate from 0 to $n-1$, this is not essential for the parallelisation of a broadcast loop nest. The only purpose of this initial assumption was to simplify the description of the new loop structure. In fact, the parallel schedules devised in the remainder of this section do not even require that the iteration space be rectangular.

Furthermore, it is possible that for one or more $j \in 1..J$, the reference to $b_j[i_2, i_3, \ldots, i_{k_j-1}, f_j(i_1), i_{k_j+1}, \ldots, i_K]$ within the body of the main computation loop is replaced

```
for i1 = 0,n-1 do
  x[i1] = a[i1]/m[i1,i1]
  for i2 = i1+1,n-1 do
    a[i2] = a[i2] - m[i2,i1]x[i1]
```

(a) the sequential algorithm

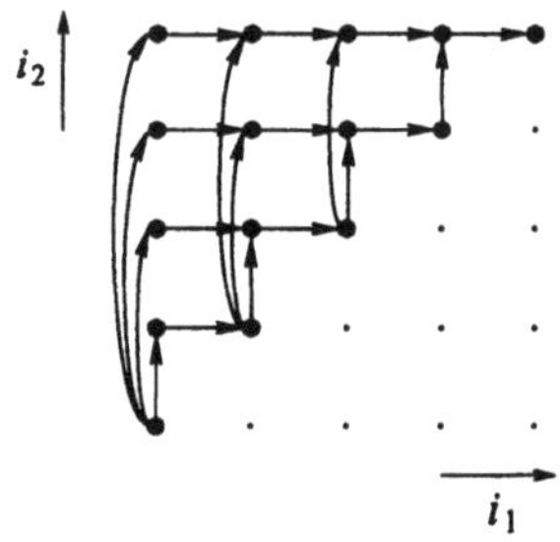

(b) the data flow for $n = 5$

Figure 5.12: Triangular linear system solution by forward substitution.

by $a[i_2, i_3, \ldots, i_{k_j-1}, f_j(i_1), i_{k_j+1}, \ldots, i_K]$. When this is the case, either the j-th broadcast initialisation loop modifies the corresponding elements from the output array a, or it is missing altogether.

Example 5.9 Figure 5.12 depicts the pseudocode and the data flow for the solution of the following triangular linear system:

$$\begin{cases} m_{0,0}x_0 & & & = a_0 \\ m_{1,0}x_0 & + m_{1,1}x_1 & & = a_1 \\ \ldots & & & \\ m_{n-1,0}x_0 & + m_{n-1,1}x_1 & + \cdots + m_{n-1,n-1}x_{n-1} & = a_{n-1} \end{cases}$$

The code in Figure 5.12(a) represents a 2-level broadcast loop nest comprising a single, degenerate broadcast initialisation loop of nesting level $K-2=0$, and a main computation loop of nesting level $K-1=1$. The iteration space of the loop nest is triangular, and array x is used instead of the auxiliary array b_1 from the standard format of a broadcast loop nest. As illustrated in Figure 5.12(b), the only broadcast initialisation loop in the code corresponds to a *broadcast data stream* in direction i_2 of the iteration space.

Example 5.10 Gaussian elimination (without pivoting) represents another instance of a broadcast loop nest. Indeed, consider the following system of linear equations:

$$\begin{cases} a_{0,0}x_0 & + a_{0,1}x_1 & + \cdots + a_{0,n-1}x_{n-1} & = a_{0,n} \\ a_{1,0}x_0 & + a_{1,1}x_1 & + \cdots + a_{1,n-1}x_{n-1} & = a_{1,n} \\ \ldots & & & \\ a_{n-1,0}x_0 & + a_{n-1,1}x_1 & + \cdots + a_{n-1,n-1}x_{n-1} & = a_{n-1,n} \end{cases}$$

The first phase of the Gaussian elimination algorithm that solves this system is shown in Figure 5.13, together with the data flow corresponding to a single execution of the main computation loop. Obviously, the code in Figure 5.13(a) is a 3-level

for $i_1 = 0, n-1$ **do**
  for $i_3 = i_1, n$ **do**
    $a[i_1, i_3] = a[i_1, i_3] / a[i_1, i_1]$
  for $i_2 = i_1 + 1, n-1$ **do**
    for $i_3 = i_1, n$ **do**
      $a[i_2, i_3] = a[i_2, i_3] - a[i_1, i_3] a[i_2, i_1]$

(a) the first phase of the sequential algorithm

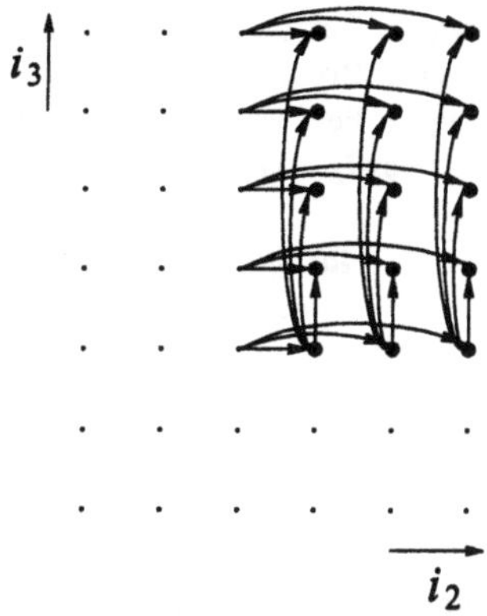

(b) the data flow for the main computation loop when $i_1 = 2$ and $n = 6$

Figure 5.13: Gaussian elimination.

broadcast loop nest whose 2-level main computation loop iteratively updates the elements of a, the augmented matrix of the linear system. Although Gaussian elimination comprises a single broadcast initialisation loop, its main computation loop uses two broadcast data streams—this can be easily seen from the data flow depicted in Figure 5.13(b). The stream whose associated broadcast initialisation loop is missing is due to the use of $a[i_2, i_1]$, i.e. to the use of data computed during the previous execution of the main computation loop.

Many other examples of broadcast loop nests exist. They include Gauss-Jordan reduction, transitive closure, and shortest paths.

Two strategies can be used to map a broadcast loop nest onto a BSP computer. In the former strategy, the multiple accesses to the same data are achieved through actual broadcasts. Accordingly, this strategy is called *scheduling through broadcast implementation*. The latter strategy, termed *scheduling through broadcast elimination*, works by converting the broadcast loop nests into fully permutable loop nests and parallelising them by means of wavefront block scheduling.

5.8.2 Scheduling Through Broadcast Implementation

The straightforward way of scheduling a broadcast loop nest is to sequentialise the execution of its outermost loop, and to evenly distribute the execution of its main computation loop among the available processors. Indeed, the instance of the main computation loop corresponding to any iteration of the outermost loop consists of fully independent iterations, and can be performed in parallel. Notice that any schedule based on this strategy must satisfy a single requirement, namely to ensure that the

for $i_1 = 0, n-1$ **do**
  Stage 1. Compute the broadcast initialisation loops
  Stage 2. Broadcast the data computed in Stage 1 and required by other processors
  Stage 3. Perform the main computation loop
    for $i_2 = me_1 n/x_2, (me_1+1)n/x_2 - 1$ **do**
      ...
      for $i_K = me_{K-1} n/x_K, (me_{K-1}+1)n/x_K - 1$ **do**
        main-computation-loop-body

Figure 5.14: Broadcast loop nest scheduling through broadcast implementation.

data computed by the broadcast initialisation loops are sent to the processors that need it before each execution of the main computation loop.

Formally, given a K-level broadcast loop nest $\mathcal{L}$ with the structure in Figures 5.10-5.11, the iteration space of each instance of its main computation loop is block-partitioned using the tiling matrix $\mathsf{T} = \text{diag}(x_2, x_3, \dots, x_K)$, $\prod_{k=2}^{K} x_k = n^{K-1}/p$.[5] Next, for each instance of the main computation loop, the p equally sized rectangular blocks obtained through this partitioning are computed in parallel by the p processors. For this purpose, the processors are regarded as arranged into a logical $(K-1)$-dimensional array of size $n/x_2 \times n/x_3 \times \cdots \times n/x_K$, and each processor is assigned the computation of the tile whose coordinates match its own coordinates in the processor array.

The parallel schedule of the broadcast loop nest comprises three stages for each iteration of its outermost loop. As shown in Figure 5.14, which depicts the code executed by a generic processor $(me_1, me_2, \dots, me_{K-1})$ from the processor array, in the first stage the broadcast initialisation loops are performed, typically in a single superstep. As concerns the partitioning of the broadcast initialisation loops, it is induced by that of the main computation loop. In other words, the iteration $(i_2, \dots, i_{k_j-1}, i_{k_j+1}, \dots, i_K)$ of the j-th broadcast initialisation loop, $1 \le j \le J$, is executed by the processor which is assigned the iteration $(i_2, \dots, i_{k_j-1}, f_j(i_1), i_{k_j+1}, \dots, i_K)$ of the main computation loop. Since each broadcast initialisation loop has nesting level $K-2$, the cost of this stage is bounded above by

$$Jn^{K-2}.$$

No synchronisation cost is charged here, because this computation can take place in the first superstep of the second stage.

The resulting data are then broadcast during the second stage of any outermost loop iteration to the processors that need them for the subsequent execution of the main computation loop. The realisation of these broadcasts using the standard BSP broadcast algorithms, as well as the analysis of their cost, will be described later.

Finally, in the third stage, which also takes a single superstep, the p tiles of the

[5] As in the case of other scheduling techniques, block-cyclic partitioning may be used to decrease the workload imbalance associated with the block partitioning of non-rectangular iteration spaces.

main computation loop are executed in parallel, at a cost of

$$\frac{n^{K-1}c}{p},$$

where c is the cost of performing the body of the main computation loop for a single point of its iteration space. Again, no synchronisation cost was taken into account because the only superstep of this stage can be merged with the first superstep in the next iteration of the schedule.

In order to determine the cost of the second stage of the schedule, we need the result provided by the following theorem.

Theorem 5.5 *Let $\mathcal{L}$ be a K-level broadcast loop nest whose main computation loop is partitioned into p rectangular tiles of size $x_2 \times x_3 \times \cdots \times x_K$, $\prod_{k=2}^{K} x_k = n^{K-1}/p$, $K \geq 2$. Also, let i_{k_j}, $2 \leq k_j \leq K$, be the index of the missing loop in the j-th broadcast initialisation loop of $\mathcal{L}$, $1 \leq j \leq J$. Then, the standard BSP broadcast algorithms can be used to distribute the data computed by the j-th broadcast initialisation loop in time*

$$broadcast\_cost(j) = \begin{cases} 0, & \text{if } x_{k_j} = n \\ O(\log p(L+g)), & \text{if } x_{k_j} < n \text{ and } K = 2 \\ 2\left(L + gn^{K-1}/(px_{k_j})\right), & \text{otherwise} \end{cases} \quad (5.15)$$

for any iteration of the outermost loop of $\mathcal{L}$.

Proof For any fixed value taken by $(i_2, \ldots, i_{k_j-1}, i_{k_j+1}, \ldots, i_K)$ across the iteration space of the main computation loop, the value of $b_j[i_2, \ldots, i_{k_j-1}, f_j(i_1), i_{k_j+1}, \ldots, i_K]$ is required for the computation of the n iteration points on the segment determined by this fixed value and by $0 \leq i_{k_j} < n$. Since the iteration space is partitioned into rectangular tiles whose size along the k_j-th direction is x_{k_j}, the iteration points on this segment are assigned to n/x_{k_j} of the p processors. Furthermore, our scheduling technique ensures that $b_j[i_2, \ldots, i_{k_j-1}, f_j(i_1), i_{k_j+1}, \ldots, i_K]$ is actually computed by one of these n/x_{k_j} processors (namely by the processor whose tile comprises the iteration point $(i_2, \ldots, i_{k_j-1}, f_j(i_1), i_{k_j+1}, \ldots, i_K)$). Hence, for any fixed value taken by $(i_2, \ldots, i_{k_j-1}, i_{k_j+1}, \ldots, i_K)$, an item of data computed by the j-th broadcast initialisation loop is required by exactly n/x_{k_j} processors, and is resident in the local memory of one of these processors.

This result can be readily extended to whole tiles. For this purpose, consider a generic set of n/x_{k_j} tiles whose coordinates differ only in the element corresponding to the k_j-th direction of the iteration space. Notice that $(i_2, \ldots, i_{k_j-1}, f_j(i_1), i_{k_j+1}, \ldots, i_K)$ takes precisely the same

$$x_2 \ldots x_{k_j-1} x_{k_j+1} \ldots x_K = \frac{1}{x_{k_j}} \prod_{k=2}^{K} x_k = n^{K-1}/(px_{k_j})$$

distinct values across each of these tiles, and all iteration points corresponding to these values belong to this set of tiles. Consequently, each of the n/x_{k_j} processors that compute these tiles needs exactly $n^{K-1}/(px_{k_j})$ items of data generated by the j-th broadcast initialisation loop. Moreover, all these items of data reside on one of the n/x_{k_j} processors, namely on the processor whose (k_j-1)-th coordinate satisfies $me_{k_j-1} = \lfloor f_j(i_1)/x_{k_j} \rfloor$.

In conclusion, the processors can be viewed as partitioned into $n^{K-2}/(x_2 \dots x_{k_j-1} x_{k_j+1} \dots x_K)$ groups of n/x_{k_j} processors, and within each group $n^{K-1}/(px_{k_j})$ items of data must be broadcast to all members of the group. All these data reside on the same processor in the group, and no other inter-processor communication is required.

When $n/x_{k_j} = 1$ (i.e. when $x_{k_j} = n$), it follows from the above result that no inter-processor communication is needed, so *broadcast_cost*$(j) = 0$. In order to analyse the other two cases of the theorem, the remainder of the proof assumes that $x_{k_j} < n$.

Firstly, if $K = 2$, the main computation loop is a simple loop, and there is a single item of data that has to be broadcast from one processor to all the others. In this case, the p processors are organised in a logical d-ary tree rooted at the source processor, $d \in 2..p-1$. The data item is then conveyed along the tree structure in $\Theta(\log_d p)$ supersteps [1]. The cost of the entire broadcast is $O(\log p(L+g))$.

Secondly, for $K > 2$, $n^{K-1}/(px_{k_j}) \gg n/x_{k_j}$ for any practical values of n and p, and the standard two-superstep broadcast procedure is used independently for each group of $p' = n/x_{k_j}$ processors. Consider one such group. In the first superstep, the processor which holds the data that need to be broadcast partitions these data into p' chunks of equal size, and sends a different chunk to each of the other $p'-1$ processors in its group, keeping a data chunk for itself. The cost of this superstep is $L+g(p'-1)(n^{K-1}/(px_{k_j}))/p' < L+gn^{K-1}/(px_{k_j})$. In the second superstep, each processor sends the chunk of data it acquired in the first superstep to all other $p'-1$ processors. Since each processor sends and receives $(p'-1)n^{K-1}/(p'px_{k_j})$ items of data, the cost of this superstep is again bounded above by $L+gn^{K-1}/(px_{k_j})$. By summing the costs of the two supersteps we obtain the final result of the theorem. □

The previous theorem allows us to complete the analysis of the parallel schedule in Figure 5.14. We start with the degenerate case when there is a non-empty subset $\mathcal{K} \subset 2..K$ such that for all $k \in \mathcal{K}$ no broadcast stream exists along the k-th direction of the iteration space. In this case, the tiling matrix $\mathsf{T} = \mathrm{diag}(x_2, x_3, \dots, x_K)$ can be chosen so as to eliminate the need for inter-processor communication during the second stage of the schedule. All we have to do to achieve this is to set $x_k = n$ for all $k \notin \mathcal{K}$. The other diagonal elements of T are chosen so as to minimise the cost of a preliminary superstep in which loop-external data required by the schedule are fetched from the appropriate locations, subject to the load balancing constraint $\prod_{k=2}^{K} x_k = n^{K-1}/p$. Under these circumstances, the second stage disappears from each iteration of the schedule, and the whole computation is executed in a single superstep. The overall cost of the resulting communication-free schedule is

$$L + \frac{n^K c}{p}(1+o(1)), \tag{5.16}$$

which is optimal in all respects. A speedup of at least $p/(1+\varepsilon)$ is obtained if $n \geq n_\varepsilon = pL/(\varepsilon\, c)$.

Nevertheless, in almost all practical situations, broadcast loop nests comprise broadcast streams along each of the $K-1$ directions of the main computation loop. When $K=2$, it follows from Theorem 5.5 that the cost of the second stage of each outermost loop iteration is $O(\log p(L+g))$. Accordingly, an entire iteration of the schedule takes

$$[O(1)]+[O(\log p(L+g))]+\left[\frac{nc}{p}\right]$$

time, and the overall cost of the schedule is

$$O(n\log p\, L)+\frac{n^2c}{p}(1+o(1))+O(gn\log p). \qquad (5.17)$$

Due to its high synchronisation and communication overheads, this schedule can achieve optimal $O(n^2/p)$ cost only if $g\le n/(p\log p), L\le n/(p\log p)$.

Finally, when $K>2$, we shall further assume that a single broadcast stream exists in each of the $K-1$ dimensions of the main computation loop; this represents by far the most common situation encountered in practice. Since the $J=K-1$ broadcasts are fully independent, the communication cost of the second stage is obtained by summing the costs of the $K-1$ broadcasts. As for the synchronisation cost, it is no larger than that of a single broadcast, because the $K-1$ broadcasts can be performed concurrently. Consequently, if $K>2$, the cost of the second stage is

$$2\left(L+\sum_{k_j\in\{2,3,\ldots,K\}}\frac{gn^{K-1}}{px_{k_j}}\right)=2L+2\,\frac{gn^{K-1}}{p}\sum_{k=2}^{K}\frac{1}{x_k}.$$

As the parameters $x_2, x_3, \ldots, x_K$ must satisfy the load balancing constraint $\prod_{k=2}^{K}x_k = n^{K-1}/p$, it follows from the mean inequality that this cost is minimised for $x_2=x_3=\cdots=x_K=n/p^{1/(K-1)}$; its minimum value is

$$2L+\frac{2(K-1)gn^{K-2}}{p^{(K-2)/(K-1)}}.$$

When this tiling is employed, the cost of an iteration of the schedule becomes:

$$[Jn^{K-2}]+\left[2L+\frac{2(K-1)gn^{K-2}}{p^{(K-2)/(K-1)}}\right]+\left[\frac{n^{K-1}c}{p}\right],$$

leading to a schedule whose overall cost is

$$2nL+\frac{n^Kc}{p}(1+o(1))+\frac{2(K-1)gn^{K-1}}{p^{(K-2)/(K-1)}}. \qquad (5.18)$$

The one-optimal computation cost of the schedule dominates the synchronisation cost as soon as $L\le n^{K-1}/p$, which, for $K>2$, represents an easily satisfiable requirement. As expected for a parallel schedule comprising $K-1$ broadcasts for every n computations, the communication cost is significantly higher. Nonetheless, the other condition that has to be fulfilled by a schedule achieving $O(n^K/p)$ time complexity (i.e. $g\le n/p^{1/(K-1)}$) is equally easily satisfied for average problem sizes.

```
for i_1 = 0, n-1 do
  p' = ⌊i_1/⌈n/p⌉⌋          /* identifier of processor that holds x[i_1] */
  if me = p' then
    x[i_1] = a[i_1]/m[i_1, i_1]
  broadcast x[i_1] from processor p' to processors p'+1, p'+2, ..., p-1
  for i_2 = max{i_1 + 1, me⌈n/p⌉}, min{n-1, (me+1)⌈n/p⌉ - 1} do
    a[i_2] = a[i_2] - m[i_2, i_1]x[i_1]
```

Figure 5.15: Parallel solution of a triangular linear system—broadcast implementation.

Example 5.11 Consider the sequential solution of a triangular linear system (Figure 5.12). Its parallel version generated by the scheduling technique devised in this section is shown in Figure 5.15. This BSP schedule assumes that the elements of the array m and those of the vectors a and x are initially distributed uniformly across the system, such that each processor holds $\lceil n/p \rceil$ successive rows of m and $\lceil n/p \rceil$ successive elements of a and x, respectively. It follows from the previous analysis (equation (5.17)) that the cost of the schedule is

$$\mathrm{O}(n \log p\, L) + \frac{n^2}{p} + \mathrm{O}(gn \log p).$$

The schedule is one-optimal in computation, and has optimal $\mathrm{O}(n^2/p)$ overall time complexity if $g \leq n/(p \log p)$, $L \leq n/(p \log p)$.

5.8.3 Scheduling Through Broadcast Elimination

This section proposes an alternative approach to the parallelisation of broadcast loop nests. This approach is based on the *pipelining* mechanism used for the normalisation of systems of recurrence equations in systolic array design [82, 83]. As we shall see, pipelining replaces broadcasts with sequences of *data movements* between pairs of neighbouring iteration points, transforming a broadcast loop nest into a uniform-dependence loop nest.

Consider again the K-level broadcast loop nest $\mathcal{L}$ in Figures 5.10-5.11, and assume that for all $1 \leq j \leq J$, $f_j(i_1) = 0$. We can then augment the j-th broadcast initialisation loop as shown in Figure 5.16, by expanding the auxiliary $(K-1)$-dimensional array b_j into a K-dimensional array and adding the loop indexed by i_{k_j}. As long as each reference $b_j[s_2, s_3, \ldots, s_K]$ is replaced with $b_j[i_1 - 1, s_2, s_3, \ldots, s_K]$ if it precedes the j-th broadcast initialisation loop, and with $b_j[i_1, s_2, s_3, \ldots, s_K]$ otherwise, the resulting loop nest performs the same computation as $\mathcal{L}$. This remains true if we additionally expand the output array a into a K-dimensional array, and replace the body of the main

```
for i_2 = 0, n-1 do
  for i_3 = 0, n-1 do
    ...
      for i_{k_j - 1} = 0, n-1 do
        for i_{k_j} = 0, n-1 do
          for i_{k_j + 1} = 0, n-1 do
            ...
              for i_K = 0, n-1 do
                if i_{k_j} = 0 then
                  b_j[i_1, i_2, i_3, ..., i_{k_j - 1}, i_{k_j}, i_{k_j + 1}, ..., i_K] = ...
                else
                  b_j[i_1, i_2, i_3, ..., i_{k_j - 1}, i_{k_j}, i_{k_j + 1}, ..., i_K] =
                           b_j[i_1, i_2, i_3, ..., i_{k_j - 1}, i_{k_j} - 1, i_{k_j + 1}, ..., i_K]
```

Figure 5.16: Augmented broadcast initialisation loop.

computation loop with

$$\begin{aligned} a[i_1,i_2,i_3,\ldots,i_K] = f(a[i_1-1,i_2,i_3,\ldots,i_K],\\ & b_1[i_1,i_2,i_3,\ldots,i_{k_1-1},i_{k_1},i_{k_1+1},\ldots,i_K],\\ & b_2[i_1,i_2,i_3,\ldots,i_{k_2-1},i_{k_2},i_{k_2+1},\ldots,i_K],\\ & \ldots,\\ & b_J[i_1,i_2,i_3,\ldots,i_{k_J-1},i_{k_J},i_{k_J+1},\ldots,i_K],\\ & \ldots), \end{aligned}$$

and any reference to $a[s_2,s_3,\ldots,s_K]$ from the broadcast initialisation loops with the reference $a[i_1-1,i_2,i_3,\ldots,i_K]$.

Under these circumstances, the J broadcast initialisation loops and the main computation loop can be fused to produce a tightly nested loop $\mathcal{L}'$ equivalent to $\mathcal{L}$—Figure 5.17. Furthermore, the data dependences of $\mathcal{L}'$ can be represented by K distance vectors that are exactly the columns of the $K\times K$ identity matrix (i.e. by the distance vectors in the set $D=\{\mathbf{d}^1;\mathbf{d}^2;\ldots;\mathbf{d}^K \mid [\mathbf{d}^1,\mathbf{d}^2,\ldots,\mathbf{d}^K]=\mathsf{I}_K\}$). Hence, $\mathcal{L}'$ is a fully permutable loop nest, and can be parallelised using wavefront block scheduling. As the iteration space of $\mathcal{L}'$ is a K-dimensional hypercube and $\sum_{\mathbf{d}\in D} d_k = 1$ for all $1\le k\le K$, it follows from the performance analysis in Section 5.4.1 that the tiling matrix employed by wavefront block scheduling is

$$\mathsf{T}=\mathsf{I}_K\left[x_1,n/p^{1/(K-1)},n/p^{1/(K-1)},\ldots,n/p^{1/(K-1)}\right]^{\mathrm{T}},$$

where $x_1\in 1..n$ is given by equation (5.8). According to (5.7), the cost of the resulting parallel schedule is bounded above by

$$\left(\frac{n}{x_1}+p-1\right)L+\left(1+\frac{(p-1)x_1}{n}\right)\frac{n^K c'}{p}+\left(1+\frac{(p-1)x_1}{n}\right)\frac{(K-1)gn^{K-1}(1+o(1))}{p^{(K-2)/(K-1)}}, \tag{5.19}$$

for $i_1 = 0, n-1$ **do**
  for $i_2 = 0, n-1$ **do**
    ...
      for $i_K = 0, n-1$ **do**
        if $i_{k_1} = 0$ **then**
          $b_1[i_1, i_2, \ldots, i_K] = \ldots$
        else
          $b_1[i_1, i_2, \ldots, i_K] = b_1[i_1, i_2, \ldots, i_{k_1-1}, i_{k_1} - 1, i_{k_1+1}, \ldots, i_K]$
        ...
        if $i_{k_J} = 0$ **then**
          $b_J[i_1, i_2, \ldots, i_K] = \ldots$
        else
          $b_J[i_1, i_2, \ldots, i_K] = b_J[i_1, i_2, \ldots, i_{k_J-1}, i_{k_J} - 1, i_{k_J+1}, \ldots, i_K]$
        $a[i_1, i_2, i_3, \ldots, i_K] = f(a[i_1 - 1, i_2, i_3, \ldots, i_K], b_1[i_1, i_2, \ldots, i_K],$
              $b_2[i_1, i_2, \ldots, i_K], \ldots, b_J[i_1, i_2, \ldots, i_K], \ldots)$

Figure 5.17: A perfect loop nest equivalent to the broadcast loop nest in Figures 5.10-5.11.

where c' denotes the cost of executing the loop body of $\mathcal{L}'$ for a single iteration point. Notice that this cost is higher than c, the cost of performing the loop body of the main computation loop of $\mathcal{L}$ for a single iteration point.

So far, we have seen how to avoid the implementation of broadcasts in the parallel schedule of a standard-format broadcast loop nest satisfying $f_j(i_1) = 0$ for all $1 \leq j \leq J$. This technique can be readily extended to the case when the iteration space of the main computation loop of $\mathcal{L}$ is not rectangular, and, for all $1 \leq j \leq J$, $f_j(i_1)$ matches the lower bound of the loop indexed by i_{k_j} in the main computation loop.

Example 5.12 In order to illustrate the application of the broadcast elimination technique, we shall address again the parallelisation of the triangular linear system solution in Figure 5.12(a). Firstly, the single, degenerate broadcast initialisation loop in the code is augmented and becomes:

for $i_2 = i_1, n-1$ **do**
  if $i_2 = i_1$ **then**
    $x[i_1, i_2] = a[i_1 - 1, i_2]/m[i_1, i_1]$
  else
    $x[i_1, i_2] = x[i_1, i_2 - 1]$

Next, the augmented broadcast initialisation loop is fused with the main computation loop, the two vectors being expanded into 2-dimensional arrays in both steps:

for $i_1 = 0, n-1$ **do**
  for $i_2 = i_1, n-1$ **do**
    if $i_2 = i_1$ **then**
      $x[i_1, i_2] = a[i_1 - 1, i_2]/m[i_1, i_1]$
    else /* $i_2 \geq i_1 + 1$ */
      $x[i_1, i_2] = x[i_1, i_2 - 1]$
      $a[i_1, i_2] = a[i_1 - 1, i_2] - m[i_2, i_1]x[i_1, i_2]$

This perfect loop nest is equivalent to the initial broadcast loop nest in a restricted but well-defined sense. Thus, if for all $0 \leq i_2 < n$, $a[-1,i_2]$ is initialised with the value of $a[i_2]$ in the original code, then $x[0,n-1], x[1,n-1], \ldots, x[n-1,n-1]$ will contain the solution of the linear system after the execution of the transformed loop.

Finally, in a third step, wavefront block scheduling is used to parallelise the execution of the transformed code, which is a fully permutable loop nest. The resulting parallel schedule is entirely similar to the one devised in Example 5.5, and has a cost of

$$\left(\frac{n}{x_1}+p-1\right)L+\left(1+\frac{(p-1)x_1}{n}\right)\frac{n^2}{p}+\left(1+\frac{(p-1)x_1}{n}\right)gn,$$

where x_1 denotes the height of the iteration space tiles computed by the processors in each superstep of the schedule. The best schedule is obtained when (equation (5.8)) the tile height takes the value

$$x_1 = \left\lceil \sqrt{\frac{pL}{(p-1)(1+gp/n)}} \right\rceil.$$

This schedule approaches one-optimality in computation, and achieves optimal $O(n^2/p)$ time complexity if $g \leq n/p, L \leq n/p$. Similar to Example 5.5, the n_ε performance metric can be shown to satisfy $n_\varepsilon \leq (g+L)p/\varepsilon$.

The same BSP solution of a triangular linear system is proposed in [35], where the tile height is fixed at $x_1 = \lceil n/p \rceil$ for simplicity. Consequently, the schedule described in [35] has a cost of $2pL + 2n^2/p + 2gn$, and attains only two-optimality in computation.

5.8.4 Comparison of the Two Approaches

As anticipated, the elimination of actual data broadcasts significantly decreases the communication and synchronisation overheads of the parallel schedule of a broadcast loop nest. For a standard-format K-level broadcast loop nest, $K > 2$ for instance, the costs of the schedules obtained through broadcast implementation and through broadcast elimination are given by expressions (5.18) and (5.19), respectively. It is noticeable that, whereas the computation cost of both schedules approaches one-optimality, the first technique leads to a communication cost almost twice as large as that induced by the second technique; the ratio of the two communication overheads corresponding to the parallelisation of a three-level broadcast loop nest on a typical BSP computer is presented in Figure 5.18. Moreover, the synchronisation overheads of the former schedule are much higher than those corresponding to the latter schedule.

These disadvantages of broadcast implementation scheduling are slightly compensated for by the increased memory complexity of the schedules obtained through broadcast elimination. However, the memory complexity of broadcast elimination scheduling can be reduced significantly by rewriting the schedule so as to reuse the array elements which are not referred by boundary iteration points from the tiles.

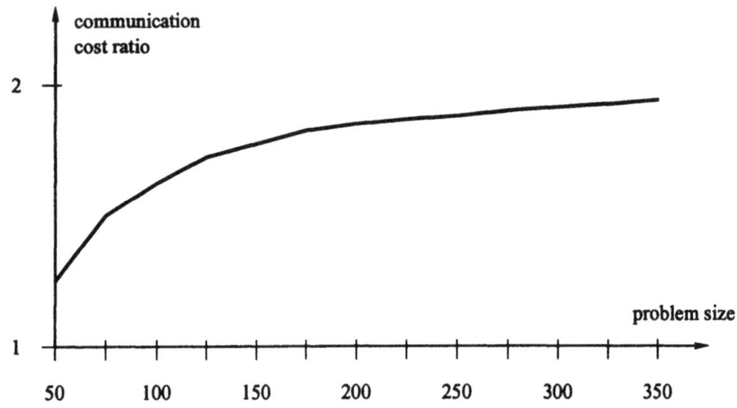

Figure 5.18: The ratio between the communication costs associated with the parallelisation of a three-level broadcast loop nest through broadcast implementation and broadcast elimination, respectively. A typical 16-processor BSP computer with $L = 1000$ and $g = 10$, and a cost of executing a single instance of the loop body of $c' = 4$ are considered.

In conclusion, the application of the broadcast elimination technique is strongly recommended whenever the broadcast loop nest can be reorganised as a fully permutable loop nest. When, on the other hand, this is not possible, the use of the broadcast implementation technique remains the only option.

5.9 Summary

In this chapter, we developed a collection of techniques for the template-matching parallelisation of nested loops. The first three techniques in this collection tackle the parallelisation of uniform-dependence loop nests, namely of perfectly nested loops whose data dependences can be encoded by distance vectors. The technique applicable to a specific loop nest depends on whether its distance vectors span the entire iteration space or not.

In the former case, wavefront block scheduling and iterative scheduling may be used. Both these techniques are extensions of the classical wavefront parallelisation method, and build the parallel version of a sequential loop nest by tiling its iteration space and executing the resulting tiles concurrently, in a sequence of supersteps. They differ, however, in their handling of tile computation, as well as in the nested loops they can parallelise without a preliminary affine transformation of the iteration space. The relative merits of the two scheduling methods are discussed in Section 5.5.3.

In the latter case, the application of communication-free scheduling is possible. The result is an optimal parallel schedule that performs the computation of the original loop nest in a single superstep, and incurs no inter-processor communication during this superstep.

A second set of scheduling techniques devised in this chapter addresses the parallelisation of three common loop structures that comprise non-uniform data dependences. The first two techniques in the set are dedicated to the parallelisation of reduction and recurrence loops, respectively. As concerns the third technique, it can be employed to parallelise a computation pattern whose instances include salient scientific computing problems such as the solution of triangular linear systems, LU decomposition, and the algebraic path problem.

6. Generic Loop Nest Parallelisation

One's first step in wisdom is to question everything—and one's last is to come to terms with everything.

Georg Christoph Lichtenberg – *Aphorisms*

6.1 Introduction

This chapter addresses the architecture-independent parallelisation of generic loop nests, i.e. of loop nests that match none of the computation patterns studied in Chapter 5. The scheduling scheme employed for the mapping of a generic, untightly nested loop on a parallel computer comprises four steps (Figure 6.1).

In the first of these steps, the data dependences of the sequential loop nest are identified, and its dependence graph is built. This dependence information is then used to expose the parallelism available in the sequential code in the second step of the scheme. In a third step, the data and the computation are partitioned among the processor/memory units of the parallel computer so as to efficiently exploit the potential parallelism of the original loop nest. Finally, in the fourth step, communication and synchronisation are inserted into the incomplete parallel code generated in step 3.

The chapter is organised as follows. First, we review other results on automatic parallelisation of generic loop nests, and compare them with our scheduling scheme. Next, the four steps of the scheme are described in detail in Sections 6.3 to 6.6. In particular, new algorithms are introduced for the last three steps. Thus, we develop a potential parallelism identification algorithm that uses loop interchange to increase the granularity of the parallelism it reveals, and employs an early termination test to eliminate the negative effects of unnecessary loop distribution. In addition, we devise a new, efficient data and computation partitioning technique, and a powerful communication and synchronisation generation algorithm. The latter algorithm takes

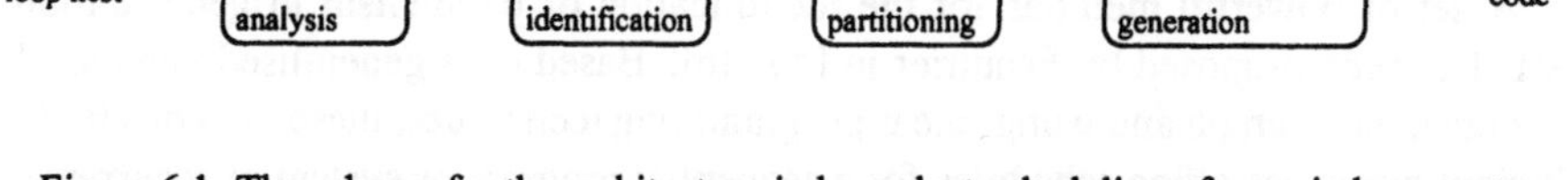

Figure 6.1: The scheme for the architecture-independent scheduling of generic loop nests.

into account the decoupling between communication and synchronisation in the BSP model—a feature unique to our parallelisation scheme.

6.2 Related Work

The current interest in the automatic parallelisation of generic loop nests was sparked by the seminal work of Allen, Callahan and Kennedy in the mid 1980s [20, 28]. Based on the loop distribution algorithm introduced by Kuck [60], and on the first developments in the area of data dependence analysis [4, 6, 84], the three researchers developed the first algorithm addressing the loop-level parallelisation of generic sequential code [20]. This algorithm partitions a sequential program into serial blocks and parallel loops separated by barrier synchronisations, and represents the basic building structure of many automatic parallelisation and vectorisation techniques.

Notwithstanding its significance, the approach of Allen, Callahan and Kennedy has two serious limitations. Firstly, while the authors emphasise the importance of loop interchange, this important code transformation technique is not taken into account by their parallelisation algorithm. Secondly, the approach in [20, 28] considers only the mapping of the potential parallelism revealed by the algorithm on vector computers. Although more recent work due to Zima and Chapman [29] extends the usage of the parallelisation algorithm in [20] to shared-memory multiprocessors, no attempt to use it in the context of scalable, distributed-memory parallel computers has been made so far.

Our scheduling scheme overcomes these limitations by using an extended version of the parallelisation algorithm in its potential parallelism identification step. The extended algorithm integrates loop interchange into the basic parallelisation technique in [20, 28, 29], succeeding to expose the coarse-grained parallelism required in a distributed-memory setting. Moreover, the subsequent steps of the scheme map this parallelism on a BSP computer, generating an architecture-independent parallel version of the original sequential code.

A different approach to the automatic parallelisation of generic loop nests has been proposed by Lim and Lam, who devised an algorithm for the parallelisation of programs consisting of sequences of untightly nested loops [18]. This algorithm works by partitioning the iteration space of the nested loops that compose the sequential program into subsets of iterations which share no common memory reference. Following the construction of this partition, the iterations from each such subset are eventually mapped on the same processor. The result is a Single-Program Multiple-Data (SPMD) parallel version of the sequential code that is communication free. However, the fact that in many practical cases suitable (e.g. well-balanced) communication-free partitions are impossible to obtain renders this parallelisation technique infeasible.

A set of powerful methods for the identification of parallelism in generic loop nests has been proposed by Feautrier in [45, 46]. Based on a generalised version of the dependence graph and using linear programming techniques, these methods build efficient piecewise affine schedules for a sequential program or system of recurrence equations. A one-dimensional such schedule θ gives, for each statement S and each iteration $\mathbf{i}$ of its surrounding loops, the *execution date* $\theta(S,\mathbf{i}) \geq 0$ when the instance of S corresponding to iteration $\mathbf{i}$ must be performed [45]. When no one-dimensional schedule exists, the Feautrier parallelisation algorithm computes a multidimensional schedule [46]. In this case, the statement instances must be performed in the lexicographical order of their multidimensional execution date.

While the affine scheduling techniques of Feautrier represent the most powerful parallelisation framework available to date, they are prone to generate extremely complicated parallel code. Thus, although the resulting schedules exhibit a high degree of parallelism, the intricacy of their practical implementations may significantly decrease the gains obtained from the exploitation of this parallelism.

In order to overcome this limitation, Darte and Vivien have devised a new parallelisation technique [27] which combines elements from the parallelisation algorithms of Allen and Kennedy [28], Wolf and Lam [16] and Feautrier [45, 46]. The technique computes an optimal multidimensional schedule of a nested loop based on the information in its *polyhedral reduced dependence graph*. This represents a dependence graph whose edges are labelled with a polyhedron that includes all the direction vectors of the associated dependence—a generalisation of the direction vector dependence abstraction.

The current version of the parallelisation technique introduced by Darte and Vivien is chiefly applicable to tightly nested loops [27]. Despite recent efforts to extend it to generic, non-perfect nested loops through loop nest "perfectisation", it is not yet clear whether this is possible [27, 85].

The parallelisation algorithms of Feautrier [45, 46] and of Darte and Vivien [27] generate efficient affine schedules that expose the fine- and medium-grained parallelism in the considered loop nest. Furthermore, little knowledge is available on how the underlying data could be partitioned in a distributed-memory setting. Therefore, the schedules they produce are only feasible for implementation on shared-memory multiprocessors, where the operations with the same execution date can be distributed easily among the available processors, and the data used by these operations can be accessed unrestrictedly.

Unlike these algorithms, the potential parallelism identification algorithm employed in the second step of our parallelisation scheme is tuned to expose the coarse-grained parallelism in regular computation structures. Therefore, while in some cases it is less powerful than the parallelisation algorithms described in [27, 45, 46], it betters these algorithms when the distributed-memory mapping of the schedules they produce is considered. In addition, our algorithm permits the exemption of *secondary* statements and/or loops from the parallelisation process. As shown in the remainder of the chapter, this feature has beneficial effects on the data and computation partitioning performed in the third step of the parallelisation scheme.

By far the most common strategy employed in automatic parallelisation for distributed-memory systems is the one described by Zima and Chapman in [30]. This strategy comprises three stages. First, the data of the sequential program are partitioned among the processors of the target parallel computer. Typically, this partition or a starting point for its automatic computation is provided by the user of the parallelising compiler or tool. Next, the computation of the sequential program is distributed using the "owner computes" rule, i.e. ensuring that each processor performs exactly the statement instances that modify locally stored data. This rule is enforced by *masks* (i.e. boolean guards) added to each statement. Also in the second stage, pairwise send/receive communication primitives are inserted into the code whenever non-local data are used by some processor. The last stage of the strategy optimises the resulting parallel code. This is done by attempting to translate statement masks into new loop bounds, to group and extract communication primitives from loops and to eliminate redundant communication, etc.

Variants of this parallelisation strategy, and parallelising tools that implement them are presented in [32, 86–88]. Many of these variants also include a preliminary stage in which various code transformation techniques are used to eliminate as many data dependences as possible before the actual parallelisation takes place.

As the above mentioned approaches lack a potential parallelism identification step, there is no guarantee whatsoever that the schedules they produce assign independent computations to different processors. Unlike these approaches, our scheduling scheme exposes first the parallelism available in the original sequential code. Therefore, the subsequent data and computation distribution step maps the execution of independent statement instances and the associated data on different processor/memory pairs, yielding efficient parallel code. In addition, the scheduling scheme introduced in this chapter automatically devises a data partition for most regular, dense computations. Finally, the scheme generates separate communication and synchronisation primitives to account for the dependences among computations scheduled on different processors. This feature simplifies the algorithms required for the last step of the scheme, enables the performance analysis of the resulting parallel code, and completely eliminates the threat of deadlocks.

6.3 Data Dependence Analysis

In the first step of the generic loop nest scheduling scheme, the data dependences of the target loop nest are identified, and its dependence graph is built as explained in Chapter 3. This dependence graph is then used as an input parameter for the algorithms that implement the other three steps of the scheduling scheme.

No new data dependence test (i.e. test for detecting the existence of a data dependence between two statement instances) is proposed in this book. Instead, we rely on the extensive collection of dependence tests devised within the last two decades [8–10, 12, 21, 28].

Example 6.1 Throughout this chapter, we shall illustrate the usage of the various algorithms employed by our scheduling scheme by applying them to the generic, untightly nested loop in Figure 6.2(a). This loop nest comprises four data dependences. The first is a flow dependence $S_1\delta S_1$ of direction vector $[<,=]^{\mathrm{T}}$, and is due to the fact that different instances of statement S_1 read and modify the elements of array a. The other three dependences, namely $S_2\delta_{[<]}S_1$, $S_2\bar{\delta}_{[<,>,=]^{\mathrm{T}}}S_2$ and $S_2\delta_{[<,=,>]^{\mathrm{T}}}S_2$, are a result of the definition and use of array b in statements S_2 and S_1. Consequently, the

```
l1    for i1 = 1,n-2 do
l2      for i2 = 0,n-1 do
S1:       a[i1,i2] = f1(a[i1-1,i2],b[i1-1,i1,i2])
l3      for i2 = 1,n-1 do
l4        for i3 = 0,n-2 do
S2:         b[i1,i2,i3] = f2(b[i1+1,i2-1,i3],b[i1-1,i2,i3+1])
```

(a)

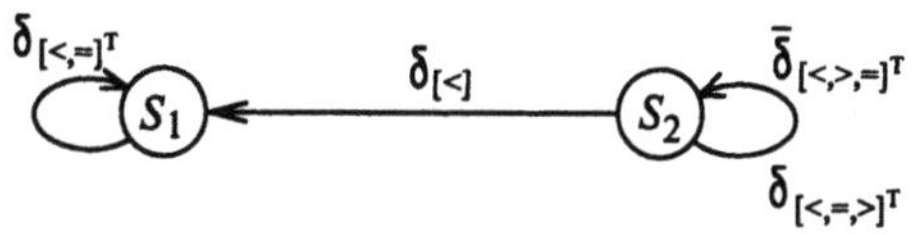

(b)

Figure 6.2: A generic, untightly nested loop (a), and its dependence graph (b).

dependence graph obtained in the first step of the scheduling scheme has the form in Figure 6.2(b).

6.4 Potential Parallelism Identification

This section presents an algorithm which exposes the potential parallelism of a generic loop nest based on the information in its dependence graph. This algorithm extends previous parallelisation techniques by Kuck [60], Allen, Callahan and Kennedy [20, 28], and Zima and Chapman [29]. The novelty of our algorithm is twofold. Firstly, it integrates loop interchange into the existing techniques. This integration leads to an important increase in the granularity of the resulting potential parallelism, with beneficial effects in a distributed-memory setting. Secondly, our algorithm employs an early termination test to eliminate the negative effects of unnecessary loop distribution.

The theory underlying the new parallelisation algorithm is introduced by the following two theorems which summarise results from [12, 17, 21, 28, 29].

Theorem 6.1 *Let S_x and S_y be two statements surrounded by $K > 0$ common loops. Assume that a generic data dependence $S_x \delta_{\mathbf{v}}^{*} S_y$ with $v_k =$ '$<$' for some $1 \le k \le K$ exists between the two statements. Then, if the k-th loop surrounding S_x and S_y is sequentially executed in the outermost position of the K loops, all the restrictions imposed by this dependence are satisfied.*

Proof Consider two generic iteration points $\mathbf{x} = (x_1, x_2, \ldots, x_K)$ and $\mathbf{y} = (y_1, y_2, \ldots, y_K)$ such that the data dependence occurs between the instance of S_x for the first iteration point and the instance of S_y for the second iteration point. As the k-th component of the direction vector characterising the considered dependence is '$<$', we necessarily have $x_k < y_k$.

Assume now that the k-th loop surrounding S_x and S_y is brought into the outermost position and executed sequentially, with the other loops executed in parallel, in an arbitrary order. Since the iterations of the k-th loop are executed sequentially, the iteration point $\mathbf{x}$ will be executed before the iteration point $\mathbf{y}$ by the transformed loop nest. Hence, this loop nest executes any interdependent iteration points in the correct order, and the restrictions imposed by the dependence $S_x\delta^*_{\mathbf{v}}S_y$ are satisfied. □

Theorem 6.1 provides the basis for the parallelisation of the inner loops of a loop nest when one of the loops that *carries* its data dependence(s) is sequentialised in the outermost position. Consider for instance the following loop nest:

$$\begin{array}{ll} & \textbf{for } i_1 = 1, n-1 \textbf{ do} \\ & \quad \textbf{for } i_2 = 2, n-1 \textbf{ do} \\ S_1: & \qquad a[i_1, i_2] = f(a[i_1 - 1, i_2 - 2]) \end{array}$$

Since both loops carry $S_1\delta_{[<,<]^T}S_1$, the only data dependence of this loop nest, the sequential execution of either loop in the outermost position enables the parallel execution of the other loop.

Theorem 6.2 *Consider two statements S_x and S_y surrounded by $K > 0$ common loops. Assume that a data dependence $S_x\delta^*_{\mathbf{v}}S_y$ with v_k='=' for some $1 \leq k \leq K$ exists between the two statements. Then, if the k-th loop surrounding S_x and S_y is concurrently executed in an arbitrarily chosen position, and the other $K-1$ loops are executed so as to satisfy the restrictions imposed by the data dependence $S_x\delta^*_{[v_1,\ldots,v_{k-1},v_{k+1},\ldots,v_K]^T}S_y$, the constraints enforced by the original dependence on the entire loop nest are also satisfied.*

Proof Let $\mathbf{x} = (x_1, x_2, \ldots, x_K)$ and $\mathbf{y} = (y_1, y_2, \ldots, y_K)$ be two generic iteration points such that the dependence occurs between the instance of S_x for the first iteration point and the instance of S_y for the second iteration point. In any legal transformation of the loop nest, the execution order of two iteration points must remain unchanged (i.e. first $\mathbf{x}$, then $\mathbf{y}$).

Consider now that the k-th common loop surrounding S_x and S_y is brought into a randomly chosen position and executed in parallel. According to the hypothesis of the theorem, $x_k = y_k$. Therefore, the fact that iteration points with different k-th components are executed simultaneously does not influence the execution order of the iteration points $\mathbf{x}$ and $\mathbf{y}$. Instead, the order in which $\mathbf{x}$ and $\mathbf{y}$ are performed depends on the other $K-1$ loops, i.e. it is given by the execution order of $\mathbf{x}' = (x_1, \ldots, x_{k-1}, x_{k+1}, \ldots, x_K)$ and $\mathbf{y}' = (y_1, \ldots, y_{k-1}, y_{k+1}, \ldots, y_K)$ when only the other $K-1$ loops are taken into account. As long as these loops are executed so as to respect the data dependence $S_x\delta^*_{[v_1,\ldots,v_{k-1},v_{k+1},\ldots,v_K]^T}S_y$, $\mathbf{x}'$ is performed before $\mathbf{y}'$. Hence, the initially considered iteration points are also executed in the correct order, and the restrictions imposed by the original data dependence are obeyed. □

Typically, the position in which a loop that satisfies the hypothesis of Theorem 6.2 is worth parallelising is the outermost level of its loop nest. Therefore, this theorem provides a way of increasing the granularity of the potential parallelism of a loop nest by parallelising certain loops in the outermost position. The application of the theorem is illustrated for the following example of a nested loop:

for $i_1 = 1, n-1$ **do**
  for $i_2 = 0, n-1$ **do**
    for $i_3 = 0, n-2$ **do**
S_1: $a[i_1, i_2, i_3] = f(a[i_1 - 1, i_2, i_3 + 1])$

The only data dependence of this loop nest is $S_1 \delta_{[<,=,>]^T} S_1$. Since the second component of the direction vector is '=', the loop indexed by i_2 can be parallelised in the outermost position as long as the execution of the other loops does not violate the constraints imposed by the data dependence $S_1 \delta_{[<,>]^T} S_1$.

Before actually presenting the potential parallelism identification algorithm, let us make clear the goals of this algorithm. First of all, note that when addressing the architecture-independent scheduling of a generic loop nest, the attempt to parallelise as many of its constituent statements and loops as possible is not always the best approach. Consider for instance the following loop nest, and assume that the problem size n is much greater than p, the number of processors available on the parallel computer:

for $i_1 = 0, n-1$ **do**
S_1: ...
  for $i_2 = 0, n-1$ **do**
S_2:   ...
    for $i_3 = 0, n-1$ **do**
S_3:   ...

As the sequential cost of executing the loop nest is $O(n^3)$, what one expects from a p-processor parallel version of this loop nest is an execution cost of $O(n^3/p)$. Obviously, this can only be achieved if the execution of statement S_3—which we term the *main statement* of the loop nest—is parallelised. The concurrent execution of the *secondary statement* S_1 and, perhaps, of S_2 is irrelevant for the successful parallelisation of the loop nest as a whole. In addition, as we shall see in the next section, the parallelisation of a statement places certain constraints on the data partition computed in the third step of the scheduling scheme. To reduce the number of such constraints, our parallelisation algorithm focuses on the identification of the potential parallelism corresponding to the main statements of the target loop nest.

The above reasoning also applies to the parallelisation of the individual loops that compose the sequential loop nest. Consider the following example of a 3-level loop nest:

for $i_1 = 0, n-1$ **do**
  for $i_2 = 0, 2$ **do**
    for $i_3 = 0, n-1$ **do**
S_1:   ...

Assuming again that the problem size n is much greater than the number of processors p, any successful parallel version of this loop nest must be able to concurrently execute the loop body for different iteration points along directions i_1 and/or i_3 of the iteration space. Indeed, the parallelisation of the loop indexed by i_2 is of little use in this case. Therefore, our parallelisation algorithm concentrates on those loops whose iteration space size depends on the problem size—these are called the *main loops* of the loop nest—rather than on the loops whose index bounds are (small) constants.

Finally, the position of a parallelised main loop is very important. If the parallel loop whose iterations are distributed across the processors of a parallel computer is in an inner position, a synchronisation may be required after every execution of this loop. Hence, the synchronisation overheads may well dominate the overall cost of the resulting parallel schedule. If, on the other hand, the parallel loop can be brought into a middle position (or, even better, in the outermost position), barrier synchronisations will be required far less often, and the generation of an efficient parallel schedule is possible. Accordingly, our algorithm pays attention to the parallelisation of loops in the outermost legal position, i.e. to the extraction of the coarsest-grained parallelism that is available.

Having clarified its aims, we can now move on to the description of the parallelisation algorithm. The algorithm is depicted in Figure 6.3, and identifies the potential parallelism of a generic loop nest $\mathcal{L}$ using the information in its dependence graph $\mathcal{G}$. In doing so, the algorithm attempts to parallelise the execution of a maximum number of main loops surrounding main statements of $\mathcal{L}$. Therefore, the set of main statements *main_stmts*, and the set of main loops *main_loops* are provided as the last two parameters of the algorithm.

The algorithm (function PARALLELISE) works as follows. In a first stage (lines 1–3), the generic loop nest $\mathcal{L}$ is parallelised as a whole, without using loop distribution. The resulting parallel version of the loop nest is accepted—and the algorithm terminates—if each main statement is completely parallelised, i.e. if each main loop whose body contains at least one main statement is parallelised. The algorithm also terminates when $\mathcal{L}$ comprises a single statement, since in this case no further loop distribution is possible.

When none of the termination conditions is fulfilled, the algorithm enters a second stage (lines 4–15), in which loop distribution is employed as in [29], in an attempt to increase the amount of available parallelism. Firstly, the strongly connected components (or π-blocks [28, 61]) of $\mathcal{G}$ are identified (line 4). Next, if $\mathcal{G}$ comprises several strongly connected components, the parallelisation algorithm is recursively applied to each such component, in topologically sorted order (lines 5–10). The distributed parallel version of the loop nest ($\mathcal{PL}_2$) is obtained by concatenating the results of the successive applications of the algorithm.

If, on the other hand, $\mathcal{G}$ comprises a single π-block, the distributed parallel version of $\mathcal{L}$ is obtained by keeping the outermost loop in the parallelised "as a whole" version of the loop nest unchanged, and applying the algorithm recursively to the body of this loop (lines 11–14). Before re-applying the algorithm, however, the edges that stand for dependences carried by the outermost loop are eliminated from $\mathcal{G}$. (Note that if the outermost loop is parallel, it carries no dependence, so no test is needed to check whether the outermost loop is sequential or parallel.)

The result returned by the parallelisation algorithm is the best choice between

```
PARALLELISE(L, G, main_stmts, main_loops)
  PL1 = PARALLELISE_AS_A_WHOLE(L, G, main_loops)
  if all main loops surrounding main statements in PL1 are parallelised
  or L comprises a single statement then
    return PL1
  identify the strongly connected components of G
  if G has several strongly connected components then
    PL2 = {}
    for each strongly connected component C, in topologically sorted order do
      L' = reduction of L to the statements in C
      G' = reduction of G to the vertices in C
      PL2 = PL2 ++ PARALLELISE(L', G', main_stmts, main_loops)
  else     /* G has a single strongly connected component */
    L' = body of loop, the outermost loop in PL1
    G' = G without the edges corresponding to dependences carried by loop
    PL2 = loop ++ PARALLELISE(L', G', main_stmts, main_loops)
  return BEST_CHOICE(PL1,PL2)

PARALLELISE_AS_A_WHOLE(L, G, main_loops)
  if L is a simple statement then
    return L
  identify loops, the set of outermost loops surrounding the statements in L
  PL = PARALLELISE_OUTERMOST_LOOPS(loops, G, main_loops)
  for each component L' in the loop body of loops do
    G' = reduction of G to the statements in L'
    PL = PL ++ PARALLELISE_AS_A_WHOLE(L', G', main_loops)
  return PL

PARALLELISE_OUTERMOST_LOOPS(loops, G, main_loops)
  V = the set of non-null direction vectors corresponding to the edges of G
  PL = {}
  while loops ≠ {} do
    identify par_loops, the set of main loops from loops with the property that
    their associated components in any direction vector in V are '='
    if par_loops ≠ {} then
      PL = PL ++ parallelised par_loops
      loops = loops \ par_loops
    else
      identify seq_loops, the set of loops from loops with the property that their
      associated components in any direction vector in V are '=' or '<'
      choose seq_loop ∈ seq_loops such that the elimination from V of the direction
      vectors whose component corresponding to seq_loop is '<' permits the
      parallelisation of most main loops in the next step; among several candidate
      loops, prefer a secondary loop
      PL = PL ++ seq_loop
      loops = loops \ {seq_loop}
      V = V \ direction vectors whose component corresponding to seq_loop is '<'
      G = G without the edges corresponding to the eliminated direction vectors
  return PL
```

Figure 6.3: The potential parallelism identification algorithm.

$\mathcal{PL}_1$, the parallelised "as a whole" version of $\mathcal{L}$, and $\mathcal{PL}_2$, the distributed parallel version of $\mathcal{L}$ (line 15). Thus, $\mathcal{PL}_2$ is chosen if it brings extra parallelism, and $\mathcal{PL}_1$ if the potential parallelism revealed by the two parallel versions of the original loop nest is identical.

For the parallelisation of a loop nest as a whole, Theorems 6.1 and 6.2 are applied to the data dependences encoded by the dependence graph $\mathcal{G}$ (function PARALLELISE_AS_A_WHOLE). First, the outermost perfectly nested loops of the loop nest are identified, and parallelised in lines 3–4. Next, the algorithm is applied recursively to each component belonging to the body of these loops (lines 5–7).

Finally, the parallelisation of a sequence of outermost loops is an iterative process (function PARALLELISE_OUTERMOST_LOOPS; as an exception, the parameter $\mathcal{G}$ of this function is an input-output parameter; all other parameters are input only). In each iteration of the while loop in lines 3–14, the algorithm attempts first to find main loops that satisfy Theorem 6.2, and thus can be parallelised in the outermost position (line 4). If such loops exist, they are brought into the outermost position and changed into parallel loops (lines 5–7).

Otherwise, in lines 9–10 an outermost sequential loop is chosen from the loops that satisfy Theorem 6.1 (at least one such loop, the current outermost loop, exists). The choice is made so as to maximise the number of parallel loops in the next iteration of the algorithm, a secondary loop taking precedence over a main loop that would reveal the same amount of parallelism in the next iteration. After establishing the outermost loop(s), they are eliminated from the set of loops to be parallelised, and the algorithm is iterated until no loop is left in this set. When a sequential loop is selected in the current iteration of the algorithm, Theorem 6.1 is applied to eliminate the dependences carried by this loop before proceeding to the next iteration (lines 13–14).

Example 6.2 To illustrate the usage of the parallelisation algorithm, let us identify the potential parallelism of the loop nest $\mathcal{L}$ in Figure 6.2(a) by calling

$$\text{PARALLELISE}(\mathcal{L}, \mathcal{G}, \{S_1, S_2\}, \{l_1, l_2, l_3, l_4\})$$

where $\mathcal{G}$ represents the dependence graph in Figure 6.2(b). In the first stage, the loop nest is parallelised as a whole, yielding the following undistributed parallel version of $\mathcal{L}$:

l_1 **for** $i_1 = 1, n-2$ **do**
l_2 **forall** $i_2 = 0, n-1$ **do in parallel**
S_1: $a[i_1, i_2] = f_1(a[i_1 - 1, i_2], b[i_1 - 1, i_1, i_2])$
l_3 **forall** $i_2 = 1, n-1$ **do in parallel**
l_4 **forall** $i_3 = 0, n-2$ **do in parallel**
S_2: $b[i_1, i_2, i_3] = f_2(b[i_1 + 1, i_2 - 1, i_3], b[i_1 - 1, i_2, i_3 + 1])$

Indeed, all the data dependences are carried by loop l_1, and the other loops can be parallelised once loop l_1 is sequentialised in the outermost position.

As one of the main loops surrounding S_1 and S_2 is sequential, the algorithm proceeds to the second stage. In this stage, the two strongly connected components of $\mathcal{G}$

$$
\begin{array}{ll}
l_1 & \textbf{for } i_1 = 1, n-2 \textbf{ do} \\
l_3 & \quad \textbf{forall } i_2 = 1, n-1 \textbf{ do in parallel} \\
l_4 & \quad\quad \textbf{forall } i_3 = 0, n-2 \textbf{ do in parallel} \\
S_2: & \quad\quad\quad b[i_1, i_2, i_3] = f_2(b[i_1+1, i_2-1, i_3], b[i_1-1, i_2, i_3+1]) \\
l_2 & \textbf{forall } i_2 = 0, n-1 \textbf{ do in parallel} \\
l_1 & \quad \textbf{for } i_1 = 1, n-2 \textbf{ do} \\
S_1: & \quad\quad a[i_1, i_2] = f_1(a[i_1-1, i_2], b[i_1-1, i_1, i_2])
\end{array}
$$

Figure 6.4: The potential parallelism of the loop nest in Figure 6.2(a).

are parallelised in topologically sorted order, i.e. first the π-block comprising statement S_2, then the π-block comprising S_1. For the first strongly connected component, the algorithm yields

$$
\begin{array}{ll}
l_1 & \textbf{for } i_1 = 1, n-2 \textbf{ do} \\
l_3 & \quad \textbf{forall } i_2 = 1, n-1 \textbf{ do in parallel} \\
l_4 & \quad\quad \textbf{forall } i_3 = 0, n-2 \textbf{ do in parallel} \\
S_2: & \quad\quad\quad b[i_1, i_2, i_3] = f_2(b[i_1+1, i_2-1, i_3], b[i_1-1, i_2, i_3+1])
\end{array}
$$

and for the second one

$$
\begin{array}{ll}
l_2 & \textbf{forall } i_2 = 0, n-1 \textbf{ do in parallel} \\
l_1 & \quad \textbf{for } i_1 = 1, n-2 \textbf{ do} \\
S_1: & \quad\quad a[i_1, i_2] = f_1(a[i_1-1, i_2], b[i_1-1, i_1, i_2])
\end{array}
$$

Since in both cases the loop nests to be parallelised comprise a single statement, the algorithm terminates. Next, $\mathcal{PL}_2$, the distributed parallel version of the original loop nest is obtained by concatenating the parallel code for the two components (Figure 6.4). This is also the final result, because the distributed parallel version of $\mathcal{L}$ reveals coarser-grained potential parallelism than the undistributed one.

6.5 Data and Computation Partitioning

In the third step of the scheduling scheme, the potential parallelism of the loop nest is mapped on the processor-memory pairs of the parallel computer. This is done by distributing the data and the computation of the loop nest so as to allocate operations that can be performed in parallel to distinct processors. Similar to other parallelisation strategies aimed at distributed-memory systems [30, 32, 88], we first build a data partition, and then apply the "owner computes" rule to distribute the associated computation.

Most of the above mentioned approaches obtain the data partition or a starting point for its computation from the user. Unlike these approaches, we provide an algorithm allowing the automatic detection of a suitable data distribution in most cases when the computation to be parallelised has a regular structure. Only when this algorithm cannot generate a data partition is user expertise required for the selection of the data distribution.

```
COMPUTE_DATA_PARTITION(PL, main_stmts)
  par_loop_layer = 0; acceptable = FALSE
  while acceptable=FALSE and par_loop_layer ≤ max_par_loop_layer do
    ready = FALSE
    PL' = PL with parallel loops in layers greater than par_loop_layer sequentialised
    while ready =FALSE do
      Step 1. Initialise the partition
        for each array a in PL' and each dimension j of a do
          distribution[a, j] = UNDEFINED
      Step 2. Partition the arrays in dimensions corresponding to parallel loops
        for each main statement S do
          for each dimension j of an array a referenced by S do
            if the j-th subscript of a has the form αi_k + β, where i_k is the index
            of a surrounding parallel loop and α ≠ 0, β are integer constants then
              if distribution[a, j] =UNDEFINED then
                distribution[a, j] = BLOCK
            else
              distribution[a, j] = SERIAL
      Step 3. Check if any parallel loop in PL' has to be sequentialised
        ready = TRUE
        for each main statement S and each parallel loop pl surrounding S in PL' do
          for each array a referenced by S do
            if a is the definition of a main statement and a has no block-partitioned
            dimension whose associated subscript has the form αi_k + β, with i_k the
            index of pl and α ≠ 0, β integer constants then
              sequentialise pl
              ready = FALSE
    Step 4. Verify if current partition is acceptable
      acceptable = TRUE
      for each main statement S do
        if def(S) is block-partitioned in no dimension then
          acceptable = FALSE
    par_loop_layer = par_loop_layer + 1
  if acceptable =TRUE then
    return distribution, with undefined elements set to SERIAL
  else
    get data partition from the user, starting from the one described by distribution
```

Figure 6.5: The data partitioning algorithm.

The data partitioning algorithm is presented in Figure 6.5. It takes two input parameters, the parallelised loop nest ($\mathcal{PL}$) and the set of the main statements in the loop (*main_stmts*), and returns a distribution of the arrays referenced within the loop body. For each array, and each of its dimensions, the algorithm decides whether the array should be partitioned into blocks, or left *serial* (i.e. unpartitioned) in that dimension. The array dimensions that are candidates for block-partitioning are those corresponding to parallel loops, namely those whose associated subscripts have the form $\alpha i_k + \beta$, where i_k is the index of a surrounding parallel loop and $\alpha \neq 0$, β are integer constants.

The algorithm is designed to exploit first the coarsest-grained parallelism that is available. Therefore, it initially takes into account only the outermost layer of parallel loops surrounding the main statements of $\mathcal{PL}$. When an acceptable distribution (the criterion used to establish the acceptability of a distribution is described later in the text) cannot be obtained at this level, inner layers of parallelism are iteratively explored. The algorithm terminates when either an acceptable distribution is found, or when no such distribution is available even when fully exploiting the potential parallelism of the loop nest.

The data partitioning algorithm works as follows. First, $\mathcal{PL}'$, a copy of the parallelised loop nest is built (line 4 of COMPUTE_DATA_PARTITION). In this copy, the parallel loops belonging to layers greater than *par_loop_layer*, the currently considered layer of parallel loops, are sequentialised. A stable data distribution is then built in steps 1 to 3. In step 1, the distribution is initialised: for each array and each dimension of that array, the way of distributing the data is marked as undefined. In step 2, the partitioning of each array referenced by a main statement is attempted. Thus, array dimensions that correspond to parallel loops in $\mathcal{PL}'$ and whose distribution is undefined are marked as block-partitioned (lines 10–12), and array dimensions that correspond to no parallel loop are marked as serial-partitioned (line 14).

Finally, in step 3, the algorithm checks if all parallel loops surrounding a main statement S correspond to at least a partitioned dimension of each array referenced by S, and which is also the *definition* of a main statement (i.e. the array written by a main statement). When this is not the case, the later use of the "owner computes" rule would map all the iterations of some parallel loop(s) on every processor—if the array is the definition of S, or the entire array block used locally by S would reside on remote processors—if the array is the definition of another main statement. To avoid these unwanted situations, such a parallel loop is sequentialised explicitly, and the flag *ready* is set to FALSE, to indicate that a stable data distribution has not been reached yet (lines 19–20). The while loop in lines 5–20 iterates the three steps until no further change of $\mathcal{PL}'$ is required.

Next, the acceptability of the resulting distribution is verified in step 4. A data distribution is deemed acceptable if for any main statement S, $def(S)$—the definition of S—is block-partitioned in at least one dimension. Indeed, if the definition of a main statement S is fully unpartitioned, S must be scheduled for sequential execution on every processor, rendering the whole parallel schedule inefficient. Hence, if such a main statement exists, the algorithm seeks an acceptable distribution using an additional layer of parallel loops.

The outer while loop in lines 2–25 iterates until either an acceptable data distribution is found, or until no such distribution can be built even by exploiting the entire potential parallelism of the loop nest. In the former case, the algorithm returns the acceptable distribution, while in the latter case user expertise is sought.

Example 6.3 Let us illustrate the application of the data partitioning algorithm by using it to build a data distribution for the parallelised loop nest in Figure 6.4. The main statements of the loop (as considered when identifying its potential parallelism) are S_1 and S_2. The loop nest has a single layer of parallel loops (namely loop l_2 surrounding S_1, and loops l_3, l_4 surrounding S_2). As a result, in the only outer iteration of the algorithm, $\mathcal{PL}'$ is initially identical to $\mathcal{PL}$. After initialising the data distribution to

$$a[\text{UNDEFINED}, \text{UNDEFINED}]$$
$$b[\text{UNDEFINED}, \text{UNDEFINED}, \text{UNDEFINED}]$$

in step 1, step 2 is performed, first on statement S_1, and then on statement S_2. After performing step 2 on statement S_1, the data distribution is changed into:

$$a[\text{SERIAL}, \text{BLOCK}]$$
$$b[\text{SERIAL}, \text{SERIAL}, \text{BLOCK}]$$

since array dimensions corresponding to the subscript i_2 are marked as block-partitioned, and those corresponding to the subscripts i_1 and $i_1 - 1$ are marked as serial-partitioned. The application of step 2 to statement S_2 brings no change into the data distribution.

However, in step 3 the algorithm identifies the fact that loop l_3 surrounding statement S_2 corresponds to no partitioned dimension of array b. Consequently, this loop is sequentialised, the distribution is marked as unstable, and a new iteration through steps 1 to 3 is performed. The new iteration yields the same data distribution, and is also found to be stable. Hence, the algorithm proceeds to step 4, and verifies the acceptability of the distribution. Since both $a = def(S_1)$ and $b = def(S_2)$ are partitioned in at least one dimension, the data distribution is acceptable and the algorithm terminates successfully. According to this data distribution, a generic processor with identifier *me*, $0 \leq me < p$, is considered to "own" the array blocks

$$a[0..n-1, me\lceil n/p \rceil..\min\{n-1, (me+1)\lceil n/p \rceil - 1\}]$$
$$b[0..n-1, 0..n-1, me\lceil n/p \rceil..\min\{n-1, (me+1)\lceil n/p \rceil - 1\}]$$

in the remaining stages of the parallelisation scheme.

Consider now the generic case when, following the application of the data partitioning algorithm, an m-dimensional array a of size $n_1 \times n_2 \times \cdots \times n_m$ is block-partitioned in Q dimensions, $1 < Q \leq m$. In this case, the p processors are considered to be arranged into a logical Q-dimensional array of size $p_1 \times p_2 \times \cdots \times p_Q$, $\prod_{q=1}^{Q} p_q = p$. The array block owned by the processor with coordinates $(me_1, me_2, \ldots, me_Q)$ in this array is $a[l_1..u_1, l_2..u_2, \ldots, l_m..u_m]$, where the lower and upper bounds along the j-th dimension, $1 \leq j \leq m$ are

$$(l_j, u_j) = \begin{cases} (0, n_j - 1) & \text{if } a \text{ is unpartitioned in dimension } j \\ (me_q\lceil n_j/p_q \rceil, \min\{n_j - 1, (me_q+1)\lceil n_j/p_q \rceil - 1\}) & \text{if dimension } j \text{ is the } q\text{-th block-partitioned dimension of } a \end{cases} \quad (6.1)$$

After building a data distribution, the third step of the scheduling scheme proceeds with the partitioning of the computation of the target loop nest. Typically, the computation partitioning algorithms based on the "owner computes" rule comprise two phases [30, 32]. In the first phase, they generate *masks* (i.e. boolean guards checking the ownership of the modified data) for each statement in the program. Then, in the latter phase, these algorithms strive to adjust the surrounding loop bounds so as to eliminate as many statement masks as possible.

Our computation partitioning algorithm (Figure 6.6) is an exception from this point of view, as it computes the new loop bounds and the statement masks in a single phase. This is achieved by translating each data ownership constraint either into a loop bound constraint or into a statement mask (step 1 of COMPUTATION_PARTITION). To understand the algorithm, note that for each statement S and for each block-partitioned dimension j of the definition of S, s_j—the j-th subscript of this definition—must satisfy the constraint:

$$l_j \leq s_j \leq u_j, \tag{6.2}$$

where l_j, u_j are given by equation (6.1). Therefore, whenever $s_j = \alpha i_k + \beta$, with i_k the index of a surrounding parallel loop pl, and $\alpha \neq 0$, β integer constants, this condition translates into

$$\lceil (l_j - \beta)/\alpha \rceil \leq i_k \leq \lfloor (u_j - \beta)/\alpha \rfloor,$$

and is stored as a pair of constraints associated with statement S and loop pl (i.e. $lower[pl,S]$, $upper[pl,S]$) in lines 7–9. If, however, s_j has a different form, constraint (6.2) is added to the mask of statement S (line 11).

The algorithm also comprises a second step in which the new loop bounds and the statement masks are inserted into the parallelised version of the loop nest (line 12). This step (function ADD_MASKS&BOUNDS) is performed by applying the following rules on each component C of the loop nest. Firstly, if C is a parallel loop pl originally iterating from $lower\_bound(pl)$ to $upper\_bound(pl)$, these bounds are replaced with loop bounds that take into account only the statement instances to be executed locally (lines 2–8). Thus, the iteration range of loop pl is changed such that its new lower bound is

$$\max\left\{lower\_bound(pl), \min_{\text{stmts } S \text{ surrounded by } pl} lower[pl,S]\right\}$$

and its new upper bound is

$$\min\left\{upper\_bound(pl), \max_{\text{stmts } S \text{ surrounded by } pl} upper[pl,S]\right\}$$

Additionally, the masks and loop bounds insertion algorithm is recursively applied to the body of the loop (line 9).

Secondly, if C is a sequential loop, the control of the loop is left unchanged, and function ADD_MASKS&BOUNDS is called recursively for the loop body (lines 10–12). Finally, when C is an assignment statement, its mask is augmented in lines 14–18 with the loop bound constraints associated with the statement and which are not

```
COMPUTATION_PARTITION(PL, data_distribution)
  Step 0. Initialise statement masks and loop bound constraints
    for each statement S do
      mask[S] = {}
      for each loop loop surrounding S do
        lower[loop,S] = {}; upper[loop,S] = {}
  Step 1. Compute loop bound constraints and statement masks
    for each statement S and each block-partitioned dimension j of def(S) do
      let s_j be the j-th subscript of def(S)
      if s_j = αi_k + β where i_k is the index of a surrounding parallel loop pl,
      and α ≠ 0, β are integer constants then
        lower[pl,S] = max{lower[pl,S], ⌈(l_j−β)/α⌉}, with l_j given by eq. (6.1)
        upper[pl,S] = min{upper[pl,S], ⌊(u_j−β)/α⌋}, with u_j given by eq. (6.1)
      else
        mask[S] = (mask[S] and l_j ≤ s_j ≤ u_j), with l_j, u_j given by eq. (6.1)
  Step 2. Add loop bounds and statement masks to PL
    ADD_MASKS&BOUNDS(PL, mask, lower, upper)
```

```
ADD_MASKS&BOUNDS(PL, mask, lower, upper)
1  for each component C of PL do
2    if C is a parallel loop pl then
3      overall_lower = {}; overall_upper = {}
4      for each statement S surrounded by loop pl do
5        overall_lower = min{overall_lower, lower[pl,S]}
6        overall_upper = max{overall_upper, upper[pl,S]}
7      replace lower_bound(pl) with max{lower_bound(pl), overall_lower}
8      replace upper_bound(pl) with min{upper_bound(pl), overall_upper}
9      call ADD_MASKS&BOUNDS for the body of the loop pl
10   else if C is a sequential loop then
11     leave loop control unchanged
12     call ADD_MASKS&BOUNDS for the body of the loop
13   else   /* C is a simple statement S */
14     for each loop loop surrounding S do
15       if lower[loop,S] ≠ {} and lower[loop,S] > lower_bound(loop) then
16         mask[S] = mask[S] and lower[loop,S] ≤ index(loop)
17       if upper[loop,S] ≠ {} and upper[loop,S] < upper_bound(loop) then
18         mask[S] = mask[S] and index(loop) ≤ upper[loop,S]
19     if mask[S] ≠ {} then
20       replace S with the statement "if mask[S] then S"
```

Figure 6.6: The computation partitioning algorithm.

enforced by the new bounds of the surrounding loops. If the resulting mask is non-empty, it is added as a guard to the statement (lines 19–20).

Example 6.4 To demonstrate the use of the algorithm, we shall partition the computation of the parallelised loop nest in Figure 6.4. Starting from the data distribution obtained in the first part of this section, the first step of the algorithm yields the constraints:

l_1 **for** $i_1 = 1, n-2$ **do**
l_3 **forall** $i_2 = 1, n-1$ **do in parallel**
l_4 **forall** $i_3 = me\lceil n/p \rceil, min\{n-2, (me+1)\lceil n/p \rceil - 1\}$ **do in parallel**
S_2: $b[i_1, i_2, i_3] = f_2(b[i_1+1, i_2-1, i_3], b[i_1-1, i_2, i_3+1])$
l_2 **forall** $i_2 = me\lceil n/p \rceil, min\{n-1, (me+1)\lceil n/p \rceil - 1\}$ **do in parallel**
l_1 **for** $i_1 = 1, n-2$ **do**
S_1: $a[i_1, i_2] = f_1(a[i_1-1, i_2], b[i_1-1, i_1, i_2])$

Figure 6.7: The partitioned parallel version of the loop nest in Figure 6.2(a).

$$
\begin{aligned}
&lower[l_1, S_1] = \{\}\\
&upper[l_1, S_1] = \{\}\\
&lower[l_2, S_1] = me\lceil n/p \rceil\\
&upper[l_2, S_1] = (me+1)\lceil n/p \rceil - 1\\
&mask[S_1] = \{\}\\
&lower[l_1, S_2] = \{\}\\
&upper[l_1, S_2] = \{\}\\
&lower[l_3, S_2] = \{\}\\
&upper[l_3, S_2] = \{\}\\
&lower[l_4, S_2] = me\lceil n/p \rceil\\
&upper[l_4, S_2] = (me+1)\lceil n/p \rceil - 1\\
&mask[S_2] = \{\}
\end{aligned}
$$

These data ownership constraints are then inserted into the parallel code in the second step of the algorithm; the resulting partitioned parallel version of the loop nest is depicted in Figure 6.7.

6.6 Communication and Synchronisation Generation

In the fourth and final step of the parallelisation scheme, the complete parallel schedule of the original loop nest is built by adding synchronisation and communication to its partitioned parallel version. Unlike other parallelisation techniques, our scheme takes into account the decoupling between communication and synchronisation that characterises the BSP model of computation. Therefore, the typical approach of generating pairs of send/receive communication primitives that solve the requirements for non-local data and synchronise the two processors involved in the data transfer is not applicable. Instead, the algorithm introduced in this section generates independent calls to both communication and synchronisation primitives, based on the information in the dependence graph of the loop nest.

Before describing the communication and synchronisation generation algorithm, let us analyse what non-local data are needed for the execution of a generic statement. Since the computation was partitioned using the "owner computes" rule, all statement definitions (i.e. variables written by statements) are local. (Note that according to this property, output dependences always occur between local statement instances and can be neglected in this step.) The only variable references that may access non-local data are the statement *uses*, namely the variables that are read by statements. As a result, the algorithm will identify the statement uses that refer to non-local data, and will generate **bsp_get** calls that bring these data into the local memories of the processors that use them.

In order to reduce the synchronisation and communication overheads, these communication primitives are inserted into the code in the outermost possible position. When a non-local use is the sink of no flow data dependence, this "outermost possible position" is before the entire computation. Hence, antidependences can be ignored by the algorithm until the very last moment: non-local data which are the source of an antidependence will be brought into the local memory before any computation takes place. The situation is entirely different if a non-local use is the sink of one or more flow dependences. In this case, the outermost loop that carries each such dependence is considered, and the non-local data will be fetched within the body of the innermost of these loops.

This approach reduces the parallelisation overheads in several ways. Firstly, it permits the *vectorisation* [87, 88] of remote data gets (i.e. the inter-processor communication of array blocks rather than that of individual array elements). Secondly, the algorithm uses this strategy to avoid the communication of multiple copies of the same data (this is called *communication coalescing* [87, 88]). Finally, the synchronisation overheads are minimised since the barrier synchronisation primitives that must follow each sequence of remote data gets will also be inserted at the outermost possible level.

The synchronisation and communication generation algorithm is presented in Figure 6.8. The algorithm takes three parameters: $\mathcal{PL}$, the partitioned parallel version of the loop nest; $\mathcal{G}$, its dependence graph; and *data_distribution*, the data partition. During its execution, calls to communication and synchronisation primitives are inserted into $\mathcal{PL}$, which is an input/output parameter. Several other parameters of the functions in Figure 6.8 are input/output parameters: the parameters $\mathcal{B}$ and *satisfied_use* of function ADD_SYNC&COMM_TO_BLOCK, and the parameters $\mathcal{L}$ and *satisfied_use* of function ADD_SYNC&COMM_TO_LOOP.

The algorithm works by initially marking each statement use in the code as not satisfied locally (lines 1–2 of GENERATE_SYNC&COMM), and solving the non-local uses in a "depth-first search" fashion. To achieve this, it first calls the function ADD_SYNC&COMM_TO_BLOCK for the entire block of code $\mathcal{PL}$, generating the communication and synchronisation required by the use of non-local data that are the sinks of flow dependences (line 3). Each statement use is then examined by the for loop in lines 4–6 and, if necessary, an additional communication superstep solving the uses that are still unsatisfied at this outermost level is added before the entire code.

In order to generate the communication and synchronisation corresponding to a block of code (i.e. to a sequence of loops and/or simple statements), function ADD_SYNC&COMM_TO_BLOCK initially tackles each component of the block (lines 1–7). Then—if the block comprises several components—communication satisfying the loop-independent flow dependences between statements in different components

```
GENERATE_SYNC&COMM(PL, G, data_distribution)
for each statement S and each variable use read by S do
   satisfied_use[S,use] = FALSE
ADD_SYNC&COMM_TO_BLOCK(PL, G, data_distribution, satisfied_use, PL)
for each statement S and each variable use read by S do
   if satisfied_use[S,use] = FALSE then
      generate a bsp_get for the non-local elements of use before the entire code
if at least one bsp_get was generated before the actual computation then
   insert a bsp_sync call before the actual computation

ADD_SYNC&COMM_TO_BLOCK(B, G, data_distribution, satisfied_use, PL)
for each component C in the block B do
   if C is a loop then
      ADD_SYNC&COMM_TO_LOOP(C, G, data_distribution, satisfied_use, PL)
   else   /* C is an assignment statement */
      for each variable use read by C do
         if use is owned by the current processor for all local instances of C then
            satisfied_use[C,use] = TRUE
if B comprises more than one component then
   taking into account all flow dependences carried by no loop in PL and whose sink
   is unsatisfied yet, topologically sort the components of B into subsets S_1, S_2, ..., S_m
   such that the components in S_k depend only on those in S_1, S_2, ..., S_{k-1}
   rearrange the components in topologically sorted order
   for k=2,m do
      for each flow dependence between a component in S_1, ...,S_{k-1} and one in S_k do
         let the variable use from statement S be the sink of the dependence
         if satisfied_use[S,use] = FALSE then
            insert a bsp_get fetching the non-local elements of use before S_k
            satisfied_use[S,use] = TRUE
      insert a bsp_sync before S_k

ADD_SYNC&COMM_TO_LOOP(L, G, data_distribution, satisfied_use, PL)
ADD_SYNC&COMM_TO_BLOCK(loop_body(L),G,data_distribution,satisfied_use,PL)
if L is a sequential loop then
   for each flow dependence between two statements in loop_body(L) do
      let the variable use from statement S be the sink of the dependence
      if satisfied_use[S,use] = FALSE and the dependence is carried by L and by no
      loop surrounding L in PL then
         insert a bsp_get for the non-local elements of use before the loop body of L
         satisfied_use[S,use] = TRUE
   if at least one bsp_get was inserted before the loop body of L then
      insert a bsp_sync before the loop body of L
else   /* L is a parallel loop */
   if L is part of a perfect loop nest and communication primitives were
   generated before the body of an inner loop then
      move L between these communication primitives and the loop body,
      adjusting the communication primitives accordingly
```

Figure 6.8: The synchronisation and communication generation algorithm.

is generated (lines 8–17).

The application of the algorithm for a single component C depends on the type of that component. If C is a loop, function ADD_SYNC&COMM_TO_LOOP is called in line 3 to generate the communication and synchronisation required by C. If, on the other hand, the component is a simple statement (i.e. an assignment), the algorithm only marks locally held uses as satisfied (lines 4–7).

Function ADD_SYNC&COMM_TO_LOOP solves the non-local uses of a loop by firstly applying the algorithm to the loop body (line 1). It then generates the communication and synchronisation accounting for the flow dependences that are carried by the loop itself and by no outer loop, and whose sink is an unsatisfied use. As indicated in lines 2–9, such dependences can only exist when the loop is sequential. When a parallel loop is reached during this depth-first search, the algorithm checks whether the loop is part of a perfect loop nest comprising an inner loop for which a communication superstep was generated. If this is the case, Theorem 6.2 is applied, and the parallel loop is moved between this communication superstep and the body of the inner loop, thus decreasing the synchronisation overheads (lines 10–12).

Here is an example of such a situation. Consider that the following loop nest is part of the code obtained after the potential parallelism identification step:

```
l1      forall i1 = 0,n-1 do in parallel
l2        for i2 = 1,n-1 do
l3          forall i3 = 2,n-1 do in parallel
S1:           a[i1,i2,i3] = f(a[i1,i2-1,i3-2])
```

and assume that the data distribution for array a is $a[\text{SERIAL},\text{SERIAL},\text{BLOCK}]$. After partitioning the computation and generating the communication and synchronisation for statement S_1 and loops l_2, l_3, the following BSP code is obtained:

```
l1   forall i1 = 0,n-1 do in parallel
l2     for i2 = 1,n-1 do
         if me > 0 then
           bsp_get a[i1,i2-1,me⌈n/p⌉-2..me⌈n/p⌉-1]
                   from processor me-1
         bsp_sync
l3       forall i3 = max{2,me⌈n/p⌉},min{n-1,(me+1)⌈n/p⌉-1} do in parallel
S1:        a[i1,i2,i3] = f(a[i1,i2-1,i3-2])
```

This BSP schedule comprises n^2 supersteps. By moving loop l_1 into an inner position as described above, the number of supersteps is decreased to n:

```
l2   for i2 = 1,n-1 do
       if me > 0 then
         bsp_get a[0..n-1,i2-1,me⌈n/p⌉-2..me⌈n/p⌉-1]
                 from processor me-1
       bsp_sync
l1     forall i1 = 0,n-1 do in parallel
l3       forall i3 = max{2,me⌈n/p⌉},min{n-1,(me+1)⌈n/p⌉-1} do in parallel
S1:        a[i1,i2,i3] = f(a[i1,i2-1,i3-2])
```

```
l1      for i1 = 1,n-2 do
          if me < p-1 then
            bsp_get b[i1-1, 1..n-1, (me+1)⌈n/p⌉] from processor me+1
          bsp_sync
l3        for i2 = 1,n-1 do
l4          for i3 = me⌈n/p⌉, min{n-2, (me+1)⌈n/p⌉-1} do
S2:           b[i1,i2,i3] = f2(b[i1+1,i2-1,i3], b[i1-1,i2,i3+1])
l2      for i2 = me⌈n/p⌉, min{n-1, (me+1)⌈n/p⌉-1} do
l1        for i1 = 1,n-2 do
S1:         a[i1,i2] = f1(a[i1-1,i2], b[i1-1,i1,i2])
```

Figure 6.9: The BSP schedule of the generic, untightly nested loop in Figure 6.2(a).

Finally, when a **bsp_get** call generated by the algorithm corresponds to a statement that acquired a mask in the computation partitioning step, this mask is automatically inherited by the **bsp_get** call. For the sake of simplicity, this rule is not included in the algorithm description in Figure 6.8.

Example 6.5 Let us complete the scheduling of the loop nest in Figure 6.2(a), by adding the necessary communication and synchronisation to its partitioned parallel version in Figure 6.7. The algorithm described in this section is first applied to the loop nest containing statement S_2. The use $b[i_1+1, i_2-1, i_3]$ in this statement is identified as locally satisfied, but the use $b[i_1-1, i_2, i_3+1]$ refers to non-local data for some values of i_3. Hence, appropriate communication and synchronisation is inserted before the body of loop l_1, the outermost loop that carries the only flow dependence whose sink is $b[i_1-1, i_2, i_3+1]$:

```
l1   for i1 = 1,n-2 do
       if me < p-1 then
         bsp_get b[i1-1, 1..n-1, (me+1)⌈n/p⌉] from processor me+1
       bsp_sync
l3     forall i2 = 1,n-1 do in parallel
l4       forall i3 = me⌈n/p⌉, min{n-2, (me+1)⌈n/p⌉-1} do in parallel
S2:        b[i1,i2,i3] = f2(b[i1+1,i2-1,i3], b[i1-1,i2,i3+1])
```

The algorithm is then applied to the second loop nest, the one surrounding statement S_1. In this case, both uses in statement S_1 are local, so no modification of the code is required. Since all statement uses are satisfied at this point, no further communication and synchronisation is added during the execution of the algorithm. The parallel schedule of the entire loop nest is depicted in Figure 6.9.

6.7 Performance Analysis

One of the salient properties of the BSP model of computation is its *predictability*, namely the possibility to assess the cost of BSP code analytically. While the performance analysis of a schedule generated by the parallelisation scheme introduced in

```
SCHEDULE_COST(S)
1  (sync_cost, comp_cost, comm_cost) = (0,0,0)
2  for each component C of S do
3    if C is a barrier synchronisation then
4      sync_cost = sync_cost + L
5    else if C is a simple assignment statement S then
6      comp_cost = comp_cost + c_S
7    else if C is a bsp_get call then
8      comm_cost = comm_cost + g·fetched_data_size
9    else     /* C is a loop */
10     (sync_cost, comp_cost, comm_cost) = (sync_cost, comp_cost, comm_cost)+
            (upper_bound(C) − lower_bound(C) + 1)·SCHEDULE_COST(loop_body(C))
11 return (sync_cost, comp_cost, comm_cost)
```

Figure 6.10: The performance analysis algorithm.

this chapter can be readily performed manually, the straightforwardness of the BSP cost model allows the automation of this analysis.

This section provides a simple algorithm for the assessment of the BSP cost associated with a schedule $\mathcal{S}$ produced by the parallelisation scheme. This algorithm (Figure 6.10) estimates the synchronisation, computation and communication costs of schedule $\mathcal{S}$ using a "depth-first search" approach. During the assessment of these costs, each barrier synchronisation is charged a (synchronisation) cost of L (line 4), each assignment statement S the (computation) cost c_S of executing a single instance of S (line 6), and each inter-processor communication of a remote word of data a (communication) cost of g (line 8).

Since statement masks are not taken into account, the algorithm provides an upper bound for the computation cost. On the other hand, the synchronisation cost of the schedule is accurately computed because each barrier synchronisation must be reached by all processors. As concerns the communication cost, its estimation is based on the assumption that, in each superstep, the maximum amount of data sent by any processor is closely approximated by the maximum amount of data received by any processor. Since this assumption is highly justified by the uniformity of the data distribution, and by the regularity of the communication pattern generated by the parallelisation scheme, the algorithm yields a good approximation of the communication overheads.

Example 6.6 Applied to the BSP schedule in Figure 6.9, the performance analysis algorithm returns

$$\left((n-2)L, \frac{(n-2)n}{p}(c_{S_1}+(n-1)c_{S_2}), g(n-1)(n-2)\right)$$

with the three components standing for the costs of synchronisation, computation and communication, respectively. It can be seen immediately that the three estimates are accurate. Accordingly, the schedule is one-optimal in computation, and achieves optimal $\mathrm{O}(n^3/p)$ time complexity if $L \leq n^2/p, g \leq n/p$.

6.8 Summary

In this chapter, we devised a four-step scheme for the architecture-independent parallelisation of generic loop nests. In its first step, the scheme employs existing dependence tests to reveal the data dependences of the considered loop nest. The second step of the scheme exposes the potential parallelism of the nested loop. Finally, the remaining two steps map this parallelism on the processor/memory units of the target parallel computer, and generate the required communication and synchronisation.

The new algorithm used in the second step of the scheme builds on parallelisation approaches previously used in a shared-memory or vector multiprocessor setting. Nevertheless, this algorithm is engineered to deliver good performance in a distributed-memory environment. By integrating loop interchange and loop distribution into the same procedure, it successfully exposes coarse-grained parallelism. Additionally, our parallelisation algorithm uses an early termination mechanism to avoid the overheads incurred by superfluous loop distribution.

The parallelisation scheme also comprises new algorithms for the distribution of the data and computation across the processors of a generic parallel computer. These algorithms exploit the coarse-grained potential parallelism of the considered loop nest. In doing so, they assign data modified by operations that can be performed concurrently and the associated operations to distinct processors/memory units. Following their application in the third step of the scheme, a partitioned version of the loop nest is obtained.

The references to non-local data are then identified in the fourth step of the parallelisation scheme. The novel algorithm employed in this step "solves" these non-local references by adding appropriate communication and synchronisation to the partitioned version of the loop nest. This represents the only BSP-specific step of the scheme, and its performance generates an architecture-independent parallel schedule of the original loop nest. Finally, the BSP cost of this parallel schedule can be investigated mechanically using the performance analysis algorithm introduced in the previous section.

7. A Strategy and a Tool for Architecture-Independent Loop Parallelisation

If to do were as easy as to know what were good to do, chapels had been churches, and poor men's cottages princes' palaces.

William Shakespeare – *The Merchant of Venice*

7.1 Introduction

Based on the two classes of parallelisation techniques described so far, this chapter proposes a novel, two-phase strategy for the parallelisation of sequential loop nests. This strategy attempts to apply template-matching scheduling in its former phase, and uses generic loop nest scheduling as a back-up parallelisation technique in its latter phase. The new parallelisation strategy is presented in Section 7.3.

Also in this chapter, we introduce BSPSCHEDULER, a research tool that implements the above mentioned parallelisation strategy. The tool accepts as input a generic nested loop described in some simple pseudocode, and produces its architecture-independent schedule. For the sake of readability, this schedule is initially described in pseudocode, but BSPSCHEDULER is able to convert it into real parallel code, ready to be incorporated into a BSP application. The parallelisation tool is described in Section 7.4.

7.2 Related Work

An important number of research groups have been implementing automatic parallelisation tools within the last decade or so. In this section, we briefly review several parallelisation systems that resemble the BSP scheduling tool introduced in this chapter. Some of these tools such as BOUCLETTES [98, 99] or LOOPO [102] are also targeted at the parallelisation of loop nests, whereas many others address the loop-level parallelisation of entire sequential programs.

PARAFRASE, the first automatic vectorising and parallelising system [89], is a Fortran source to source translator. In a sequence of phases, PARAFRASE applies various code transformations to the original program, generating a code representation of the intermediate program at the end of each phase. Additional analysis is applied after each phase to update the dependence information for the entire program.

The speed and capabilities of PARAFRASE are substantially improved by its successor, PARAFRASE-2 [90]. PARAFRASE-2 is a complex restructuring compiler able to handle both C and Fortran sequential programs. It works by translating the input sequential code into an internal representation, and performing successive user-guided *passes* of code transformations on this representation. It performs thorough inter-procedural and symbolic analysis, and comprises an advanced graphical interface allowing the user interaction in the dependence analysis phase. The code transformations implemented by the tool are available as menu options in this interface and must be selected by the user. The original program is partitioned into tasks which are assigned to processors at execution time: each idle processor performs the next available task from the ready tasks queue. Hence, the resulting parallel program is suitable for execution on shared-memory multiprocessors.

The SUPERB interactive restructuring tool described in [86] translates Fortran 77 programs into several variants of architecture-specific message-passing Fortran code. While the tool performs extensive dependence analysis, it requires a user-specified data partition prior to generating the parallel version of the input program. Once such a data partition is available, SUPERB automatically partitions the computation, inserting pairwise send/receive communication primitives into the parallel code. Additionally, it employs powerful optimisation techniques to extract communication from loops, and to reduce the communication overheads by combining individual communication statements [30].

An important ongoing project pursued by a large research team from Rice University has led to the development of the PARASCOPE parallel programming environment [78, 91]. PARASCOPE comprises a set of complex and powerful tools for the interactive parallelisation of entire programs, and is intended for the experienced parallel programmer. The PARASCOPE EDITOR [78] combines automatic and interactive parallelisation in a unique way, taking advantage of both the most advanced dependence analysis techniques and the skilled parallel programmer's expertise. Following an automatic parallelisation step, the knowledgeable user can attempt to expose additional parallelism by specifying assertions that invalidate conservatively assumed dependences and by explicitly applying a wide variety of loop transformations. Since this attempt may well lead to the neglect of valid dependences, the PARASCOPE environment also comprises a powerful debugger able to reveal the *data races* induced by such parallelisation errors.

While PARASCOPE tackles the development of shared-memory parallel applications, the same research team from Rice University has also addressed the automatic generation of parallel code for distributed-memory multiprocessors [87, 92]. To achieve this goal, they developed FORTRAN D, an extension of Fortran which permits the explicit specification of data decompositions. Based on the data decomposition specified by the programmer, sequential FORTRAN D programs are parallelised by assigning the execution of each statement instance to the processor that stores in its local memory the variable modified by that statement instance [92, 93]. The Rice University project—currently known as the FORTRAN TOOLS project—continues with work on automatic data partitioning, HPF (High Performance Fortran) compiler development, irregular problem parallelisation, etc.

POLARIS, the result of many years of work at the supercomputing research centre of the University of Illinois [94, 95], is an advanced parallelising system for the manipulation of Fortran programs. Similar to PARAFRASE-2, it operates in a sequence of analysis and transformation passes performed on an internal representation of the original program. POLARIS uses techniques such as reduction and recurrence scheduling [96] in a way similar to that implemented by our scheduling tool [97]. Much of its power is also based on the sophisticated use of new techniques such as array and scalar privatisation, and symbolic and inter-procedural analysis. The current version of the restructuring compiler is targeted at parallel systems comprising a global address space.

The BOUCLETTES system [98, 99] addresses the automatic parallelisation of uniform-dependence perfect loop nests. The tool implements a series of template-matching parallelisation techniques based on the hyperplane method of Lamport [62], and generates High Performance Fortran (HPF) code. As a result, the BOUCLETTES loop paralleliser is unable to tackle the parallelisation of generic, untightly nested loops.

CAPTOOLS, a semi-automatic parallelisation system developed at the University of Greenwich [32, 100], guides the user-supervised scheduling of computational mechanics Fortran software. It automatically builds an array partition starting from a user specification, and employs the "owner computes" rule to generate the parallel code. CAPTOOLS uses sophisticated dependence analysis techniques (including symbolic and inter-procedural dependence analysis [101]) to accurately assess the dependences in the sequential program, and to optimise the parallel code generation process. The tool produces portable and scalable PVM or MPI versions of the input sequential program.

The LOOPO paralleliser [102] represents a prototype system for conducting research on loop parallelisation techniques. For the parallelisation of a nested loop, these techniques are regarded as space-time mappings of its iteration space in the polytope model introduced by Lengauer in [26]. LOOPO implements a broad range of scheduling techniques, including the hyperplane method of Lamport [62], the affine scheduling strategy of Feautrier [45, 46] and the multi-dimensional scheduling algorithm of Darte and Vivien [27]. The tool generates a C or Fortran parallel schedule in which calls to pseudo-functions are used for parallel loops and for communication and synchronisation primitives.

7.3 A Two-Phase Strategy for Loop Nest Parallelisation

The previous chapters studied two different approaches to loop nest parallelisation. The former approach—which we termed *template-matching scheduling*—comprises techniques dedicated to the parallelisation of specific computation patterns. These

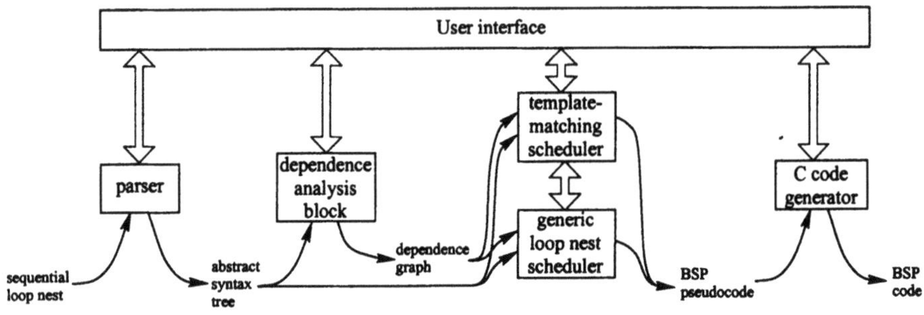

Figure 7.1: The structure of the architecture-independent scheduling tool.

techniques build the parallel version of a sequential loop nest starting from a predefined, highly optimised schedule. Therefore, they present the advantage of inexpensively generating efficient parallel code. However, when faced with the parallelisation of a nested loop whose structure matches none of the recognised computation patterns, template-matching scheduling is unable to deliver any parallel schedule whatsoever.

The latter approach to architecture-independent loop parallelisation was considered in Chapter 6, where a scheme for the *scheduling of generic loop nests* was developed. While it tackles the parallelisation of any nested loop structure, generic loop nest scheduling has two important disadvantages. Firstly, it is significantly more complex than any template-matching scheduling technique. Secondly, generic loop nest parallelisation is prone to yield sub-optimal schedules even when dealing with very simple nested loops.

In order to take advantage of the benefits of both parallelisation approaches, we propose a two-phase, hybrid strategy for the architecture-independent scheduling of nested loops. In the first phase of this strategy, the application of template-matching scheduling is attempted. If this attempt is successful (i.e. if the loop nest to be parallelised matches one of the computation patterns for which a predefined, efficient parallel schedule is known), the parallelisation is complete. Otherwise, the generic loop nest scheduling scheme described in the previous chapter is employed in the second phase of the strategy. This two-phase strategy is implemented by BSPSCHEDULER, the research parallelisation tool presented in the remainder of the chapter.

7.4 BSPscheduler: an Architecture-Independent Loop Paralleliser

7.4.1 The Structure of the Parallelisation Tool

The structure of BSPSCHEDULER is depicted in Figure 7.1. First, the tool has a user interface that transfers information between its other modules and the user. Next, it comprises a parser block which analyses the sequential loop nest fed into the tool and

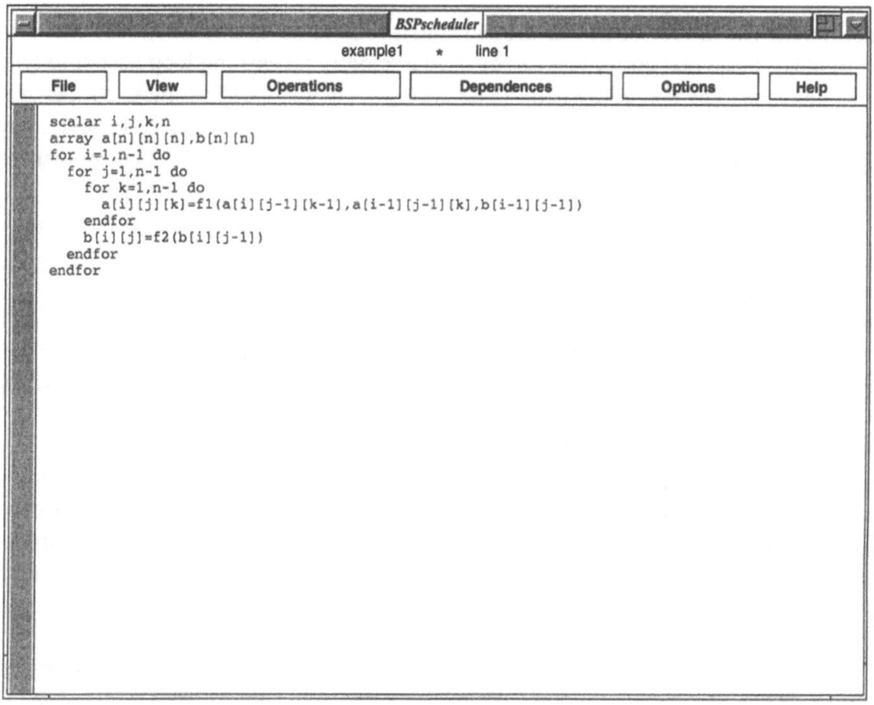

Figure 7.2: The BSPSCHEDULER user interface; a sample loop nest is loaded into the tool.

builds its abstract syntax tree. The other modules operate on this abstract syntax tree rather than on the original sequential code. The parser also generates a symbol table and other compiler-like data structures, and performs minor changes into the original code in order to bring it to a normalised form.

The dependence analysis block applies a series of dependence tests on the internal, abstract syntax tree representation of the loop nest, building the adjacency matrix of its dependence graph. The information conveyed by the dependence graph is then passed on to two scheduler modules, one for each type of scheduling implemented by the tool. At this level, a decision is taken on which scheduling block is in charge of the parallelisation, and this block generates the BSP version of the original loop nest. The BSP schedule is described in simple pseudocode, and can be converted into real C code comprising BSP primitive calls by a C code generator module.

7.4.2 The User Interface

The scheduling tool was implemented as an X Window application, with the user interface (Figure 7.2) developed on top of the X Toolkit Intrinsics and the Athena widget set [103]. The commands of the tool are organised under five categories.

The file–related commands provide the usual facilities for loading or saving a source file (i.e. a file containing the sequential code to be parallelised). The tool also provides a basic text editor that can be used to modify an existing loop nest or to type in a new one. The text editor is disabled during the actual parallelisation, but the user can return to the edit mode at any moment (command File/Modify). However, any BSP schedule or intermediate parallelisation result computed up to that moment is discarded before re-enabling the text editor.

At any time, the BSPSCHEDULER window can show one or several panes comprising various scheduling information. The following panes are available:

- the source pane containing the original sequential code;
- the normalised source pane containing a *normalised* version of the loop;
- the data dependence pane listing the dependences of the nested loop;
- the intermediate results pane providing details of the potential parallelism of the nested loop and of the distribution of data;
- the BSP pseudocode pane comprising the BSP schedule of the loop nest.

The user can include a new pane among those shown by the BSPSCHEDULER window or hide a visible pane using the View commands. Clearly, some of the panes are only available after several (or all) steps of the parallelisation process have been performed. For instance, the BSP pseudocode pane is created after the entire scheduling process is completed. To distinguish between these panes, all but the source pane comprise a title line.

The commands that guide the parallelisation are gathered under the Operations group. They can be used to start the parser module and to initiate the dependence analysis step, as well as to activate the scheduling modules and the C code generation block. The last two operations can be performed repeatedly, for different scheduling options and output files, respectively.

As the dependence analysis is conservative (see Section 7.4.4), delete/undelete dependence commands are provided by the tool in the dependence-related command group. At the same time, the user can tune the parallelisation process by using the commands grouped under the Options heading. Thus, the user is allowed to enable or disable the usage of template-matching scheduling, to check and/or modify the data partition automatically generated by the tool, etc. Finally, on–line help information on BSPSCHEDULER can be obtained using the Help group of commands.

7.4.3 The Parser Module

The parser module has the role of analysing the input loop nest, and of building several compiler-like data structures used by the other modules of the tool. These data structures include the abstract syntax tree of the loop nest and its symbol table, as well as a loop table and a statement table. The last two tables comprise important information about each loop and each assignment statement in the original code, respectively.

The sequential loop nest must be described in a simple, Fortran-style pseudocode (Figure 7.2). A formal description of the BSPSCHEDULER input language is provided in Appendix B. In addition to the syntactic rules of this minimal imperative language, the parser checks the following semantic rules:

Rule 1: Loop indices cannot be modified (i.e. assigned to) within the loop body;

```
scalar i, j, n
array a[n][n], b[n][n]
for i = 0,n-1 do
  for j = 1,n-1 do
    if a[i][j-1] < 0 then
      a[i][j] = ...
      b[i][j] = ...
    else
      a[i][j] = ...
    endif
  endfor
endfor
```

a

```
scalar i, j, n
array a[n][n], b[n][n], _cond1[n][n]
for i = 0,n-1 do
  for j = 1,n-1 do
    _cond1[i][j] = a[i][j-1] < 0
    if _cond1[i][j] then a[i][j] = ... endif
    if _cond1[i][j] then b[i][j] = ... endif
    if not _cond1[i][j] then a[i][j] = ... endif
  endfor
endfor
```

b

Figure 7.3: A nested loop (a), and its normalised version generated by the parser (b).

Rule 2: Any identifier used to define the size of an array in an array declaration is a symbolic constant, and cannot be used as the left-hand side of an assignment or as a loop index.

The tool allows the use of user functions, but requires that function parameters are scalars passed as values, function executions have no side effects, and functions return a scalar value. Under these circumstances, the definitions of user functions are irrelevant for the parallelisation of the loop nest, and therefore not required by the tool.

When analysing a sequential loop nest, the parser stops at the first error it encounters, issuing a message that specifies the type of the error and the line in the input code where the error was found. The user can then restart the parser after correcting the error.

During the analysis of the input code, the parser brings the loop nest to a normalised form. This is a form in which control dependences are converted into data dependences [104], and conditional statement controls are distributed over the statements in the body of the conditional statement (Figure 7.3). In the normalisation process, auxiliary array variables are used to eliminate control dependences. These variables are automatically introduced by the parser, but their declarations have to be completed by the user. To form their names, the parser adds a number generated by a special counter to the prefix '*_cond*'.

Example 7.1 The usage of the parser module for the analysis of the sample loop nest in Figure 7.2 is illustrated in Figure 7.4. As shown in this example, in addition to the normalisation of the input code, the parser assigns a unique identifier to each loop and statement in the code. These identifiers are then used by the tool whenever it needs to refer to a specific loop or statement during the remainder of the parallelisation process.

Figure 7.4: The usage of the parser module.

7.4.4 The Dependence Analysis Module

Using the information in the abstract syntax tree and in the other data structures generated by the parser block, the dependence analysis module identifies the data dependences of the input loop nest. The following dependence tests are employed by the current version of the dependence analysis block:

- the *separability test* [30], an exact test used to compare two array subscripts with the form $xi+y, x'i+y'$, where x, x', y, y' are integer constants and i is a surrounding loop index;
- the *gcd test* [28, 30], an approximate test used to compare two array subscripts which are linear combinations of the surrounding loop indices;
- the *Banerjee test* [8, 12, 28], another approximate test applicable to two array subscripts that are linear combinations of the surrounding loop indices.

Due to the modular structure of BSPSCHEDULER, additional dependence tests can be easily added at any time, without modifying any of the other blocks of the tool.

As a result of the dependence analysis, the adjacency matrix of the dependence graph of the loop nest is built. Each entry in this matrix describes all the data dependences involving the two statements associated with the entry. For every data dependence, the following information is provided:

- the type of the dependence (i.e. flow, anti-, or output dependence);
- the variable references that form the source and the sink of the data dependence;

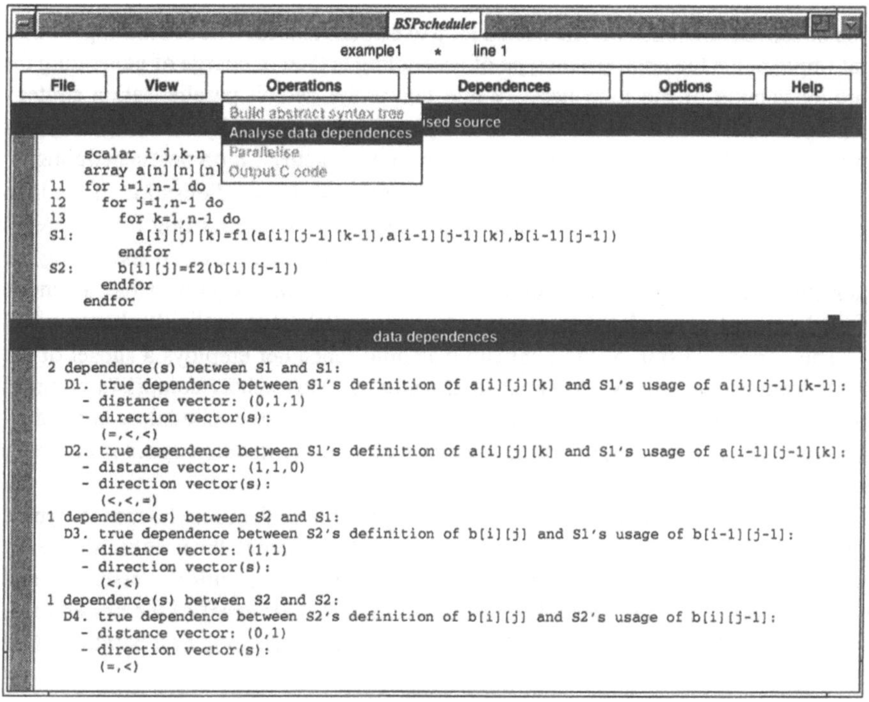

Figure 7.5: The dependence analysis step.

- the distance vector and the direction vector representations of the data dependence.

The dependence analysis process is conservative: whenever the dependence tests fail to prove that two data references are independent, dependence is unconditionally assumed. Therefore, the user is shown a list presenting all the data dependences identified in the input code, and is allowed to delete any of these dependences. Based on the dependence information, the user may also decide to modify the original loop nest in order to eliminate a real data dependence that limits or even prohibits the parallelisation of the loop nest.

Example 7.2 Consider again the sample loop nest in Figure 7.2. Following the parsing step, the tool can identify the data dependences of this untightly nested loop (command Operations/Analyse data dependences). The result of the dependence analysis is shown in Figure 7.5. Three of the four entries of the dependence graph adjacency matrix are non-empty. These entries correspond to the two dependences between statement S_1 and S_1, to the only data dependence between S_2 and S_1, and to the only dependence between S_2 and S_2, respectively.

7.4.5 The Scheduling Modules

Based on the dependence information provided by the dependence analysis block, and on the structure of the abstract syntax tree built by the parser, the tool decides on the type of scheduling that suits the nested loop to be parallelised. The scheduling module that implements the appropriate type of scheduling is then in charge of generating the parallel version of the loop nest. While this is the default parallelisation strategy employed by BSPSCHEDULER, the user is permitted to alter it, by choosing to bypass template-matching scheduling and to rely entirely on generic loop nest scheduling.

When the template-matching scheduler is assigned the parallelisation of the loop nest, it builds the abstract syntax tree of the parallel schedule starting from a predefined skeleton. Additionally, the scheduler generates a data partition specifying the distribution of all arrays used within the loop body, and, whenever possible, a version of the loop nest in which the available potential parallelism is explicitly shown.

The current version of the template-matching scheduler employs a subset of the parallelisation techniques presented in Chapter 5. This subset comprises communication-free scheduling, wavefront block scheduling, iterative scheduling and reduction scheduling. However, no affine transformation of the iteration space is currently implemented by the scheduler.

When template-matching scheduling is not possible or the user chooses to bypass it, the generic loop nest scheduler becomes active. At this point, the user has to specify the *main statements* (i.e. the statements whose concurrent execution is essential) and the *main loops* (i.e. the loops whose parallelisation makes sense) of the nested loop. For details on the role of these two parameters of the generic loop nest parallelisation scheme, see Section 6.4.

Next, the scheduler uses the parallelisation algorithm described in Section 6.4 to expose the potential parallelism of the loop nest, concentrating on the parallelisation of main loops that surround main statements. The resulting intermediate parallel version of the loop nest is then used in the automatic generation of a data partition. Block distribution of array elements, in one or several dimensions, is implemented in the current version of the tool.

As described in Section 6.5, the "owner computes" rule is subsequently applied to partition the computation. Hence, the data partition is considered *acceptable* if the definition (i.e. the left-hand side) of each main statement is block-distributed in at least one dimension. If an acceptable data partition cannot be generated automatically, the user is shown the potential parallelism of the loop nest and the data partition reached by the tool, and is asked to use his or her expertise to derive a final data partition.

To decrease the synchronisation overheads of the resulting parallel schedule, the tool is tuned to minimise the number of loop distributions used in the potential parallelism identification step. However, the user can override this setting and ask that a maximum number of loops are distributed over the statements in their loop body, thus increasing the chance of an acceptable data partition being derived automatically. Furthermore, the user has the option of checking and modifying the automatically generated data partition before the tool proceeds to the distribution of computation, even when this partition is acceptable.

Once the abstract syntax tree of the parallel schedule is generated by one of the scheduling modules, the user interface translates this internal representation into BSP pseudocode. While the language used to describe the BSP pseudocode is similar to the BSPSCHEDULER input language, it also includes new types of statement for the spec-

Table 7.1: The auxiliary functions and variables used by the scheduling tool. An underscore prefixes the name of each of these identifiers in order to differentiate them from the user-defined symbols.

identifier	type	description
`_p`	variable	the number of processors executing the parallel schedule
`_me`	variable	the identifier of the current processor, 0 ≤`_me`<`_p`
`_px_y`	variable	when the processors are organised into a logical x–dimensional array, the number of processors in the $(y+1)$-th dimension of the array
`_mex_y`	variable	when the processors are organised into a logical x–dimensional array, the $(y+1)$-th coordinate of the current processor in the array
`_ceil`	function	returns the ceiling of its single parameter
`_floor`	function	returns the floor of its single parameter
`_min`	function	returns the minimum over its set of arguments
`_max`	function	returns the maximum over its set of arguments

ification of BSP primitive calls. The syntax of these new statement types is formally defined in Appendix C. Beyond the new types of statement, the tool introduces several new functions and auxiliary scalar variables in the parallel pseudocode it generates. An account of these functions and variables is presented in Table 7.1.

In addition to the BSP schedule, the user can examine the data partition used by the tool, and, whenever possible, an intermediate parallel version revealing the potential parallelism of the original loop nest. The data partition is presented by indicating, for each array and each of its dimensions, whether the array is partitioned or not in that dimension. For instance, if a two-dimensional array a is block-partitioned in its first dimension and is unpartitioned in its second dimension, the entry describing the distribution of array a will be:

$$a(\text{block}, *)$$

Accordingly, if the array size is $n_1 \times n_2$, a generic processor with identifier me, $0 \leq me < p$, will own the rectangular array block:

$$a[me\lceil n_1/p\rceil..\min\{n_1-1,(me+1)\lceil n_1/p\rceil-1\}][0..n_2-1]$$

and will execute all statements that modify these elements of a. As for the case when an array is block-partitioned in $Q>1$ dimensions, the array block owned by a generic processor is computed as described in Section 6.5.

Example 7.3 Let us return to the untightly nested loop used to illustrate the preceding steps of a BSPSCHEDULER parallelisation session. The parallel pseudocode generated by the tool for this loop nest (command Operations/Parallelise) is depicted in Figure 7.6. The potential parallelism of the loop nest, and the data partition used to generate this schedule can be examined in the intermediate results pane—Figure 7.7.

Figure 7.6: The actual parallelisation step.

The sequential cost of computing the original loop nest is $n^3(\text{cost}(f1)+\text{o}(1))$, where $\text{cost}(f_1)$ represents the cost of a single execution of function f_1. The BSP cost of the resulting schedule is

$$n(1+\text{o}(1))L+\frac{n^3(\text{cost}(f_1)+\text{o}(1))}{p}+gn^2(1+\text{o}(1)).$$

As a result, the automatically generated schedule is one-optimal in computation, and $\text{O}(n^3/p)$ time complexity can be achieved if $L \leq n^2/p, g \leq n/p$. Furthermore, the parallel schedule is one-optimal in its space complexity, requiring $n^3(1+\text{o}(1))/p$ space on each processor/memory unit compared to the $n^3(1+\text{o}(1))$ space complexity of the sequential loop nest.

7.4.6 The Code Generation Module

During a BSPSCHEDULER parallelisation session, the user can repeatedly modify the various parallelisation options and/or the input code in order to generate and compare several parallel schedules. When the user decides on one of these schedules, the C code generator can be used to translate the parallel pseudocode into real code. The

Figure 7.7: The intermediate results of the parallelisation.

resulting code is written in C and comprises calls to functions from the standard BSP library *BSPlib* [36]. It is generated into a file and consists of the following parts:

- a header comprising a description of the data partition and of the array blocks stored on each processor;
- a part comprising `#include` directives and macro definitions;
- a function (`initialise_data`) for initialising the data owned by each processor, and a function (`output_data`) for collecting the results after the entire computation is over;
- the user functions;
- a function implementing the BSP schedule (`parallel_code`).

The remainder of this section provides a brief description of each of these elements.

For each array in the loop nest, the header of the output file lists the array distribution and the array block stored on a generic processor. The array distribution is the one generated during the parallelisation of the loop nest. As concerns the array block stored locally, it represents the smallest rectangular block containing all the array elements referred to by the considered processor during the entire computation. This array block includes the block owned by the current processor, and all the non-local elements whose value is used locally. Whenever a processor stores in its memory only a part of an array, the subscripts of each array reference must be adjusted accordingly.

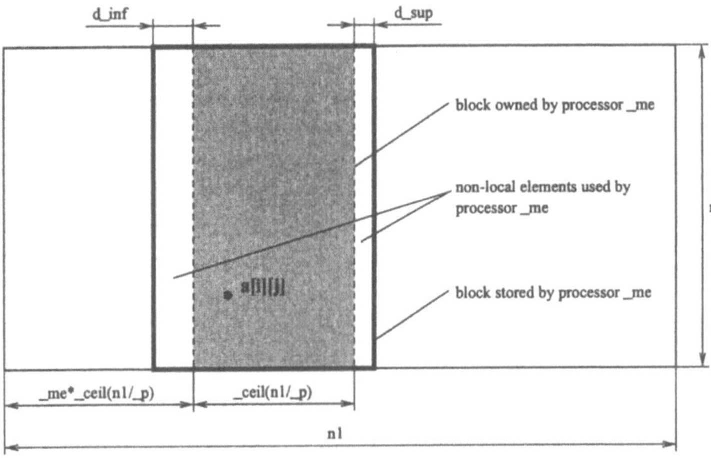

Figure 7.8: The adjustment of array subscripts in the code generation step.

Example 7.4 To demonstrate the subscript adjustment process, consider a two-dimensional array a of size $n_1 \times n_2$, and assume that the array is block-partitioned in its first dimension and unpartitioned in its second dimension. Under these assumptions, the diagram in Figure 7.8 depicts the array block owned by a generic processor with identifier me, $0 \leq me < p$ (i.e. $a[me\lceil n_1/p\rceil..(me+1)\lceil n_1/p\rceil - 1][0..n_2 - 1]$) and the array block actually stored on processor me. With the notations in this diagram, a reference to a generic array element $a[i][j]$ is converted into $a[i - me\lceil n_1/p\rceil + d\_inf][j]$.

Furthermore, the arrays used in the loop nest are vectorised in the output code in order to simplify the manipulation of array references. Consequently, a reference $a[s_1][s_2]\dots[s_m]$ to a generic element of an m-dimensional array a is further replaced with $a[s_1 n_2 n_3 \dots n_m + s_2 n_3 \dots n_m + \dots + s_m]$, where the size of the array block stored locally is $n_1 \times n_2 \times \cdots \times n_m$.

The second part of the output code comprises directives that include the BSPlib header file and several ANSI C header files into the code, as well as a series of macro definitions. These macros define the auxiliary functions introduced by the tool (Table 7.1), and the array vectorisation primitives used to translate multidimensional array coordinates into linear coordinates (e.g. `_lin2(i1,i2,n2)=i1*n2+i2`).

The body of the input/output functions in the third part of the code, and the body of the user functions in its fourth part are left empty by the tool. Before actually including the automatically generated code into a BSP application, the user has the responsibility of writing the code for these functions. In doing so, the user must ensure that the input function correctly initialises the data owned by each processor, and that the output function saves all the computation results that are required.

Finally, the actual computation is implemented as a C function that forms the last part of the code. This function takes as arguments the symbolic constants used in array declarations, and the number of processors on which the code is executed. When

Table 7.2: The speedup of the parallel schedule in Appendix D.

	$p=1$	$p=2$	$p=3$	$p=4$
$n=50$	1.00	1.37	1.50	1.51
$n=100$	1.00	1.78	2.30	3.08
$n=150$	1.00	1.89	2.66	3.48
$n=200$	1.00	1.92	2.77	3.62
$n=250$	1.00	1.93	2.80	3.72
$n=300$	1.00	1.95	2.89	3.76

an array is block-partitioned in more than one dimension, the processors are viewed as if arranged into a logical array. In this case, the function also takes as arguments the size of this processor array (i.e. the appropriate _px_y variables described in Table 7.1). The user is responsible for calling this function with appropriate arguments, after initialising the BSP application.

Example 7.5 The parallel code produced by the code generation module for the BSP pseudocode in Figure 7.6 is shown in Appendix D. This code was enclosed into a BSP application and tested on a 4-processor SGI Power Challenge multiprocessor. The speedups of the parallel schedule for several problem sizes are depicted in Table 7.2. The experimental data show that the performance of the schedule approaches one-optimality starting from average problem sizes, validating the result of the complexity analysis conducted in Example 7.3.

7.5 Summary

This chapter has introduced a loop parallelisation strategy that combines template-matching and generic loop nest scheduling in a unique way. The new strategy is implemented by BSPSCHEDULER, a research tool which employs many of the parallelisation techniques developed in the previous chapters of this book.

As described in Section 7.4, BSPSCHEDULER accepts as input a generic, untightly nested loop, and builds its parallel schedule in a sequence of steps. For increased readability, the user is initially presented with a pseudocode description of this parallel schedule. Nevertheless, the tool is able to translate this pseudocode into real parallel code, ready to be incorporated into an architecture-independent parallel application.

While BSPSCHEDULER is mainly intended for conducting research into the effectiveness of automatic loop nest parallelisation, its usefulness extends beyond this scope. Indeed, due to its friendly graphical interface and to its step-by-step parallelisation policy, the tool can be of great help to the beginner learning architecture-independent parallel programming. Furthermore, its fine tuning facilities make BSPSCHEDULER convenient for obtaining and comparing various schedules of the same sequential computation, a feature that recommends the tool to the experienced parallel software designer.

8. The Effectiveness of Architecture-Independent Loop Parallelisation

If I have told you these details about Asteroid B-612 and revealed its number to you, it is on account of grown-ups. Grown-ups love figures ... That is the way they are. One must not hold it against them. Children should show great understanding towards grown-ups.

Antoine de Saint-Exupéry – *The Little Prince*

8.1 Introduction

In the previous chapters, we introduced a series of techniques for the architecture-independent parallelisation of loop computations, and we described a scheduling tool that implements a subset of these techniques. In order to assess the effectiveness as well as the limitations of our approach, this chapter studies its applicability to a number of real scientific computing problems.

For each of the case studies, we first assess the possibility of using one of the template-matching scheduling techniques devised in Chapter 5. When this is not possible, we analyse the result of applying generic loop nest parallelisation. In either situation, the resulting parallel schedule is then compared with the best known BSP algorithm that solves the same problem. Finally, we discuss the parallel code produced by the BSP scheduling tool for the considered problem.

8.2 Matrix-Vector and Matrix-Matrix Multiplication

The BSP parallelisation of dense matrix-vector and matrix-matrix multiplication—two of the most important problems in scientific computing—has been extensively studied within the last few years [1, 34, 35, 52]. The optimal parallel algorithms proposed in these papers are briefly described below.

Consider first the multiplication of an $n \times n$ matrix A by an n-dimensional vector $\mathbf{x}$. The optimal BSP algorithm introduced by McColl and Bisseling [35, 52] assumes that the matrix is initially block-block distributed across the p processors, i.e. that each processor holds an $n/\sqrt{p} \times n/\sqrt{p}$ block of A.[1] The elements of $\mathbf{x}$ are also uniformly distributed among the processors in blocks of size n/p. The algorithm comprises three supersteps. In its first superstep, each processor gets the $n/\sqrt{p}$ elements of $\mathbf{x}$ to be multiplied with the locally held matrix block, at a cost of $L+gn/\sqrt{p}$. In the next superstep, the n^2/p local multiplications are performed, and the partial results are sent to the processors that will compute the elements of the result vector $\mathbf{y}$ in the third superstep. Since each processor is assigned the computation of n/p elements of $\mathbf{y}$ starting from $\sqrt{p}$ partial results for every element, the costs of these two supersteps are $L+n^2/p+gn/\sqrt{p}$ and $L+n/\sqrt{p}$, respectively. Consequently, the overall cost of the optimal BSP algorithm from [35, 52] is $3L+n^2/p+2gn/\sqrt{p}$. This algorithm attains $O(n^2/p)$ time complexity if $L \leq n^2/p, g \leq n/p^{1/2}$.

The optimal BSP algorithm based on the standard $O(n^3)$ $n \times n$ matrix multiplication is due to McColl and Valiant [35], and uses a similar strategy to achieve a cost of $3L+n^3/p+3gn^2/p^{2/3}$; hence, $O(n^3/p)$ cost can be obtained if $L \leq n^3/p, g \leq n/p^{1/3}$. The algorithm assumes that the elements of A and B, the two $n \times n$ matrices to be multiplied, are uniformly but arbitrarily partitioned among the p local memories, and the processors are arranged into a logical $p^{1/3} \times p^{1/3} \times p^{1/3}$ cubic array. The coordinates of a generic processor in this array are (me_1, me_2, me_3), $0 \leq me_1, me_2, me_3 < p^{1/3}$.

In a possible instance of the algorithm in [35], processor (me_1, me_2, me_3) is assigned the multiplication of the matrix blocks A^{me_1,me_2} and B^{me_2,me_3}, where for any $n \times n$ matrix $M=[m_{ij}]$, $M^{x,y}=\{m_{ij} \mid xn/p^{1/3} \leq i < (x+1)n/p^{1/3} \wedge yn/p^{1/3} \leq j < (y+1)n/p^{1/3}\}$. The algorithm comprises three supersteps. In the first superstep, the two $n/p^{1/3} \times n/p^{1/3}$ matrix blocks are brought into the local memory at a cost of $L+2gn^2/p^{2/3}$. Next, the matrix block multiplication is performed, and n^2/p disjoint sets of $p^{1/3}$ partial results each are sent to every processor in a superstep whose cost is $L+n^3/p+gn^2/p^{2/3}$. Finally, every processor adds the $p^{1/3}$ elements in each of its n^2/p sets of partial results in $L+n^2/p^{2/3}$ time.

The parallelisation strategy employed by the previously described algorithms has been developed into a BSP scheduling technique by Ding and Stefanescu [43]. This technique is applicable to a class of problems that includes dense matrix-vector and matrix-matrix multiplication, and can be used to mechanically construct the two optimal BSP schedules.

As it does not implement the template-matching scheduling technique in [43], the current version of the parallelisation tool is unable to generate the optimal schedules for the two problems. Instead, it exploits the fact that the computation of different elements of the result can be performed concurrently, and uses communication-free scheduling to produce the straightforward sub-optimal schedules in both cases. The costs of these schedules are $2L+n^2/p+gn$ and $2L+n^3/p+2gn^2/p^{1/2}$ for matrix-vector and matrix-matrix multiplication, respectively. The conditions under which optimal $O(n^2/p)$ time complexity is achieved for the matrix-vector multiplication schedule are $L \leq n^2/p$, $g \leq n/p$; for the matrix-matrix multiplication schedule, optimal $O(n^3/p)$ execution time can be attained if $L \leq n^3/p, g \leq n/p^{1/2}$.

---

[1] For ease of exposition, the algorithms presented in this chapter assume that $\sqrt{p}$, $p^{1/3}$, n/p, $n/\sqrt{p}$, $n/p^{1/3}$ and $n/p^{2/3}$ denote integer quantities.

8.3 LU Decomposition

This section studies the architecture-independent parallelisation of the LU decomposition of an $n \times n$ matrix $\mathsf{A} = [a_{ij}]$. A technique for the BSP scheduling of LU decomposition and related problems has been developed by McColl [35]. Here, we shall follow the same steps as in [35], but we shall use wavefront block scheduling, the parallelisation technique introduced in Section 5.4.

The sequential approach to LU decomposition uses *Gaussian elimination* to build a lower triangular matrix L and an upper triangular matrix U such that A = LU [105]. (Hence, the discussion in this section also applies to linear system solution through Gaussian elimination.) The sequential algorithm is best described recursively. If $n = 1$, we choose $\mathsf{L} = \mathsf{I}_1$ and $\mathsf{U} = \mathsf{A}$. Otherwise (i.e. when $n > 1$), the A matrix can be written as

$$\mathsf{A} = \left[\begin{array}{c|ccc} a_{0,0} & a_{0,1} & \cdots & a_{0,n-1} \\ \hline a_{1,0} & a_{1,1} & \cdots & a_{1,n-1} \\ \vdots & \vdots & \ddots & \vdots \\ a_{n-1,0} & a_{n-1,1} & \cdots & a_{n-1,n-1} \end{array}\right] = \begin{bmatrix} a_{0,0} & \mathbf{w}^{\mathrm{T}} \\ \mathbf{v} & \mathsf{A}' \end{bmatrix} =$$

$$\begin{bmatrix} 1 & \mathbf{0}^{\mathrm{T}} \\ \mathbf{v}/a_{0,0} & \mathsf{I}_{n-1} \end{bmatrix} \begin{bmatrix} a_{0,0} & \mathbf{w}^{\mathrm{T}} \\ \mathbf{0} & \mathsf{A}' - \mathbf{v}\mathbf{w}^{\mathrm{T}}/a_{0,0} \end{bmatrix},$$

where $\mathbf{v}$ and $\mathbf{w}$ are $(n-1)$-dimensional vectors. Thus, if $\mathsf{L}'\mathsf{U}' = \mathsf{A}' - \mathbf{v}\mathbf{w}^{\mathrm{T}}/a_{0,0}$ is the recursively computed LU decomposition of the $(n-1) \times (n-1)$ matrix $\mathsf{A}' - \mathbf{v}\mathbf{w}^{\mathrm{T}}/a_{0,0}$, the LU decomposition of A is given by

$$\mathsf{A} = \begin{bmatrix} 1 & \mathbf{0}^{\mathrm{T}} \\ \mathbf{v}/a_{0,0} & \mathsf{I}_{n-1} \end{bmatrix} \begin{bmatrix} a_{0,0} & \mathbf{w}^{\mathrm{T}} \\ \mathbf{0} & \mathsf{L}'\mathsf{U}' \end{bmatrix} = \begin{bmatrix} 1 & \mathbf{0}^{\mathrm{T}} \\ \mathbf{v}/a_{0,0} & \mathsf{L}' \end{bmatrix} \begin{bmatrix} a_{0,0} & \mathbf{w}^{\mathrm{T}} \\ \mathbf{0} & \mathsf{U}' \end{bmatrix} = \mathsf{LU}.$$

The pseudocode corresponding to the iterative version of this tail recursion is shown in Figure 8.1(a).

According to the definition in Section 5.8.1, this pseudocode represents a 3-level broadcast loop nest. Moreover, the conditions in which scheduling through broadcast elimination can be applied are satisfied. Consequently, we first expand the original pseudocode into a perfect loop nest using the broadcast elimination technique presented in Section 5.8.3 (Figure 8.1(b)). As the three data dependences in the transformed sequential pseudocode are described by the distance vectors in the set $D = \{[1,0,0]^{\mathrm{T}}, [0,1,0]^{\mathrm{T}}, [0,0,1]^{\mathrm{T}}\}$, we then build its BSP version using wavefront block scheduling.

The analysis in Section 5.4.1 shows that the optimal schedule is obtained when the p processors are organised into a logical $\sqrt{p} \times \sqrt{p}$ array, and the iteration space is partitioned using the tiling matrix $\mathsf{T} = \mathrm{diag}(x_1, n/\sqrt{p}, n/\sqrt{p})$, with the tile height x_1 given by equation (5.8). In this schedule, a generic processor with coordinates (me_1, me_2) computes the tiles of coordinates $(0, me_1, me_2)$, $(1, me_1, me_2)$, ..., $(\lceil n/x_1 \rceil, me_1, me_2)$ in supersteps $me_1 + me_2$, $me_1 + me_2 + 1$, ... $me_1 + me_2 + \lceil n/x_1 \rceil$ (Figure 8.2). The

```
for k = 0,n-1 do
  for j = k,n-1 do
    u[k,j] = a[k,j]
  for i = k,n-1 do
    l[i,k] = a[i,k]/u[k,k]
  for i = k+1,n-1 do
    for j = k+1,n-1 do
      a[i,j] = a[i,j] - l[i,k]u[k,j]
```

(a) straightforward pseudocode

```
for k = 0,n-1 do
  for i = k,n-1 do
    for j = k,n-1 do
      if i = k then u[k,i,j] = a[k-1,i,j] else u[k,i,j] = u[k,i-1,j]
      if j = k then l[i,k,j] = a[k-1,i,j]/u[k,i,j] else l[i,k,j] = l[i,k,j-1]
      a[k,i,j] = a[k-1,i,j] - l[i,k,j]u[k,i,j]
```

(b) pseudocode after broadcast elimination

Figure 8.1: Sequential LU decomposition.

schedule cost is

$$\left\lceil \frac{n}{x_1} + 2(\sqrt{p}-1) \right\rceil L + \left\lceil 1 + \frac{2(\sqrt{p}-1)x_1}{n} \right\rceil \frac{n^3}{p} + 2g \left\lceil 1 + \frac{2(\sqrt{p}-1)x_1}{n} \right\rceil n^2,$$

with the minimum attained for $x_1 = \left\lceil \sqrt{pL/(2(\sqrt{p}-1)(n+2gp))} \right\rceil$. Therefore, the schedule approaches one-optimality in computation, and has $O(n^3/p)$ cost if $L \leq n^2/p, g \leq n/p$.

The same BSP version of LU decomposition is proposed in [35], where the tile height is fixed at $x_1 = n/\sqrt{p}$ for simplicity. Hence, the cost of the schedule in [35] is $3\sqrt{p}L + 3n^3/p + 6gn^2$, i.e. the schedule is only three-optimal in computation.

BSP Gaussian elimination is extensively studied by Tiskin [106], who proposes a parallel algorithm of cost

$$O(p^\alpha)L + O(n^3/p) + gO(n^2/p^\alpha),$$

with $1/2 \leq \alpha \leq 2/3$. Due to its asymptotic performance (i.e. optimal $O(n^3/p)$ time complexity attained for $L \leq n^3/p^{1+\alpha}, g \leq n/p^{1-\alpha}$), this algorithm represents the best known BSP solution for Gaussian elimination. However, being based on a recursive restructuring of the original sequential algorithm, the algorithm described in [106] is intricate and less practical than the BSP schedule in Figure 8.2.

Finally, the parallel solution in Figure 8.2 also represents the code automatically produced by the BSP scheduling tool for the sequential loop nest in Figure 8.1(b).

```
for t = 0, ⌈n/x1⌉ + 2√p − 3 do
  c1 = t − (me1 + me2)
  if 0 ≤ c1 < ⌈n/x1⌉ and me1 > 0 then
    bsp_get u[c1x1..min{n−1, (c1+1)x1−1}, me1n/√p−1,
              max{k, me2n/√p}..(me2+1)n/√p−1] from processor (me1−1, me2)
  if 0 ≤ c1 < ⌈n/x1⌉ and me2 > 0 then
    bsp_get l[max{k, me1n/√p}..(me1+1)n/√p−1, c1x1..min{n−1, (c1+1)x1−1},
              me2n/√p−1] from processor (me1, me2−1)
  bsp_sync
  for k = max{0, c1x1}, min{n−1, (c1+1)x1 − 1} do
    for i = max{k, me1n/√p}, (me1+1)n/√p − 1 do
      for j = max{k, me2n/√p}, (me2+1)n/√p − 1 do
        if i = k then u[k,i,j] = a[k−1,i,j] else u[k,i,j] = u[k,i−1,j]
        if j = k then l[i,k,j] = a[k−1,i,j]/u[k,i,j] else l[i,k,j] = l[i,k,j−1]
        a[k,i,j] = a[k−1,i,j] − l[i,k,j]u[k,i,j]
```

Figure 8.2: Parallel LU decomposition.

8.4 Algebraic Path Problem

The algebraic path problem (APP) was originally proposed as a means of describing several graph algorithms (e.g. shortest paths and transitive closure) in a formal and unitary way [107]. Its applicability, however, has been found to extend to many additional problems, including some which are not directly related to the theory of graphs. Consequently, APP represents a very important primitive in the development of many computer applications. A formal definition of the algebraic path problem follows.

Let $(S,+,\cdot,0,1)$ be a *closed semiring*, i.e. an algebraic structure with $(S,+,0)$ a commutative and idempotent monoid, $(S,\cdot,1)$ a monoid, $\cdot$ right and left distributive over $+$, and 0 annihilator for $\cdot$. Then, given an $n \times n$ matrix $\mathsf{C} = [c_{ij}]$ with $c_{ij} \in S$ for all $0 \leq i,j < n$, the algebraic path problem is to compute the transitive closure $\mathsf{C}^* = [c^*_{ij}] = \sum_{k=0}^{\infty} \mathsf{C}^k$, where $\mathsf{C}^0 = [c^0_{ij}] = \mathrm{diag}(1,1,\ldots,1)$.

Based on the properties of a closed semiring, and assuming that $s^* = \sum_{k=0}^{\infty} s^k$ can be computed in $\mathrm{O}(1)$ time for all $s \in S$, the Floyd-Warshall shortest paths algorithm [108] can be extended to compute C^* in $\mathrm{O}(n^3)$ time [105]. The resulting algorithm (Figure 8.3) uses an auxiliary $(n+1) \times n \times n$ array a, and comprises a 2-level initialisation loop nest, a 3-level actual computation loop nest, and a 2-level result extraction loop nest.

Since the initialisation and result extraction loop nests are fully parallel and require only $\mathrm{O}(n^2)$ time to complete, we shall concentrate on the parallelisation of the actual computation loop. It follows from the definition of a broadcast loop nest in Section 5.8.1 that the actual computation of the sequential APP algorithm is a 3-level broadcast loop nest. This broadcast loop nest comprises a broadcast stream along each direction of its main computation loop, and the two associated broadcast initialisation loops are missing.

From the two techniques for the scheduling of broadcast loop nests devised in

for $i = 0, n-1$ **do**
  for $j = 0, n-1$ **do**
    $a[0,i,j] = c[i,j] + c^0[i,j]$
for $k = 1, n$ **do**
  for $i = 0, n-1$ **do**
    for $j = 0, n-1$ **do**
      $a[k,i,j] = a[k-1,i,j] + a[k-1,i,k] \cdot (a[k-1,k,k])^* \cdot a[k-1,k,j]$
for $i = 0, n-1$ **do**
  for $j = 0, n-1$ **do**
    $c^*[i,j] = a[n,i,j]$

Figure 8.3: The sequential solution of the algebraic path problem.

for $k = 1, n$ **do**
  broadcast $a[k-1, me_1 n/\sqrt{p}..(me_1+1)n/\sqrt{p}-1, k]$ from processor
    $(me_1, \lfloor k/(n/\sqrt{p}) \rfloor)$ to the processors in $\{(me_1, p_2) \in \mathbf{N}^2 \mid 0 \le p_2 < \sqrt{p}\}$
  broadcast $a[k-1, k, me_2 n/\sqrt{p}..(me_2+1)n/\sqrt{p}-1]$ from processor
    $(\lfloor k/(n/\sqrt{p}) \rfloor, me_2)$ to the processors in $\{(p_1, me_2) \in \mathbf{N}^2 \mid 0 \le p_1 < \sqrt{p}\}$
  broadcast $a[k-1,k,k]$ from processor $(\lfloor k/(n/\sqrt{p}) \rfloor, \lfloor k/(n/\sqrt{p}) \rfloor)$
    to the processors in $\{(p_1, p_2) \in \mathbf{N}^2 \mid 0 \le p_1, p_2 < \sqrt{p}\}$
  for $i = me_1 n/\sqrt{p}, (me_1+1)n/\sqrt{p}-1$ **do**
    for $j = me_2 n/\sqrt{p}, (me_2+1)n/\sqrt{p}-1$ **do**
      $a[k,i,j] = a[k-1,i,j] + a[k-1,i,k] \cdot (a[k-1,k,k])^* \cdot a[k-1,k,j]$

Figure 8.4: The BSP version of the APP computation loop.

Section 5.8, only the one based on broadcast implementation is applicable here. Indeed, the conditions in which the broadcast elimination technique can be used are not satisfied by the APP computation loop (see Section 5.8.3 for details).

Following the application of the parallelisation technique based on broadcast implementation, the p processors are arranged into a logical $\sqrt{p} \times \sqrt{p}$ array. Each processor in this array is assigned the computations corresponding to a different $(n+1) \times n/\sqrt{p} \times n/\sqrt{p}$ block of the auxiliary array a. The BSP schedule takes n stages, with a generic processor with coordinates (me_1, me_2) executing the BSP pseudocode in Figure 8.4. Every stage corresponds to an iteration of the outer loop of the broadcast loop nest, and consists of three broadcasts and the associated local computation.

As indicated in Section 5.8.2, the first two broadcasts—which correspond to the two broadcast streams of the loop nest—can be superposed and performed in two successive supersteps. Since the third broadcast distributes a single array element across the p processors, it is performed in the first of these supersteps, and has a cost which is negligible as long as $n > p\sqrt{p}$. Finally, the local computation of each stage is executed in the first superstep of the subsequent stage of the schedule. According to equation (5.18), the overall cost is:

$$2nL + \frac{n^3}{p} + \frac{4gn^2}{\sqrt{p}}.$$

Hence, the BSP schedule is one-optimal in computation and achieves $O(n^3/p)$ time complexity if $L \leq n^2/p, g \leq n/p^{1/2}$.

The best known BSP algorithm for the algebraic path problem [109] uses recursion to achieve a time complexity of

$$O(p^{\alpha})L + O(n^3/p) + gO(n^2/p^{\alpha}),$$

where the parameter α takes a real value in the interval $[1/2, 2/3]$. Since this algorithm achieves $O(n^3/p)$ cost for $L \leq n^3/p^{1+\alpha}, g \leq n/p^{1-\alpha}$, the BSP schedule in Figure 8.4 is asymptotically sub-optimal. Nevertheless, it is efficient in the sense described in Section 2.5. Furthermore, as the multiplicative constant associated with the $O(n^3/p)$ computation complexity of the asymptotically optimal algorithm in [109] is greater than one, the schedule in Figure 8.4 will have a smaller actual execution time for large problem sizes. Finally, unlike any implementation of the APP algorithm in [109], our schedule leads to parallel code which is very simple and resembles the original sequential code.

The current version of the BSP parallelisation tool does not implement the two techniques for the scheduling of broadcast loop nests. Therefore, it parallelises the APP computation loop using generic loop nest scheduling. The result is a BSP schedule similar to the one in Figure 8.4, but with the broadcasts implemented using the straightforward, one-superstep approach. Thus, the cost of this schedule is $nL + n^3/p + 2gn^2$, with $O(n^3/p)$ time complexity achieved for $L \leq n^2/p$, $g \leq n/p$. It is worth mentioning that the structure of the data dependences does not permit the automatic detection of an appropriate data partition. Instead, the data partition must be specified by the user, based on the automatically provided information that the inner loops of the APP computation can be parallelised.

To conclude the section, we note that a problem entirely equivalent to APP is the solution of linear systems by Gauss-Jordan reduction (without pivoting). Indeed, let M be an $n \times n$ matrix and $\mathbf{b}$ an n-dimensional vector, and consider the linear system $\mathsf{M}\mathbf{x} = \mathbf{b}$. Gauss-Jordan reduction solves this system by iteratively constructing the sequence of $n \times (n+1)$ matrices $\mathsf{A}^{-1} = [\,\mathsf{M} \mid \mathbf{b}\,], \mathsf{A}^0, \mathsf{A}^1, \ldots, \mathsf{A}^{n-2}, \mathsf{A}^{n-1} = [\,\mathsf{I}_n \mid \mathbf{x}\,]$ as follows:

for $k = 0, n-1$ **do**
  for $i = 0, n-1$ **do**
    for $j = k, n$ **do**
      if $i = k$ **then**
        $a[k,i,j] = a[k-1,i,j]/a[k-1,k,k]$
      else
        $a[k,i,j] = a[k-1,i,j] - a[k-1,i,k]a[k-1,k,j]/a[k-1,k,k]$

Therefore, the parallelisation strategy employed for the algebraic path problem can be used to produce a similar BSP version of Gauss-Jordan reduction.

for $k = 1, KMAX$ **do**
  for $i = 1, n-2$ **do**
    for $j = 1, n-2$ **do**
      $u[k,i,j] = (u[k-1,i-1,j] + u[k-1,i,j-1] + u[k-1,i+1,j] + u[k-1,i,j+1])/4$

(a) Jacobi iteration

for $k = 1, KMAX$ **do**
  for $i = 1, n-2$ **do**
    for $j = 1, n-2$ **do**
      $u[k,i,j] = (u[k,i-1,j] + u[k,i,j-1] + u[k-1,i+1,j] + u[k-1,i,j+1])/4$

(b) Gauss-Seidel iteration

Figure 8.5: Sequential finite difference iteration.

8.5 Finite Difference Iteration on a Cartesian Grid

Finite difference iteration is a numerical analysis technique which is widely used in the solution of partial differential equations. Consider for instance Laplace's equation:

$$\frac{\partial^2 u}{\partial^2 x} + \frac{\partial^2 u}{\partial^2 y} = 0,$$

where $u : \mathbf{R}^2 \to \mathbf{R}$. The discretisation of this equation at the nodes of an $n \times n$ Cartesian grid yields the set of discrete equations:

$$4u_{i,j} - u_{i-1,j} - u_{i,j-1} - u_{i+1,j} - u_{i,j+1} = 0,$$

for $0 < i,j < n-1$. Given a set of boundary conditions $\{u^0_{i,j} \mid i \in \{0, n-1\} \vee j \in \{0, n-1\}\}$, the system of discrete equations is solved iteratively. The method starts with an approximate solution u^0 built by setting the non-boundary elements of u to arbitrary values. In a sequence of iterations $k = 1, 2, \ldots, KMAX$, it then generates an approximation u^k that refines u^{k-1}. Two approximation refinement techniques—called Jacobi iteration and Gauss-Seidel iteration, respectively—are shown in Figure 8.5.

The sequential code corresponding to the Jacobi finite difference iteration (Figure 8.5(a)) is merely a variant of the nested loop whose iterative scheduling was studied in Example 5.6. Hence, its BSP version can be readily obtained using the iterative scheduling technique described in Section 5.5. The cost of a single iteration of the resulting BSP schedule is:

$$L + \frac{n^2}{p} + \frac{4gn}{\sqrt{p}}.$$

This cost is one-optimal in computation, attaining $O(n^2/p)$ time complexity for $L \leq n^2/p, g \leq n/p^{1/2}$. The schedule is identical to the one generated automatically by the

```
for k = 1,KMAX do
  if me < p-1 then
    bsp_get u[k-1,1..n-2,(me+1)n/p] from processor me+1
  for t = 0,⌈n/x1⌉+p-2 do
    c1 = t-me
    if me > 0 then
      bsp_get u[k,max{1,c1x1}..min{n-2,(c1+1)x1-1},me n/p-1]
              from processor me-1
    bsp_sync
    for i = max{1,c1x1},min{n-2,(c1+1)x1-1} do
      for j = max{1,me n/p},min{n-2,(me+1)n/p-1} do
        u[k,i,j] = (u[k,i-1,j]+u[k,i,j-1]+u[k-1,i+1,j]+u[k-1,i,j+1])/4
```

Figure 8.6: The BSP version of Gauss-Seidel finite difference iteration.

BSP parallelisation tool, and to the straightforward BSP code that a parallel programmer would use for the Jacobi iteration method.

The situation is different for the Gauss-Seidel finite difference iteration, as none of the template-matching scheduling techniques can be applied directly. Furthermore, the generic loop nest parallelisation technique is unable to expose any potential parallelism in the loop nest in Figure 8.5(b). Accordingly, the scheduling tool presented in the previous chapter cannot produce a BSP version of Gauss-Seidel iteration.

Despite the above mentioned difficulties, a BSP schedule can be obtained using template-matching parallelisation in two different ways. Firstly, it is possible to use wavefront block scheduling after an appropriate affine transformation is applied to the 3-dimensional iteration space as shown in Section 5.4.2. The resulting schedule, however, involves a non-rectangular 3-dimensional iteration space and is extremely intricate.

Secondly, iterative and wavefront block scheduling can be applied together to generate a better BSP schedule as follows. Initially, iterative scheduling is applied to the outermost loop of the loop nest, thus eliminating the two flow dependences carried by this loop. Wavefront block scheduling is then used to parallelise the computation of the two inner loops in Figure 8.5(b) in a way that is entirely similar to the one employed in Example 5.5. The BSP code assigned to a generic processor me, $0 \leq me < p$ is depicted in Figure 8.6. The cost of a single iteration is

$$\left\lceil \frac{n}{x_1}+p-1 \right\rceil L + \left\lceil 1+\frac{(p-1)x_1}{n} \right\rceil \frac{n^2}{p} + \left\lceil 2+\frac{(p-1)x_1}{n} \right\rceil gn.$$

This cost is minimised when x_1, the height of the blocks computed in the successive supersteps of the iteration, has the value $x_1 = \left\lceil \sqrt{pL/((p-1)(1+gp/n))} \right\rceil$. The schedule corresponding to this value of x_1 approaches one-optimality in computation, achieving $O(n^2/p)$ overall cost when $g \leq n/p$, $L \leq n/p$. Once again, the BSP code generated using automatic parallelisation techniques coincides with the parallel programmer's straightforward version of Gauss-Seidel iteration.

```
i1 = 0, i2 = 0
for i = 0,n-1 do
  if i1 < n1 and i2 < n2 then
    if a[i1] < b[i2] then
      c[i] = a[i1], i1 = i1 + 1
    else
      c[i] = b[i2], i2 = i2 + 1
  else
    if i1 = n1 then
      c[i] = b[i2], i2 = i2 + 1
    else
      c[i] = a[i1], i1 = i1 + 1
```

Figure 8.7: The sequential merging of two sequences sorted in increasing order.

8.6 Merging

In this section, we consider the problem of merging two sorted sequences $A = \langle a_0, a_1, \ldots, a_{n_1-1}\rangle$ and $B = \langle b_0, b_1, \ldots, b_{n_2-1}\rangle$ into the sorted sequence $C = \langle c_0, c_1, \ldots, c_{n-1}\rangle$, $n = n_1 + n_2$. Efficient BSP algorithms for merging (including an optimal algorithm) have been proposed by Gerbessiotis and Siniolakis [81]. However, none of the scheduling techniques introduced in the previous chapters is able to expose any parallelism in the sequential merging algorithm depicted in Figure 8.7. As parallel merging algorithms do not preserve the structure of the sequential algorithm, this is far from being surprising. In fact, the scheduling of the sequential solution of many other related problems (including, for instance, sorting) cannot be tackled by the existing parallelisation techniques.

8.7 Summary

The parallelisation results obtained for the scientific computing problems studied in this chapter are summed up in Table 8.1. We also include in the table results for the inner product of two vectors and for the solution of a triangular linear system, problems whose parallelisation was addressed in Example 5.7 and Example 5.12, respectively.

For each problem, Table 8.1 compares the cost of the algorithm that achieves the best time complexity among all known solutions, the cost of the schedule obtained using the parallelisation techniques described in this book, and the cost of the solution generated automatically by the BSP scheduling tool. Whenever possible, the multiplicative constants introduced by the scheduling technique employed are made explicit. The execution of the underlying loop body for a single iteration point, however, is assumed to take unit time. In addition, Table 8.2 presents the conditions when the three solutions of same set of problems are optimal. (Recall that a parallel schedule is deemed optimal if its overall cost has order $O(T(n)/p)$, where $T(n)$ is the cost of the associated sequential algorithm.)

Table 8.1: The parallelisation of a set of scientific computing problems.

problem	best known solution†	parallelisation-based solution	BSPSCHEDULER solution
inner product	$\log_d p\, L + \frac{n}{p} + gd \log_d p$ $d \in 2..p-1$	$\log_d p\, L + \frac{n}{p} + gd \log_d p$ $d \in 2..p-1$	$\log_d p\, L + \frac{n}{p} + gd \log_d p$ $d \in 2..p-1$
matrix-vector multiplication	$3L + n^2/p + 2gn/\sqrt{p}$	$3L + n^2/p + 2gn/\sqrt{p}$	$2L + n^2/p + gn$
matrix-matrix multiplication	$3L + n^3/p + 3gn^2/p^{2/3}$	$3L + n^3/p + 3gn^2/p^{2/3}$	$2L + n^3/p + 2gn^2/p^{1/2}$
Triangular linear system solution	$(\frac{n}{x} + p - 1)L +$ $(1 + \frac{(p-1)x}{n})\frac{n^2}{p} +$ $(1 + \frac{(p-1)x}{n})gn,$ $x = \left\lceil \sqrt{\frac{pL}{(p-1)(1+gp/n)}} \right\rceil$	$(\frac{n}{x} + p - 1)L +$ $(1 + \frac{(p-1)x}{n})\frac{n^2}{p} +$ $(1 + \frac{(p-1)x}{n})gn$ $x = \left\lceil \sqrt{\frac{pL}{(p-1)(1+gp/n)}} \right\rceil$	$(\frac{n}{x} + p - 1)L +$ $(1 + \frac{(p-1)x}{n})\frac{n^2}{p} +$ $(1 + \frac{(p-1)x}{n})gn$ $x = \left\lceil \sqrt{\frac{pL}{(p-1)(1+gp/n)}} \right\rceil$
LU decomposition/ Gaussian elimination	$O(p^\alpha)L + O(\frac{n^3}{p}) + gO(\frac{n^2}{p^\alpha})$ $\frac{1}{2} \leq \alpha \leq \frac{2}{3}$	$(\frac{n}{x} + 2(\sqrt{p} - 1))L +$ $\left(1 + \frac{2(\sqrt{p}-1)x}{n}\right)\frac{n^3}{p} +$ $2g\left(1 + \frac{2(\sqrt{p}-1)x}{n}\right)n^2$ $x = \left\lceil \sqrt{\frac{pL}{2(\sqrt{p}-1)(n+2gp)}} \right\rceil$	$(\frac{n}{x} + 2(\sqrt{p} - 1))L +$ $\left(1 + \frac{2(\sqrt{p}-1)x}{n}\right)\frac{n^3}{p} +$ $2g\left(1 + \frac{2(\sqrt{p}-1)x}{n}\right)n^2$ $x = \left\lceil \sqrt{\frac{pL}{2(\sqrt{p}-1)(n+2gp)}} \right\rceil$
algebraic path problem/ Gauss-Jordan reduction	$O(p^\alpha)L + O(\frac{n^3}{p}) + gO(\frac{n^2}{p^\alpha})$ $\frac{1}{2} \leq \alpha \leq \frac{2}{3}$	$2nL + \frac{n^3}{p} + \frac{4gn^2}{\sqrt{p}}$	$nL + \frac{n^3}{p} + 2gn^2$
Cartesian grid Jacobi iteration	$L + n^2/p + 4gn/\sqrt{p}$	$L + n^2/p + 4gn/\sqrt{p}$	$L + n^2/p + 4gn/\sqrt{p}$
Cartesian grid Gauss-Seidel iteration	$(\frac{n}{x} + p - 1)L +$ $(1 + \frac{(p-1)x}{n})\frac{n^2}{p} +$ $(2 + \frac{(p-1)x}{n})gn$ $x = \left\lceil \sqrt{\frac{pL}{(p-1)(1+gp/n)}} \right\rceil$	$(\frac{n}{x} + p - 1)L +$ $(1 + \frac{(p-1)x}{n})\frac{n^2}{p} +$ $(2 + \frac{(p-1)x}{n})gn$ $x = \left\lceil \sqrt{\frac{pL}{(p-1)(1+gp/n)}} \right\rceil$	—
merging	see [81]	—	—

† with respect to the time complexity

For most problems listed in Tables 8.1 and 8.2, the parallelisation techniques described in the previous chapters were able to produce either the best known or an efficient parallel solution. Although the current version of the BSP scheduling tool implements only a subset of the existing parallelisation techniques, it can be used for the automatic derivation of many of these parallel solutions. These results show that architecture-independent loop parallelisation is indeed applicable to a large number of scientific computing problems.

At the same time, automatic parallelisation cannot match the best parallel schedule designed by the human programmer when this schedule involves a significant restructuring of the original sequential code. As illustrated in Section 8.4, this happens for instance in the case of the algebraic path problem, whose optimal parallel solution is

Table 8.2: Optimality conditions for the parallel solutions in Table 8.1.

problem	best known solution†	parallelisation-based solution	BSPSCHEDULER solution
inner product	$g,L \leq n/(p\log p)$	$g,L \leq n/(p\log p)$	$g,L \leq n/(p\log p)$
matrix-vector multiplication	$L \leq n^2/p, g \leq n/p^{1/2}$	$L \leq n^2/p, g \leq n/p^{1/2}$	$L \leq n^2/p, g \leq n/p$
matrix-matrix multiplication	$L \leq n^3/p, g \leq n/p^{1/3}$	$L \leq n^3/p, g \leq n/p^{1/3}$	$L \leq n^3/p, g \leq n/p^{1/2}$
Triangular linear system solution	$g,L \leq n/p$	$g,L \leq n/p$	$g,L \leq n/p$
LU decomposition/ Gaussian elimination	$L \leq n^3/p^{1+\alpha}, g \leq n/p^{1-\alpha}$ $1/2 \leq \alpha \leq 2/3$	$L \leq n^2/p, g \leq n/p$	$L \leq n^2/p, g \leq n/p$
algebraic path problem/ Gauss-Jordan reduction	$L \leq n^3/p^{1+\alpha}, g \leq n/p^{1-\alpha}$ $1/2 \leq \alpha \leq 2/3$	$L \leq n^2/p, g \leq n/p^{1/2}$	$L \leq n^2/p, g \leq n/p$
Cartesian grid Jacobi iteration	$L \leq n^2/p, g \leq n/p^{1/2}$	$L \leq n^2/p, g \leq n/p^{1/2}$	$L \leq n^2/p, g \leq n/p^{1/2}$
Cartesian grid Gauss-Seidel iteration	$g,L \leq n/p$	$g,L \leq n/p$	—
merging	see [81]	—	—

† with respect to the time complexity

totally unrelated to the standard sequential algorithm. Furthermore, whereas for the algebraic path problem an efficient parallel solution could still be achieved automatically, for other problems (e.g. merging and sorting) this was no longer possible.

Finally, it is worth noticing that automatic parallelisation is sensitive to changes in the sequential code that are perceived as minor by the human programmer. Assume for example that, in order to decrease the memory complexity of the APP sequential algorithm, the programmer replaces the standard computation loop in Figure 8.3 with:

$s = 0$
for $k = 1, n$ **do**
  for $i = 0, n-1$ **do**
    for $j = 0, n-1$ **do**
      $a[1-s,i,j] = a[s,i,j] + a[s,i,k] \cdot (a[s,k,k])^* \cdot a[s,k,j]$
  $s = 1 - s$

This apparently slight change in the sequential code is sufficient to make the current version of the BSP scheduling tool unable to produce a parallel schedule. This limitation can be partly overcome by using techniques such as symbolic dependence analysis and enhanced template recognition. However, it is unlikely that automatic parallelisation will ever be able to tackle all the variants of an otherwise easy parallelisable sequential algorithm.

In conclusion, architecture-independent automatic parallelisation represents a feasible approach to the scheduling of regular computations on general purpose parallel computers. With a certain amount of caution, and possibly following some sequential code pre-processing, it can be applied successfully to most scientific computations that involve dense data structures.

9. Conclusions

We have convictions only if we studied nothing thoroughly.

Emil Cioran – *The Trouble with Being Born*

9.1 Summary of Contributions and Concluding Remarks

Architecture-independent programming and automatic parallelisation have long been regarded as two different ways of alleviating the prohibitive costs of parallel software development. Building on recent advances in both areas, this book has proposed a unified approach to the parallelisation of scientific computing code. This novel approach is based on the bulk-synchronous parallel model of computation, and succeeds in automatically generating parallel code which is architecture-independent, scalable, and of analytically predictable performance. The remainder of this section summarises the main contributions and conclusions of the book.

1. An extensive collection of BSP parallelisation techniques has been developed for the template-matching scheduling of loop computations. A subset of these techniques addresses the parallelisation of uniform-dependence perfect loop nests:

- Communication-free scheduling permits the generation of optimal BSP schedules when the original loop nest can be partitioned into fully independent subproblems.
- Wavefront block scheduling represents the extension of the wavefront scheduling method to the BSP model. This technique tackles the efficient parallelisation of tightly nested loops whose data dependences are described by distance vectors that span the entire iteration space.
- Iterative scheduling is a new parallelisation technique that copes successfully with many of the cases when the application of wavefront block scheduling produces intricate schedules due to its preliminary skewing of the iteration space.

The other techniques in the collection address the scheduling of several non-uniform dependence computation patterns that occur frequently in scientific computer code:

- Perfect loop nests describing reductions can be efficiently parallelised using a two-stage technique. This technique combines the concurrent computation of independent sub-reductions in its first stage with the inverse of a broadcast operation in its last stage.

- An important class of recurrences which includes (but is not limited to) linear recurrences can also be parallelised effectively. This class comprises the recurrences whose evaluation can be concurrently started at p equally distanced iteration points after some sublinear time pre-processing.
- The parallelisation of broadcast loop nests—a computation pattern defined in this book and comprising among its instances the algebraic path problem and Gaussian elimination—can be realised in two different ways. The straightforward approach preserves the structure of the sequential code, and employs actual broadcasts to satisfy its non-uniform data dependences. As a result, it works under all circumstances and generates simple but sub-optimal parallel schedules. The alternative approach produces faster schedules by expanding the original code into a uniform-dependence loop nest and using wavefront block scheduling for its parallelisation. The latter technique, however, can only be applied to a restricted category of broadcast loop nests.

The case studies presented in the book demonstrate that template-matching scheduling can be utilised successfully in the mechanical parallelisation of dense scientific computations described by regular loop structures.

2. For sequential computations whose structure is not recognised by any of the template-matching scheduling techniques, we have devised a generic loop nest parallelisation scheme. The scheme comprises four steps—data dependence analysis, potential parallelism identification, data and computation partitioning, and communication and synchronisation generation—and this book has introduced new algorithms for the last three steps:

- The algorithm applied in the second step of the scheme improves the existing parallelisation algorithms by integrating loop interchange into its code transformation procedure. This integration translates into an important increase in the granularity of the resulting potential parallelism, with beneficial effects in the BSP setting. Moreover, the new algorithm employs an original early termination test to eliminate the negative effects of unnecessary loop distribution.
- New partitioning algorithms are used for the mapping of the data and computation of a generic loop nest on the processor-memory units of a parallel computer. These algorithms are independent of the BSP model, and are applicable within any framework for distributed-memory parallel programming.
- A novel, BSP-specific algorithm is employed in the last step of the scheme. The algorithm takes into account the decoupling of communication and synchronisation that characterises the BSP model of computation. Consequently, it generates separate calls to communication and synchronisation primitives. This approach represents a radical departure from the typical generation of pairwise send/receive communication primitives that solve the requirements for non-local data, and synchronise the two processors involved in the data transfer.

The generic parallelisation scheme has been shown to produce reasonably efficient parallel code for many scientific computations that are not tackled by template-matching scheduling.

3. The performance of the schedules generated by various parallelisation methods can be assessed using the communication cost analysis framework devised in the

book. This theoretical framework permits the evaluation of the input and inter-tile communication overheads associated with loop nest tiling, and can be used to tune a parallel schedule for best performance. Furthermore, its usefulness extends to other research areas such as optimisation of cache usage in shared-memory multiprocessors and analysis of the space complexity of parallel code.

4. This book has also introduced an automatic parallelisation strategy which is unique in its combination of template-matching and generic scheduling. The hybrid parallelisation strategy comprises two phases:

- In the first phase, it attempts to build the parallel version of a sequential loop nest using template-matching scheduling. When the attempt is successful, an efficient parallel schedule is devised with very low cost.
- Otherwise, the more expensive generic loop nest parallelisation scheme is applied to the atypical sequential loop. An acceptable parallel schedule is thus obtained in most cases when the original sequential code comprises any inherent loop parallelism.

The application of this strategy in a number of case studies has produced better results than those obtained when either template-matching or generic scheduling have been used alone.

5. Based on the loop nest parallelisation strategy described above, we have implemented BSPSCHEDULER—an architecture-independent paralleliser with the following features:

- The current version of the tool implements a subset of the template-matching scheduling techniques, and the generic parallelisation scheme proposed in this book.
- The tool has been designed and used to conduct research into the effectiveness of automatic loop parallelisation, the results of this investigation being provided in the book.
- Due to its easy-to-use graphical interface and to its step-by-step parallelisation policy, BSPSCHEDULER can be of great help to the beginner learning architecture-independent parallel programming. The tool has been successfully used to teach scalable parallel programming to graduate students reading for an M.Sc. degree in software engineering.
- Its fine tuning facilities make BSPSCHEDULER convenient for obtaining and comparing various schedules of the same sequential computation. This feature recommends the tool to the experienced parallel software designer interested in increasing the speed and quality of parallel application development.

6. In order to assess the effectiveness of our approach to automatic parallelisation, we have performed a number of case studies involving common scientific computing problems. The conclusions drawn from these tests are as follows:

- First, and most important, architecture-independent loop parallelisation is able to reproduce the best known parallel solutions or to generate efficient schedules for many scientific computing problems.
- Although the current version of BSPSCHEDULER implements only a subset of the proposed parallelisation techniques, it can be used for the mechanical derivation of most of these schedules.

- The main limitation of automatic parallelisation is its sensitiveness to changes in the sequential code that are perceived as minor by the human programmer. This limitation can be partly overcome by using symbolic dependence analysis and advanced template-variant recognition.
- For some problems whose parallel solution differs completely from their sequential solution (e.g. merging, sorting), automatic parallelisation does not produce any results.

9.2 Future work directions

There are a number of ways in which architecture-independent automatic parallelisation could be refined and extended. The most significant research directions requiring further investigation are as follows:

1. The development of additional template-matching scheduling techniques could increase the success rate of automatic parallelisation. The case studies presented in this book demonstrate that the parallel version of some important computations bears no resemblance to the associated sequential version. As a result, the parallelisation of these computations can be automated only by means of template-matching scheduling.

2. A powerful template-variant recognition mechanism is required to deal with the minor changes that make the sequential code depart from the standard format recognised by the template-matching scheduling techniques. At present, the performance of the BSP parallelisation tool is constrained by its inability to identify some template variants for which an appropriate scheduling technique is available.

3. As indicated in the previous chapter, there are computation patterns whose parallelisation necessitates the iterative application of more than one scheduling technique. The development of a method for selecting the appropriate scheduling techniques and deciding on their application order remains an open problem.

4. The generic loop nest parallelisation scheme could be improved in several respects:

- The data partitioning algorithm used in the third step of the scheme may be augmented to allow the block-cyclic distribution of arrays in dimensions corresponding to variable-length loops. This extension would significantly decrease the workload imbalance that occurs when the loop nest to be parallelised presents a non-rectangular iteration space.
- The parallelisation scheme tiles the data space starting at the origin, and distributes the resulting array blocks to processors so as to match the array block and the processor coordinates. The amount of statement masking and communication induced by this data distribution policy could be decreased using a technique called *array alignment*. In array alignment, the arrays are tiled starting at a non-null displacement, and the array block coordinates are permuted before the assignment of array blocks to processors.
- The communication and synchronisation generation algorithm designed for the last step of the scheme inserts basic communication primitives in the parallel code. In some cases, subsets of these primitives implement inefficiently collective com-

munications such as broadcasts or scatters. The communication overheads may be decreased by identifying these subsets and replacing them with optimal implementations of the associated collective communications.

5. While the hybrid template-matching/generic loop parallelisation approach proposed in this book can readily tackle sequences of loop nests, an extended version of this approach is needed for the parallelisation of entire sequential programs. The main challenges in the development of this extended approach include:

- Applying different scheduling techniques to different parts of the sequential code in a consistent manner.
- Trading-off data redistribution for computation optimality. When the computationally optimal parallelisation of a particular loop nest involves serious data redistributions, a better overall schedule may be obtainable by choosing a data distribution that leads to local sub-optimality.
- Handling the inter-procedural data dependences. The strategy used to analyse these dependences has a major impact on the parallelising transformations that can be performed at intra-procedural level.

6. The effectiveness of our parallelisation tool could also be increased in several ways:

- The addition of exact and symbolic dependence tests to its dependence analysis module would significantly reduce the number of conservatively assumed nonexistent dependences. This effect may be enhanced by the use of appropriate assertions in the input sequential code.
- As the current version of the tool implements only a subset of the template-matching scheduling techniques introduced in this book, the inclusion of the other techniques would also boost its performance. In particular, the incorporation of broadcast loop nest scheduling would have a beneficial effect on the number of scientific computations handled efficiently by the tool.
- Finally, the usefulness of the architecture-independent parallelisation tool could be enhanced by providing it with a performance assessment module that implements the schedule cost analysis algorithm described in the book.

Appendix A. Theorem proofs

Theorem 4.3 *Let* $\mathsf{G} = [\mathbf{g}_1, \mathbf{g}_2, \ldots, \mathbf{g}_K]$ *be an* $m \times K$ *matrix with integer elements, and* $\mathbf{x} = [x_1, x_2, \ldots, x_K]^{\mathrm{T}}$ *a K-dimensional vector with positive integer elements. Assume that* $m < K$, *and that the m rows of* G *are linearly independent. Then, the following rules hold:*

Rule 1 (Ding and Stefanescu [43]): *If* G *is unimodular in the sense that the determinant of any* $m \times m$ *submatrix of* G *is 0 or* ± 1,

$$F(\mathsf{I}_K\mathbf{x}, \mathsf{G}) = \sum_{\substack{\{k_1,k_2,\ldots,k_m\} \in \mathbf{P}1..K \\ \det[\mathbf{g}_{k_1}, \mathbf{g}_{k_2}, \ldots, \mathbf{g}_{k_m}] \neq 0}} x_{k_1} x_{k_2} \ldots x_{k_m} \tag{4.7}$$

Rule 2: *If the k-th column of* G, $1 \leq k \leq K$ *is zero,*

$$F(\mathsf{I}_K\mathbf{x}, \mathsf{G}) = F(\mathsf{I}_{K-1}[x_1, x_2, \ldots, x_{k-1}, x_{k+1}, \ldots, x_K]^{\mathrm{T}}, [\mathbf{g}_1, \mathbf{g}_2, \ldots, \mathbf{g}_{k-1}, \mathbf{g}_{k+1}, \ldots, \mathbf{g}_K]) \tag{4.8}$$

Rule 3: *If* $g_{j,k}$, $1 \leq j \leq m$, $1 \leq k \leq K$, *is the only non-zero element in the j-th row of* G,

$$F(\mathsf{I}_K\mathbf{x}, \mathsf{G}) = x_k F(\mathsf{I}_{K-1}[x_1, x_2, \ldots, x_{k-1}, x_{k+1}, \ldots, x_K]^{\mathrm{T}}, [\mathbf{g}_1, \mathbf{g}_2, \ldots, \mathbf{g}_{k-1}, \mathbf{g}_{k+1}, \ldots, \mathbf{g}_K]) \tag{4.9}$$

Rule 4: *Let* $g_{j,1}$, $g_{j,2}$, $\ldots$, $g_{j,K}$ *be the elements of the j-th row of* G, $1 \leq j \leq m$, *and* $\alpha = \gcd(g_{j,1}, g_{j,2}, \ldots, g_{j,K})$. *Then for any tiling matrix* T, $F(\mathsf{T}, \mathsf{G}) = F(\mathsf{T}, \mathsf{G}')$, *where* G' *is the* $m \times K$ *matrix whose j-th row has the elements* $g_{j,1}/\alpha$, $g_{j,2}/\alpha$, $\ldots$, $g_{j,K}/\alpha$, *and whose other rows are copied from* G.

Rule 5: *Let* g_{j,k_1}, g_{j,k_2}, $\ldots$, g_{j,k_r}, $r \geq 1$, $1 \leq k_1 < k_2 < \cdots < k_r \leq K$, *be the only non-null elements in the j-th row of* G, $1 \leq j \leq m$. *Then,*

$$F(\mathsf{I}_K\mathbf{x}, \mathsf{G}) \leq \left(|g_{j,k_1}|x_{k_1} + |g_{j,k_2}|x_{k_2} + \cdots + |g_{j,k_r}|x_{k_r}\right) F(\mathsf{I}_K\mathbf{x}, \mathsf{G}'), \tag{4.10}$$

where G' *is the* $(m-1) \times K$ *matrix obtained by eliminating the j-th row from* G. *Furthermore, if* $|g_{j,k_1}| = |g_{j,k_2}| = \cdots = |g_{j,k_r}| = 1$ *and for any row* $j' \neq j$ $g_{j',k_1} = g_{j',k_2} = \cdots = g_{j',k_r} = 0$,

$$F(\mathsf{I}_K\mathbf{x}, \mathsf{G}) = (x_{k_1} + x_{k_2} + \cdots + x_{k_r} - r + 1) F(\mathsf{I}_{K-r}\mathbf{x}', \mathsf{G}'), \tag{4.11}$$

where $\mathbf{x}' = [x_1,\dots,x_{k_1-1},x_{k_1+1},\dots,x_{k_2-1},x_{k_2+1},\dots,x_{k_r-1},x_{k_r+1},\dots,x_K]^{\mathrm{T}}$ *and* G' *is the* $(m-1)\times(K-r)$ *matrix obtained by eliminating the columns* $\mathbf{g}_{k_1}$, $\mathbf{g}_{k_2}$, $\dots$, $\mathbf{g}_{k_r}$ *and the* j*-th row from* G.

Proof The proof of the Ding and Stefanescu's result in Rule 1 can be found in [43]. Here, we shall prove the other four rules, for an array reference with the generic form in (4.4) and for the generic rectangular tile T of coordinates $(c_1,c_2,\dots,c_K)$ described by (4.3).

In order to prove the second rule, we consider the $(K-1)$-level loop nest $\mathcal{L}'$ obtained by eliminating the k-th loop from the original loop nest $\mathcal{L}$. The tile induced by T on the iteration space of $\mathcal{L}'$ is tile T' of coordinates $(c_1,\dots,c_{k-1},c_{k+1},\dots,c_K)$, generated by the tiling matrix $\mathsf{I}_{K-1}\mathbf{x}'$, where $\mathbf{x}' = [x_1,x_2,\dots,x_{k-1},x_{k+1},\dots,x_K]^{\mathrm{T}}$.

Since the k-th column of G is $\mathbf{g}_k = \mathbf{0}$, the loop index i_k does not appear in any subscript of the array reference $a[\mathsf{G}\mathbf{i}+\mathbf{v}]$ whose footprint size we analyse. Consequently, the corresponding array reference within the loop body of $\mathcal{L}'$ is $a[\mathsf{G}'\mathbf{i}'+\mathbf{v}]$, where G' is the $m\times(K-1)$ matrix obtained by eliminating the k-th column from G and $\mathbf{i}' = [i_1,\dots,i_{k-1},i_{k+1},\dots,i_K]^{\mathrm{T}}$. The footprints of the two array references across T and T', respectively, are the same:

$$\forall \mathbf{i}=[i_1,i_2,\dots,i_K]^{\mathrm{T}}\in T \bullet \exists \mathbf{i}'=[i_1,\dots,i_{k-1},i_{k+1},\dots,i_K]^{\mathrm{T}}\in T' \bullet \mathsf{G}\mathbf{i}+\mathbf{v}=\mathsf{G}'\mathbf{i}'+\mathbf{v}$$

and

$$\forall \mathbf{i}'=[i_1,\dots,i_{k-1},i_{k+1},\dots,i_K]^{\mathrm{T}}\in T' \bullet$$
$$\exists \mathbf{i}=[i_1,\dots,i_{k-1},c_kx_k,i_{k+1},\dots,i_K]^{\mathrm{T}}\in T \bullet \mathsf{G}'\mathbf{i}'+\mathbf{v}=\mathsf{G}\mathbf{i}+\mathbf{v}$$

As a result, the left and right terms of relation (4.8), which stand for the size of these two footprints, are equal.

For Rule 3, we shall write the footprint of $a[\mathsf{G}\mathbf{i}+\mathbf{v}]$ across tile T as

$$\text{footprint}(a[\mathsf{G}\mathbf{i}+\mathbf{v}]) = \bigcup_{i_k^0=c_kx_k}^{(c_k+1)x_k-1} \{a[\mathsf{G}\mathbf{i}+\mathbf{v}] \mid \mathbf{i}\in T \wedge i_k = i_k^0\}.$$

For each of the x_k sets in this set union, the j-th subscript of a—which depends only on i_k—has a different value. Accordingly, these x_k sets are disjoint, and the footprint size of $a[\mathsf{G}\mathbf{i}+\mathbf{v}]$ can be obtained by summing their sizes:

$$F(\mathsf{I}_K\mathbf{x},\mathsf{G}) = \#\text{footprint}(a[\mathsf{G}\mathbf{i}+\mathbf{v}]) = \sum_{i_k^0=c_kx_k}^{(c_k+1)x_k-1} \#\{a[\mathsf{G}\mathbf{i}+\mathbf{v}] \mid \mathbf{i}\in T \wedge i_k = i_k^0\}.$$

Furthermore, for any $c_kx_k \le i_k^0 \le (c_k+1)x_k - 1$,

$$a[\mathsf{G}\mathbf{i}+\mathbf{v}]\Big|_{i_k=i_k^0} = a[\mathsf{G}'\mathbf{i}+\mathbf{v}'],$$

where $G' = [\mathbf{g}_1, \mathbf{g}_2, \ldots, \mathbf{g}_{k-1}, \mathbf{0}, \mathbf{g}_{k+1}, \ldots, \mathbf{g}_K]$ and $\mathbf{v}' = [v_1 + g_{1,k} i_k^0, v_2 + g_{2,k} i_k^0 \ldots, v_m + g_{m,k} i_k^0]^T$. Consequently,

$$\forall i_k^0 \in c_k x_k..(c_k+1)x_k - 1 \bullet \#\{a[G\mathbf{i}+\mathbf{v}] \mid \mathbf{i} \in T \wedge i_k = i_k^0\} = F(\mathsf{I}_K \mathbf{x}, G').$$

Since the k-th column of G' is zero, it follows from Rule 2 that

$$\forall i_k^0 \in c_k x_k..(c_k+1)x_k - 1 \bullet \#\{a[G\mathbf{i}+\mathbf{v}] \mid \mathbf{i} \in T \wedge i_k = i_k^0\} =$$
$$F(\mathsf{I}_{K-1}[x_1, x_2, \ldots, x_{k-1}, x_{k+1}, \ldots, x_K]^T, [\mathbf{g}_1, \mathbf{g}_2, \ldots, \mathbf{g}_{k-1}, \mathbf{g}_{k+1}, \ldots, \mathbf{g}_K]).$$

Finally, by summing the size of the x_k disjoint sets that compose the footprint of $a[G\mathbf{i}+\mathbf{v}]$, we obtain exactly the result stated in Rule 3.

Rule 4 expresses the obvious fact that by multiplying an array subscript with an arbitrary integer factor, the number of different values taken by the resulting subscript across any set of iteration points does not change. This is mostly an enabling rule for Rules 1 and 5.

To prove the first part of Rule 5, it is enough to show that $s_j = g_{j,k_1} i_{k_1} + g_{j,k_2} i_{k_2} + \ldots + g_{j,k_r} i_{k_r} + v_j$, the j-th subscript of the analysed array reference, can take at most $|g_{j,k_1}| x_{k_1} + |g_{j,k_2}| x_{k_2} + \cdots + |g_{j,k_r}| x_{k_r}$ values across the generic tile T. By multiplying the inequalities (4.3) satisfied by the iteration points in T with $g_{j,k}$, $1 \le k \le K$, we obtain

$$\begin{array}{rcccll} |g_{j,k}| c_k x_k & \le & g_{j,k} i_k & \le & |g_{j,k}|((c_k+1)x_k - 1), & \text{if } g_{j,k} \ge 0 \\ -|g_{j,k}|((c_k+1)x_k - 1) & \le & g_{j,k} i_k & \le & -|g_{j,k}| c_k x_k, & \text{if } g_{j,k} < 0 \end{array}$$

Summing the above inequalities for all k_l, $1 \le l \le r$, we get:

$$\sum_{\substack{l=1 \\ g_{j,k_l}>0}}^{r} |g_{j,k_l}| c_{k_l} x_{k_l} - \sum_{\substack{l=1 \\ g_{j,k_l}<0}}^{r} |g_{j,k_l}|((c_{k_l}+1)x_{k_l} - 1) \le s_j - v_j \le$$
$$\le \sum_{\substack{l=1 \\ g_{j,k_l}>0}}^{r} |g_{j,k_l}|((c_{k_l}+1)x_{k_l} - 1) - \sum_{\substack{l=1 \\ g_{j,k_l}<0}}^{r} |g_{j,k_l}| c_{k_l} x_{k_l}$$

Consequently, the length of the interval in which s_j may take only integer values is

$$\sum_{\substack{l=1 \\ g_{j,k_l}>0}}^{r} |g_{j,k_l}|((c_{k_l}+1)x_{k_l} - 1) - \sum_{\substack{l=1 \\ g_{j,k_l}<0}}^{r} |g_{j,k_l}| c_{k_l} x_{k_l} -$$
$$- \sum_{\substack{l=1 \\ g_{j,k_l}>0}}^{r} |g_{j,k_l}| c_{k_l} x_{k_l} + \sum_{\substack{l=1 \\ g_{j,k_l}<0}}^{r} |g_{j,k_l}|((c_{k_l}+1)x_{k_l} - 1) + 1 =$$
$$= \sum_{l=1}^{r} |g_{j,k_l}|(x_{k_l} - 1) + 1 \le |g_{j,k_1}| x_{k_1} + |g_{j,k_2}| x_{k_2} + \cdots + |g_{j,k_r}| x_{k_r},$$

so s_j can take at most $|g_{j,k_1}|x_{k_1} + |g_{j,k_2}|x_{k_2} + \cdots + |g_{j,k_r}|x_{k_r}$ values, and the first part of Rule 5 is correct.

It is immediate to see that when $|g_{j,k_1}| = |g_{j,k_2}| = \cdots = |g_{j,k_r}| = 1$, the subscript s_j takes all the $\sum_{l=1}^{r} \mid g_{j,k_l} \mid (x_{k_l} - 1) + 1 = x_{k_1} + x_{k_2} + \cdots + x_{k_r} - r + 1$ integer values in the above interval. Therefore, in order to prove the second part of Rule 5, it is enough to demonstrate that for any fixed value s_j^0 of s_j, the footprint of the analysed array reference comprises exactly $F(\mathsf{I}_{K-r}\mathbf{x}', \mathsf{G}')$ array elements, with $\mathbf{x}'$ and G' given in Rule 5.

For this demonstration, let $\mathbf{i} = [i_1^0, i_2^0, \ldots, i_K^0]^{\mathrm{T}} \in T$ be a fixed iteration point for which the array subscript s_j attains the value s_j^0 and $\mathcal{L}'$ the $(K-r)$-level loop nest obtained by eliminating the loops indexed by i_{k_1}, i_{k_2}, ..., i_{k_r} from $\mathcal{L}$. In this loop nest, we replace $a[\mathsf{G}\mathbf{i} + \mathbf{v}]$, the analysed array reference, with the $(m-1)$-dimensional reference $a'[\mathsf{G}'\mathbf{i}' + \mathbf{v}']$, where $\mathbf{i}'$ is the $(K-r)$-dimensional vector whose elements are the loop indices of $\mathcal{L}'$, $\mathbf{v}'$ is obtained by eliminating the j-th element from $\mathbf{v}$, and a' is defined by

$$a'[\mathsf{G}'[i_1, \ldots, i_{k_1-1}, i_{k_1+1}, \ldots, i_{k_2-1}, i_{k_2+1}, \ldots, i_{k_r-1}, i_{k_r+1}, \ldots, i_K]^{\mathrm{T}} + \mathbf{v}'] =$$
$$= a[\mathsf{G}[i_1, \ldots, i_{k_1-1}, i_{k_1}^0, i_{k_1+1}, \ldots, i_{k_2-1}, i_{k_2}^0, i_{k_2+1}, \ldots, i_{k_r-1}, i_{k_r}^0, i_{k_r+1}, \ldots, i_K]^{\mathrm{T}} + \mathbf{v}].$$

The tile induced by T on the iteration space of the loop nest $\mathcal{L}'$ is T', the tile of coordinates $(c_1, \ldots, c_{k_1-1}, c_{k_1+1}, \ldots, c_{k_2-1}, c_{k_2+1}, \ldots, c_{k_r-1}, c_{k_r+1}, \ldots, c_K)$ generated by $I_{K-r}\mathbf{x}'$. The size of the footprint of the new array reference across T' is exactly $F(I_{K-r}\mathbf{x}', \mathsf{G}')$. We shall now prove that this is also the number of elements from the original data footprint when $s_j = s_j^0$, by showing that the set $\{a[\mathsf{G}\mathbf{i} + \mathbf{v}] \mid \mathbf{i} \in T \wedge s_j = s_j^0\}$ and the footprint $\{a'[\mathsf{G}'\mathbf{i}' + \mathbf{v}'] \mid \mathbf{i}' \in T'\}$ are identical. Indeed, since s_j is the only array subscript that depends on the loop indices i_{k_1}, i_{k_2}, ..., i_{k_r}, we have

$$\forall \mathbf{i} = [i_1, i_2, \ldots, i_K]^{\mathrm{T}} \in T \bullet (g_{j,k_1} i_{k_1} + g_{j,k_2} i_{k_2} + \cdots + g_{j,k_r} i_{k_r} + v_j = s_j^0) \Rightarrow$$
$$\Rightarrow (\exists \mathbf{i}' = [i_1, \ldots, i_{k_1-1}, i_{k_1+1}, \ldots, i_{k_2-1}, i_{k_2+1}, \ldots, i_{k_r-1}, i_{k_r+1}, \ldots, i_K]^{\mathrm{T}} \in T' \bullet$$
$$a[\mathsf{G}[i_1, \ldots, i_{k_1-1}, i_{k_1}, i_{k_1+1}, \ldots, i_{k_2-1}, i_{k_2}, i_{k_2+1}, \ldots, i_{k_r-1}, i_{k_r}, i_{k_r+1}, \ldots, i_K]^{\mathrm{T}} + \mathbf{v}] =$$
$$= a[\mathsf{G}[i_1, \ldots, i_{k_1-1}, i_{k_1}^0, i_{k_1+1}, \ldots, i_{k_2-1}, i_{k_2}^0, i_{k_2+1}, \ldots, i_{k_r-1}, i_{k_r}^0, i_{k_r+1}, \ldots, i_K]^{\mathrm{T}} + \mathbf{v}] =$$
$$= a'[\mathsf{G}'[i_1, \ldots, i_{k_1-1}, i_{k_1+1}, \ldots, i_{k_2-1}, i_{k_2+1}, \ldots, i_{k_r-1}, i_{k_r+1}, \ldots, i_K]^{\mathrm{T}} + \mathbf{v}']).$$

Furthermore,

$$\forall \mathbf{i}' = [i_1, \ldots, i_{k_1-1}, i_{k_1+1}, \ldots, i_{k_2-1}, i_{k_2+1}, \ldots, i_{k_r-1}, i_{k_r+1}, \ldots, i_K]^{\mathrm{T}} \in T' \bullet$$
$$\exists \mathbf{i} = [i_1, \ldots, i_{k_1-1}, i_{k_1}^0, i_{k_1+1}, \ldots, i_{k_2-1}, i_{k_2}^0, i_{k_2+1}, \ldots, i_{k_r-1}, i_{k_r}^0, i_{k_r+1}, \ldots, i_K]^{\mathrm{T}} \in T \bullet$$
$$(g_{j,k_1} i_{k_1}^0 + g_{j,k_2} i_{k_2}^0 + \cdots + g_{j,k_r} i_{k_r}^0 + v_j = s_j^0 \wedge a'[\mathsf{G}'\mathbf{i}' + \mathbf{v}'] = a[\mathsf{G}\mathbf{i} + \mathbf{v}]),$$

and the proof is complete. □

Theorem 5.3 *The function* BUILD_POSITIVE_BASIS *in Figure 5.1 computes a positive basis of a set of $R \geq 1$ K-dimensional distance vectors $\mathbf{x}^1$, $\mathbf{x}^2$, ..., $\mathbf{x}^R$ in* $O(K^2R)$ *time.*

Proof For convenience, the algorithm in Figure 5.1 is reproduced below:

BUILD_POSITIVE_BASIS $(\mathbf{x}^1, \mathbf{x}^2, \ldots, \mathbf{x}^R)$
1 $k = 1, J = \text{rank}[\mathbf{x}^1, \mathbf{x}^2, \ldots, \mathbf{x}^R], X = \{\mathbf{x}^1, \mathbf{x}^2, \ldots, \mathbf{x}^R\}$
2 **for** $j = 1, J$ **do**
3   **while** $\forall \mathbf{x} \in X \bullet x_k = 0$ **do**
4     $k = k + 1$
5   $\mathbf{v}^j = \mathbf{x}$, with $\mathbf{x} \in X$ and $x_k > 0 \vee (x_k < 0 \wedge \forall \mathbf{x} \in X \bullet x_k \leq 0)$
6   **for** $r = 1, R$ **do**
7     $\alpha_{r,j} = x_k^r / v_k^j$
8     $\mathbf{x}^r = \mathbf{x}^r - \alpha_{r,j} \mathbf{v}^j$
9 **return** $\{\mathbf{v}^1, \mathbf{v}^2, \ldots, \mathbf{v}^J\}$

For all $r \in 1..R$, let $\mathbf{x}^{r,j}$ denote the value of $\mathbf{x}^r$ after the execution of the j-th iteration of the for loop in lines 2–8. Also, assume that the function BUILD_POSITIVE_BASIS is called with the actual arguments $\mathbf{d}^1$, $\mathbf{d}^2$, ..., $\mathbf{d}^R$, at least one of which is not null. It follows from line 8 that, for any $r \in 1..R$, and for any iteration j of the for loop in lines 2–8,

$$\mathbf{d}^r = \mathbf{x}^{r,j} + \sum_{j'=1}^{j} \alpha_{r,j'} \mathbf{v}^{j'}. \tag{A.1}$$

Using the notation $\mathrm{D} = [\mathbf{d}^1, \mathbf{d}^2, \ldots, \mathbf{d}^R]$, we shall prove by induction on the value of j that, for any $j \in 1..\text{rank}\,\mathrm{D}$, the following propositions hold:

$P_1(j)$: in the j-th iteration of the outer for loop, the while loop in lines 3–4 terminates for some $k = k_j \leq K$, and $k_1 < k_2 < \cdots < k_j$;

$P_2(j)$: $v_1^j = v_2^j = \cdots = v_{k_j-1}^j = 0$ and $v_{k_j}^j \neq 0$;

$P_3(j)$: for all $r \in 1..R$, $x_1^{r,j} = x_2^{r,j} = \cdots = x_{k_j}^{r,j} = 0$.

Since not all R distance vectors are null, there is a vector $\mathbf{d} \in D = \{\mathbf{d}^1, \mathbf{d}^2, \ldots, \mathbf{d}^R\}$ such that $d_1 = d_2 = \cdots = d_{k_1-1} = 0$, $d_{k_1} > 0$, and $\forall \mathbf{d}' \in D \bullet d'_1 = d'_2 = \cdots = d'_{k_1-1} = 0$. Hence, $P_1(1)$ and $P_2(1)$ are true. In addition, for any $1 \leq r \leq R$ the first $k_1 - 1$ elements of $\mathbf{x}^r$ are null, and the for loop in lines 6–8 zeros the k_1-th element of $\mathbf{x}^r$. Thus, $P_3(1)$ is also true.

Assume now that for some $j \in 1..\text{rank}\,\mathrm{D} - 1$ the propositions $P_1(j)$, $P_2(j)$, and $P_3(j)$ are true. We shall prove that the three propositions also hold for $j+1$. First, if $P_1(j+1)$ were false, it would follow from the structure of $\mathbf{x}^{r,j}$, $1 \leq r \leq R$, described by $P_3(j)$ that $\mathbf{x}^{r,j} = \mathbf{0}$ for any $1 \leq r \leq R$. Hence, according to (A.1), the R distance vectors could be written as linear combinations of $\mathbf{v}^1$, $\mathbf{v}^2$, ..., $\mathbf{v}^j$, i.e. as linear combinations of less than $\text{rank}\,\mathrm{D}$ vectors. As this is not possible, $P_1(j+1)$ is necessarily true. Furthermore, $\mathbf{v}^{j+1}$ is one of the vectors $\mathbf{x}^{r,j}$, $1 \leq r \leq R$, for which $d_{k_{j+1}}^{x,j} \neq 0$, and $P_2(j+1)$ is true. Finally, after the execution of the for loop in lines 6–8, $\mathbf{x}^{r,j+1} = [0, 0, \ldots, 0, x_{k_j+1}^{r,j+1}, x_{k_j+2}^{r,j+1}, \ldots, x_K^{r,j+1}]^{\mathrm{T}}$ for all $1 \leq r \leq R$, and $P_3(j+1)$ is also true.

As $P_1(j)$ is true for $j = 1, 2, \ldots, \text{rank}\,\mathrm{D}$, the algorithm terminates, and returns a set of $\text{rank}\,\mathrm{D}$ vectors. We shall demonstrate that these vectors represent a positive basis for span$\{\mathbf{d}^1,\mathbf{d}^2,\ldots,\mathbf{d}^R\}$. Given that $k_1 < k_2 < \cdots < k_{\text{rank D}}$, it follows from the generic form of $\mathbf{v}^1, \mathbf{v}^2, \ldots, \mathbf{v}^{\text{rank D}}$ described by $P_2(1), P_2(2), \ldots, P_2(\text{rank D})$ that these vectors are linearly independent. Let now $r_1, r_2, \ldots, r_{\text{rank D}}$ be the (different) values of r such that $\mathbf{v}^1 = \mathbf{d}^{r_1}$, $\mathbf{v}^2 = \mathbf{x}^{r_2,1}, \ldots, \mathbf{v}^{\text{rank D}} = \mathbf{x}^{r_{\text{rank D}},\text{rank D}-1}$. Then, according to (A.1),

$$\mathbf{d}^{r_1} = \mathbf{v}^1, \quad \mathbf{d}^{r_2} = \alpha_{r_2,1}\mathbf{v}^1 + \mathbf{v}^2, \quad \ldots, \quad \mathbf{d}^{r_{\text{rank D}}} = \sum_{j=1}^{\text{rank D}-1} \alpha_{r_{\text{rank D}},j}\mathbf{v}^j + \mathbf{v}^{\text{rank D}}.$$

Since $\mathbf{v}^1$, $\mathbf{v}^2$, ..., $\mathbf{v}^{\text{rank D}}$ are linearly independent, so are the above rank D distance vectors. Furthermore, any other distance vector can be written as a linear combination of these distance vectors, and, ultimately, as a linear combination of $\mathbf{v}^1, \mathbf{v}^2, \ldots, \mathbf{v}^{\text{rank D}}$. As a result, the set of vectors returned by BUILD_POSITIVE_BASIS represents a basis for span$\{\mathbf{d}^1,\mathbf{d}^2,\ldots,\mathbf{d}^R\}$.

In order to prove that this basis is positive, consider a generic distance vector $\mathbf{d}^r$, $1 \le r \le R$. This vector can be written as

$$\mathbf{d}^r = [0,0,\ldots,0,d^r_l,d^r_{l+1},\ldots,d^r_K]^{\mathrm{T}} = \sum_{j=1}^{\text{rank D}} \alpha_{r,j}\mathbf{v}^j,$$

where $d^r_l > 0$, $1 \le l \le K$ is its first non-zero element. Let now $j' \in 1..\text{rank D}$ be the unique value such that $k_{j'} \le l$ and either $j' = \text{rank D}$ or $l < k_{j'+1}$. Due to the form of the vectors in the basis, it follows that $\alpha_{r,1} = \alpha_{r,2} = \cdots = \alpha_{r,j'-1} = 0$ and $\mathbf{d}^r = \mathbf{x}^{r,1} = \cdots = \mathbf{x}^{r,j'-1}$.

Moreover, when the outer for loop is performed for $j = j'$, the while loop in lines 3–4 terminates with $k = k_{j'} = l$ because $x^{r,j'-1}_l = d^r_l \neq 0$. Since $x^{r,j'-1}_l = d^r_l$ is also positive, so is $v^{j'}_{k_{j'}}$, the first non-null element of $\mathbf{v}^{j'}$. Consequently, $\alpha_{r,j'} = x^{r,j'-1}_{k_{j'}}/v^{j'}_{k_{j'}}$, the first non-zero element of $[\alpha_{r,1},\alpha_{r,2},\ldots,\alpha_{r,\text{rank D}}]^{\mathrm{T}}$, is also positive, and the basis returned by BUILD_POSITIVE_BASIS is indeed a positive basis for span$\{\mathbf{d}^1,\mathbf{d}^2,\ldots,\mathbf{d}^R\}$.

The for loop in lines 2–8 is executed at most K times. For each outer loop iteration, the body of the while loop in lines 3–4 requires less than KR time, the choice of the vector $\mathbf{v}^j$ in line 5 takes $O(R)$ time, and the updating of the $\mathbf{x}$ vectors in lines 6–8 $O(KR)$ time. As a result, the overall running time of the algorithm is $O(K^2R)$. □

Appendix B. Syntax of the BSPscheduler input language

The following notation is used to define the syntax of the BSPSCHEDULER input language. Non-terminal symbols are indicated by *italic* type. Terminal symbols are indicated by **bold** type. A colon : following a non-terminal introduces its definition. Alternative definitions are separated by a vertical line |.

BSPscheduler-input : *variable-declarations loop-nest*

variable-declarations : *variable-declaration* |
variable-declaration variable-declarations

variable-declaration : *array-declaration* |
scalar-declaration

array-declaration : **array** *array-decl-list*

array-decl-list : *array-decl* |
array-decl **,** *array-decl-list*

array-decl : *identifier size-decl-list*

identifier : *letter* |
identifier letter |
identifier digit

letter : **a** | **b** | **c** | **d** | **e** | **f** | **g** | **h** | **i** | **j** | **k** | **l** | **m** |
n | **o** | **p** | **q** | **r** | **s** | **t** | **u** | **v** | **w** | **x** | **y** | **z** |
A | **B** | **C** | **D** | **E** | **F** | **G** | **H** | **I** | **J** | **K** | **L** | **M** |
N | **O** | **P** | **Q** | **R** | **S** | **T** | **U** | **V** | **W** | **X** | **Y** | **Z**

digit : **0** | **1** | **2** | **3** | **4** | **5** | **6** | **7** | **8** | **9**

size-decl-list : *size-decl* |
size-decl size-decl-list

size-decl : **[** *pos-integer-const* **]** |
[*identifier* **]**

pos-integer-const : *nonzero-digit* |
nonzero-digit digits

nonzero-digit : **1** | **2** | **3** | **4** | **5** | **6** | **7** | **8** | **9**

digits : *digit* |
digit digits

scalar-declaration : **scalar** *scalar-decl-list*

scalar-decl-list : *identifier* |
identifier **,** *scalar-decl-list*

loop-nest : *for-stmt*

for-stmt : **for** *identifier* **=** *arithm-expr* **,** *arithm-expr* **do** *stmts* **endfor**

arithm-expr : *arithm-term* |
– *arithm-term* |
arithm-expr **+** *arithm-term* |
arithm-expr **–** *arithm-term*

arithm-term : *arithm-factor* |
arithm-term ***** *arithm-factor* |
arithm-term **/** *arithm-factor*

arithm-factor : *integer-const* |
float-const |
variable |
(*arithm-expr* **)** |
function-call

integer-const : **0** |
pos-integer-const |
– *pos-integer-const*

float-const : *integer-const* **.** *digits*

variable : *identifier* |
identifier subscript-list

subscript-list : [*integer-arithm-expr*] |
[*integer-arithm-expr*] *subscript-list*

integer-arithm-expr : *integer-arithm-term* |
– *integer-arithm-term* |
integer-arithm-expr + *integer-arithm-term* |
integer-arithm-expr – *integer-arithm-term*

integer-arithm-term : *integer-arithm-factor* |
integer-arithm-term * *integer-arithm-factor* |
integer-arithm-term / *integer-arithm-factor*

integer-arithm-factor : *integer-const* |
variable |
(*integer-arithm-expr*) |
function-call

function-call : *identifier* ( ) |
identifier (*parameter-list*)

parameter-list : *expr* |
expr , *parameter-list*

expr : **not** *expr* |
logic-term |
logic-term **or** *expr*

logic-term : *logic-factor* |
logic-factor **and** *logic-term*

logic-factor : *rel-expr*|
(*expr*)

rel-expr : *arithm-expr* |
arithm-expr *rel-operator* *arithm-expr*

rel-operator : < | > | = | <= | >= | <>

stmts : *stmt* |
stmt *stmts*

stmt : *for-stmt* |
if-stmt |
assign-stmt

if-stmt	:	**if** *expr* **then** *assign-stmts* **endif** | **if** *expr* **then** *assign-stmts* **else** *assign-stmts* **endif**
assign-stmts	:	*assign-stmt* | *assign-stmt assign-stmts*
assign-stmt	:	*variable* = *expr*

Appendix C. Syntax of the BSPscheduler output language

The language used to describe the parallel pseudocode generated by BSPSCHEDULER differs from the input language of the tool in its definition of the *stmt* non-terminal symbol. The notation introduced in Appendix B is used to define the modified syntax of this non-terminal symbol. Non-terminal symbols whose definitions are identical to the definitions provided in Appendix B are no longer defined here.

stmt	:	*for-stmt* | *if-stmt* | *assign-stmt* | **BSP_sync** | *BSP-get-stmt* | *BSP-combine-stmt*
if-stmt	:	**if** *expr* **then** *assign-stmt* **endif** | **if** *expr* **then** *BSP-get-stmt* **endif**
BSP-get-stmt	:	**BSP_get** *variable* **for** (*index-list*) **in** (*index-range-list*) **from** *processor*
index-list	:	*identifier* | *identifier* , *index-list*
identifier	:	*letter* | *identifier letter* | *identifier digit* | _ *identifier*
index-range-list	:	*index-range* | *index-range* , *index-range-list*
index-range	:	*integer-arithm-expr* .. *integer-arithm-expr* | *integer-arithm-expr* .. *integer-arithm-expr* ; *pos-integer-const*

processor	:	**_proc** *processor-array-dim* **(** *processor-coordinates* **)**
processor-array-dim	:	*pos-integer-const*
processor-coordinates	:	*integer-arithm-expr* | *integer-arithm-expr* **,** *processor-coordinates*
BSP-combine-stmt	:	**BSP_combine (** *variable* **,** *combine-operator* **)**
combine-operator	:	**PLUS | MULT | OR | AND**

Appendix D. Automatically generated code for Example 7.5

```
/*****************************************************************************
 *
 * This code was generated by BSPscheduler 1.0
 *
 * Here is an account of the array distributions and of the locally stored
 * array blocks:
 *
 * > a[block][*][*]:
 *   - processor _me owns (and, if necessary, must initialise)
 *     a[_me*_ceil(n,_p)..(_me+1)*_ceil(n,_p)-1]
 *      [0..n-1]
 *      [0..n-1]
 *   - element a[i1][i2][i3] can be referred to as
 *     a[_lin3(i1-_me*_ceil(n,_p)+1,
 *             i2,
 *             i3,
 *             n,
 *             n)]
 *
 * > b[block][*]:
 *   - processor _me owns (and, if necessary, must initialise)
 *     b[_me*_ceil(n,_p)..(_me+1)*_ceil(n,_p)-1]
 *      [0..n-1]
 *   - element b[i1][i2] can be referred to as
 *     b[_lin2(i1-_me*_ceil(n,_p)+1,
 *             i2,
 *             n)]
 *
 *****************************************************************************/

#include <stdlib.h>

#include "bsp.h"

#define _floor(x) ((int)(x))
#define _ceil(x,y)  ((x+y-1)/(y))
#define _min2(x1,x2) (((x1)<(x2))?(x1):(x2))
#define _max2(x1,x2) (((x1)>(x2))?(x1):(x2))
#define _lin2(i1,i2,n2) ((i1)*(n2)+(i2))
#define _lin3(i1,i2,i3,n2,n3) (((i1)*(n2)+(i2))*(n3)+(i3))
```

```
void initialise_data(int* i,int* j,int* k,float* a,float* b,int n,
int _p,int _me){

}

void output_data(int i,int j,int k,const float* a,const float* b,
int n,int _p,int _me){

}

float f1(float _x1,float _x2,float _x3){

}

float f2(float _x1){

}

void parallel_code(int n,int _p){
  int i,j,k,_me,_s1,_s2,_aux;
  float *a,*b;
  _me=bsp_pid();
  a=(float*)calloc((_ceil(n,_p)+1)*n*n,sizeof(float));
  b=(float*)calloc((_ceil(n,_p)+1)*n,sizeof(float));
  initialise_data(&i,&j,&k,a,b,n,_p,_me);
  bsp_push_reg(a,(_ceil(n,_p)+1)*n*n*sizeof(float));
  bsp_push_reg(b,(_ceil(n,_p)+1)*n*sizeof(float));
  bsp_sync();
  for(i=_max2(1,_me*_ceil(n,_p));i<=_min2(n-1,(_me+1)*_ceil(n,_p)-1);i++)
    for(j=1;j<=n-1;j++)
      b[_lin2(i-_me*_ceil(n,_p)+1,j,n)]=
           f2(b[_lin2(i-_me*_ceil(n,_p)+1,j-1,n)]);

  for(_s1=_max2(0,_me*_ceil(n,_p)-1);_s1<=_me*_ceil(n,_p)-1;_s1++)
    bsp_get(_floor(_s1/_ceil(n,_p)),
            b,
            (_lin2(_s1-(_floor(_s1/_ceil(n,_p)))*_ceil(n,_p)+1,0,n))
              *sizeof(float),
            &b[_lin2(_s1-_me*_ceil(n,_p)+1,0,n)],
            (n-2+1)*sizeof(float));
  bsp_sync();
  for(j=1;j<=n-1;j++){
    for(_s1=_max2(0,_me*_ceil(n,_p)-1);_s1<=_me*_ceil(n,_p)-1;_s1++)
      bsp_get(_floor(_s1/_ceil(n,_p)),
              a,
              (_lin3(_s1-(_floor(_s1/_ceil(n,_p)))*_ceil(n,_p)+1,j-1,1,n,n))
                *sizeof(float),
              &a[_lin3(_s1-_me*_ceil(n,_p)+1,j-1,1,n,n)],
              (n-1)*sizeof(float));
    bsp_sync();
    for(i=_max2(1,_me*_ceil(n,_p));i<=_min2(n-1,(_me+1)*_ceil(n,_p)-1);i++)
      for(k=1;k<=n-1;k++)
        a[_lin3(i-_me*_ceil(n,_p)+1,j,k,n,n)]=
             f1(a[_lin3(i-_me*_ceil(n,_p)+1,j-1,k-1,n,n)],
                a[_lin3(i-1-_me*_ceil(n,_p)+1,j-1,k,n,n)],
                b[_lin2(i-1-_me*_ceil(n,_p)+1,j-1,n)]);
  }
```

```
  output_data(i,j,k,a,b,n,_p,_me);
  bsp_pop_reg(a);
  bsp_pop_reg(b);
  bsp_sync();
  free(a);
  free(b);
}
```

Bibliography

[1] Valiant LG. A bridging model for parallel computation. *Communications of the ACM*, 33(8):103–111, August 1990.

[2] Culler D, Karp R, Patterson D, Sahay A, Schauser KE, Santos E, et al. LogP: Towards a realistic model of parallel computation. In *Proceedings of the 4th ACM SIGPLAN Symposium on Principles and Practice of Parallel Programming*, pages 19–22. ACM Press, 1993.

[3] Nash JM, Dew PM, Davy JR, Dyer ME. Scalable and portable computing using the WPRAM model. In *Abstract Machine Models for Parallel and Distributed Computing*, IOS Press series on Concurrent Systems Engineering, pages 47–62. IOS Press, 1996.

[4] Banerjee U. Data dependence in ordinary programs. Technical Report 76-837, Department of Computer Science, University of Illinois at Urbana-Champaign, November 1976.

[5] Towle RA. *Control and data dependence for program transformations*. PhD thesis, University of Illinois at Urbana-Champaign, 1976.

[6] Wolfe M. *Optimizing supercompilers for supercomputers*. PhD thesis, Department of Computer Science, University of Illinois at Urbana-Champaign, October 1982.

[7] Wolfe M, Banerjee U. Data dependence and its application to parallel processing. *International Journal of Parallel Programming*, 16(2):137–178, 1987.

[8] Banerjee U. *Dependence Analysis for Supercomputing*. Kluwer Academic Publishers, 1988.

[9] Li Z, Yew P, Zhu C. Data dependence analysis on multi-dimensional array references. *IEEE Transactions on Parallel and Distributed Systems*, 1(1):26–34, January 1990.

[10] Pugh W. A practical algorithm for exact array dependence analysis. *Communications of the ACM*, 35(8):102–114, August 1992.

[11] Yang Y-Q, Ancourt C, Irigoin F. Minimal data dependence abstractions for loop transformations. In Pingali K, Banerjee U, Gelernter D, Nicolau A, Padua D, editors, *Languages and Compilers for Parallel Computing*, Lecture Notes in Computer Science 892, pages 201–216. Springer-Verlag, 1995.

[12] Banerjee U. *Dependence Analysis*. Kluwer Academic Publishers, 1997.

[13] Padua DA, Wolfe MJ. Advanced compiler optimizations for supercomputers. *Communications of the ACM*, 29(12):1184–1201, December 1986.

[14] Polychronopoulos CD. Loop coalescing: A compiler transformation for parallel machines. In *Proceedings of the International Conference on Parallel Processing*, pages 235–242. Pennsylvania State University Press, 1987.

[15] Banerjee U. A theory of loop permutations. In Gelernter D, Nicolau A, Padua D, editors, *Languages and Compilers for Parallel Computing*, Research Monographs in Parallel and Distributed Computing, pages 54–74. MIT Press 1989.

[16] Wolf ME, Lam MS. A loop transformation theory and an algorithm to maximize parallelism. *IEEE Transactions on Parallel and Distributed Systems*, 2(4):452–470, October 1991.

[17] Bacon DF, Graham SL, Sharp OJ. Compiler transformations for high-performance computing. *ACM Computing Surveys*, 26(4):346–420, December 1994.

[18] Lim AW, Lam MS. Communication-free parallelization via affine transformations. In Pingali K, Banerjee U, Gelernter D, Nicolau A, Padua D, editors, *Languages and Compilers for Parallel Computing*, Lecture Notes in Computer Science 892, pages 92–106. Springer-Verlag, 1995.

[19] Xue J. Communication-minimal tiling of uniform dependence loops. *Journal of Parallel and Distributed Computing*, 42(1):42–59, April 1997.

[20] Allen R, Callahan D, Kennedy K. Automatic decomposition of scientific programs for parallel execution. In *Proceedings of the 14th Annual ACM Symposium on Principles of Programming Languages*, pages 63–76. ACM Press, 1987.

[21] Wolfe MJ. *Optimizing Supercompilers for Supercomputers*. Research Monographs in Parallel and Distributed Computing. MIT Press, 1989.

[22] Wolfe MJ. More iteration space tiling. In *Proceedings Supercomputing '89*, pages 655–664. ACM Press, 1989.

[23] Schreiber R, Dongarra JJ. Automatic blocking of nested loops. Technical Report 90-38, University of Tennessee at Knoxville, May 1990.

[24] Ramanujam J, Sadayappan P. Tiling multidimensional iteration spaces for multicomputers. *Journal of Parallel and Distributed Computing*, 16(2):108–120, October 1992.

[25] Banerjee U, Eigenmann R, Nicolau A, Padua DA. Automatic program parallelisation. *Proceedings of the IEEE*, 81(2):211–243, February 1993.

[26] Lengauer C. Loop parallelization in the polytope model. In Best E, editor, *CONCUR'93*, Lecture Notes in Computer Science 715, pages 398–416. Springer–Verlag, 1993.

[27] Darte A, Vivien F. Optimal fine and medium grain parallelism detection in polyhedral reduced dependence graphs. *International Journal of Parallel Programming*, 25(6):447–497, 1997.

[28] Allen JR, Kennedy K. Automatic translation of Fortran programs to vector form. *ACM Transactions on Programming Languages and Systems*, 9(4):491–542, October 1987.

[29] Zima HP, Chapman BM. *Supercompilers for Parallel and Vector Computers*. Addison-Wesley, 1990.

[30] Zima HP, Chapman BM. Compiling for distributed-memory systems. *Proceedings of the IEEE*, 81(2):264–287, February 1993.

[31] Hall MW, Anderson JM, Amarasinghe SP, Murphy BR, Shih-Wei-Liao, Bugnion E, et al. Maximizing multiprocessor performance with the SUIF compiler. *Computer*, 29(12):84–89, December 1996.

[32] Johnson SP, Ierotheou CS, Cross M. Automatic parallel code generation for message passing on distributed memory systems. *Parallel Computing*, 22(2):227–258, 1996.

[33] Wolfe M. *High Performance Compilers for Parallel Computing*. Addison-Wesley, 1996.

[34] McColl WF. General purpose parallel computing. In Gibbons A, Spirakis P, editors, *Lectures on Parallel Computation*, Cambridge International Series on Parallel Computation: 4, pages 337–391. Cambridge University Press, 1993.

[35] McColl WF. Scalable computing. In Van Leeuwen J, editor, *Computer science today: recent trends and developments*, Lecture Notes in Computer Science 1000, pages 46–61. Springer-Verlag, 1995.

[36] Hill JMD, McColl WF, Stefanescu DC, Goudreau MW, Lang K, Rao SB, et al. BSPlib: The BSP programming library. Technical Report, Oxford University Computing Laboratory, May 1997.

[37] Hill JMD, Crumpton PI, Burgess DA. Theory, practice, and a tool for BSP performance prediction. In Bouge L, Fraigniaud P, Mignotte A, Robert Y, editors, *Euro-Par'96. Parallel Processing. Vol. II*, Lecture Notes in Computer Science 1124, pages 697–705. Springer–Verlag, 1996.

[38] Hill JMD, Jarvis S, Siniolakis C, Vasilev VP. Portable and architecture independent parallel performance tuning using a call-graph profiling tool. In *Proceedings of the 6th EuroMicro Workshop on Parallel and Distributed Processing (PDP'98)*, pages 286–292. IEEE Computer Society Press, January 1998.

[39] Geist A, Beguelin A, Dongarra J, Jiang W, Manchek R, Sunderam V. *PVM: Parallel Virtual Machine*. The MIT Press, 1994.

[40] Snir M, Otto S, Huss-Lederman S, Walker D, Dongarra J. *MPI: the complete reference*. MIT Press, 1996.

[41] Skillicorn D, Hill JMD, McColl WF. Questions and answers about BSP. *Scientific Programming*, 6(3):249–274, Fall 1997.

[42] Boulet P, Darte A, Risset T, Robert Y. (Pen)-ultimate tiling? *Integration, the VLSI Journal*, 17(1):33–51, August 1994.

[43] Ding Y-Z, Stefanescu D. Efficient scheduling of loop nests for BSP programs. Technical Report TR-04-95, Center for Research in Computing Technology, Harvard University, 1995.

[44] Calinescu R. A BSP approach to the scheduling of tightly-nested loops. In *Proceedings of the 11th International Parallel Processing Symposium (IPPS'97), 1–5 April 1997, Geneva, Switzerland*, pages 549–553. IEEE Computer Society Press, 1997.

[45] Feautrier P. Some efficient solutions to the affine scheduling problem. Part I, one-dimensional time. *International Journal of Parallel Programming*, 21(5):313–348, October 1992.

[46] Feautrier P. Some efficient solutions to the affine scheduling problem. Part II, multi-dimensional time. *International Journal of Parallel Programming*, 21(6):389–420, December 1992.

[47] Calinescu R. Automatic loop parallelization in the BSP model. In Bukhres O, El-Rewini H, editors, *Proceedings of the 2nd European Parallel and Distributed Systems Conference (Euro-PDS'98), 1-3 July 1998, Vienna, Austria*, pages 215–220. IASTED/ACTA Press, 1998.

[48] Gerbessiotis AV, Valiant LG. Direct bulk-synchronous parallel algorithms. *Journal of Parallel and Distributed Computing*, 22(2):251–267, August 1994.

[49] Cheatham T, Fahmy A, Stefanescu DC, Valiant LG. Bulk synchronous parallel computing – a paradigm for transportable software. Technical Report TR-36-94, Center for Research in Computing Technology, Harvard University, Cambridge, Massachusetts, December 1994.

[50] McColl WF. Scalability, portability and predictability: The BSP approach to parallel programming. *Future Generation Computer Systems*, 12(4):265–272, December 1996.

[51] Valiant LG. General purpose parallel architectures. In Van Leeuwen J, editor, *Handbook of Theoretical Computer Science. Volume A: Algorithms and Complexity*, pages 943–971. North Holland, 1990.

[52] Bisseling RH, McColl WF. Scientific computing on bulk synchronous parallel architectures. Technical Report 836, Department of Mathematics, Utrecht University, December 1993.

[53] Miller R. *Two approaches to architecture-independent parallel computation*. PhD thesis, Oxford University Computing Laboratory, 1994.

[54] Lecomber DS, Sujithan KR, Siniolakis CJ. PRAM programming in theory and in practice. *Concurrency: Practice and Experience*, 12(1):1–16, April 2000.

[55] McColl WF. The challenge of general purpose parallel computing. In Fincham AE, Ford B, editors, *Parallel Computation*, pages 37–80. Institute of Mathematics and its Applications, Oxford University Press, September 1991.

[56] Gerbessiotis AV, Valiant LG. Direct bulk-synchronous parallel algorithms. Technical Report TR-10-92, Harvard University, Computer Science Department, 1992.

[57] Miller R, Reed JL. The Oxford BSP library: Users guide version 1.0. Technical Report, Oxford Parallel, Oxford University Computing Laboratory, 1994.

[58] Goudreau MW, Lang K, Rao SB, Tsantilas T. The Green BSP library. Technical Report CS-TR-95-11, Department of Computer Science, University of Central Florida, Orlando, August 1995.

[59] Muraoka Y. *Parallelism exposure and exploitation in programs*. PhD thesis, University of Illinois at Urbana-Champaign, 1971.

[60] Kuck DJ. A survey of parallel machine organization and programming. *ACM Computing Surveys*, 9(1):29–59, March 1977.

[61] Kuck DJ. *The Structure of Computers and Computations*. John Wiley and Sons, 1978.

[62] Lamport L. The parallel execution of do loops. *Communications of the ACM*, 17(2):83–93, February 1974.

[63] Darte A, Robert Y. Constructive methods for scheduling uniform loop nests. *IEEE Transactions on Parallel and Distributed Systems*, 5(8):814–822, August 1994.

[64] Irigoin F, Triolet F. Supernode partitioning. In *Conference Record of the 15th ACM Symposium on Principles of Programming Languages*, pages 319–329. ACM Press, 1988.

[65] Calinescu R. Bulk synchronous parallel scheduling of uniform dags. In Bouge L, Fraigniaud P, Mignotte A, Robert Y, editors, *Euro-Par'96. Parallel Processing. Vol. II*, Lecture Notes in Computer Science 1124, pages 555–562. Springer–Verlag, 1996.

[66] Ershov AP. ALPHA—an automatic programming system of high efficiency. *Journal of the ACM*, 13(1):17–24, January 1966.

[67] Wedel D. FORTRAN for the Texas Instruments ASC system. *SIGPLAN Notes*, 10(3):119–132, March 1975.

[68] O'Keefe MT, Dietz HG. Loop coalescing and scheduling for barrier MIMD architectures. *IEEE Transactions on Parallel and Distributed Systems*, 4(9):1060–1063, September 1993.

[69] Dongarra J, Hind AR. Unrolling loops in FORTRAN. *Software Practice and Experience*, 9(3):219–226, March 1979.

[70] Rau B, Ficher JA. Instruction-level parallel processing: History, overview and perspective. *Journal of Supercomputing*, 7(1–2):9–50, May 1993.

[71] Thiebaut D, Stone HS. Footprints in the cache. *ACM Transactions on Computer Systems*, 5(4):305–329, November 1987.

[72] Agarwal A, Kranz DK, Natarajan V. Automatic partitioning of parallel loops for cache-coherent multiprocessors. Technical Report TM-481, Laboratory for Computer Science, Massachusetts Institute of Technology, December 1992.

[73] Agarwal A, Kranz DK, Natarajan V. Automatic partitioning of parallel loops and data arrays for distributed shared-memory multiprocessors. *IEEE Transactions on Parallel and Distributed Systems*, 6(9):943–962, September 1995.

[74] Ramanujam J, Sadayappan P. Iteration space tiling for distributed memory machines. In Saltz J, Mehrotra P, editors, *Languages, Compilers and Run-Time Environments for Distributed Memory Machines*, pages 255–269. Elsevier Science Publishers B.V., 1992.

[75] Andonov R, Rajopadhye S. Optimal orthogonal tiling of 2-D iterations. *Journal of Parallel and Distributed Computing*, 45(2):159–165, 1997.

[76] Wolfe M. Loop rotation. In Gelernter D, Nicolau A, Padua D, editors, *Languages and Compilers for Parallel Computing*, Research Monographs in Parallel and Distributed Computing, pages 531–553. Pitman Publishers, 1990.

[77] Webb JRL. *Functions of several real variables*. Ellis Horwood series in mathematics and its applications. Statistics and operational research. Ellis Horwood, 1991.

[78] Kennedy K, McKinley KS, Tseng C-W. Analysis and transformation in an interactive parallel programming tool. *Concurrency: Practice and Experience*, 5(7):575–602, October 1993.

[79] Kogge PM, Stone HS. A parallel algorithm for the efficient solution of a general class of recurrence equations. *IEEE Transactions on Computers*, C-22(8):786–793, August 1973.

[80] Greenberg AC, Ladner RE, Paterson MS, Galil Z. Efficient parallel algorithms for linear recurrence computation. *Information Processing Letters*, 15(1):31–35, August 1982.

[81] Gerbessiotis AV, Siniolakis CJ. Primitive operations on the BSP model. Technical Report PRG-TR-23-96, Programming Research Group, Oxford University Computing Laboratory, 1996.

[82] Fortes JAB, Moldovan DI. Data broadcasting in linearly scheduled array processors. In *Proceedings of the 2nd Annual Symposium on Computer Architecture*, pages 224–231. IEEE Press, 1984.

[83] Megson GM. *An Introduction to Systolic Algorithm Design*. Oxford University Press, 1992.

[84] Allen JR. *Dependence analysis for subscripted variables and its application to program transformation*. PhD thesis, Department of Mathematical Sciences, Rice University, Houston, TX, April 1983.

[85] Darte A, Silber G-A, Vivien F. Combining retiming and scheduling techniques for loop parallelization and loop tiling. *Parallel Processing Letters*, 7(4):379–392, 1998.

[86] Zima H, Bast H, Gerndt M. Superb: A tool for semiautomatic MIMD/SIMD parallelization. *Parallel Computing*, 6:1–18, 1988.

[87] Hiranandani S, Kennedy K, Tseng C-W. Compiling FORTRAN D for MIMD distributed-memory machines. *Communications of the ACM*, 35(8):66–80, August 1992.

[88] Banerjee P, Chandy JA, Gupta M, Hodges EW IV, Holm JG, Lain A, et al. The PARADIGM compiler for distributed-memory multiprocessors. *Computer*, 28(10):37–47, October 1995.

[89] Kuck DJ, Kuhn RH, Leasure B, Wolfe M. The structure of an advanced vectorizer for pipelined processors. In *Proceedings of the IEEE Computer Science Society Fourth International Computer Software and Applications Conference, Chicago, Oct. 1980*. IEEE, New York, 1980.

[90] Polychronopoulos CD, Girkar MB, Haghighat MR, Lee CL, Leung BP, Schouten DA. The structure of Parafrase-2: an advanced parallelizing compiler

for C and Fortran. In Gelernter D, Nicolau A, Padua D, editors, *Languages and Compilers for Parallel Computing*, Research Monographs in Parallel and Distributed Computing, pages 423–453. MIT Press, 1990.

[91] Cooper KD, Hall MW, Hood RT, Kennedy K, McKinley KS, Mellor-Crummey JM, et al. The ParaScope parallel programming environment. *Proceedings of the IEEE*, 81(2):244–262, February 1993.

[92] Hiranandani S, Kennedy K, Tseng C. Evaluating compiler optimizations for Fortran D. *Journal of Parallel and Distributed Computing*, 21(1):27–45, April 1994.

[93] Tseng C-W. Performance of the prototype Fortran D compiler. *Software—Practice and Experience*, 27(7):763–796, July 1997.

[94] Blume W, Eigenmann R, Faigin K, Grout J, Hoeflinger J, Padua D, et al. Polaris: Improving the effectiveness of parallelizing compilers. In Pingali K, Banerjee U, Gelernter D, Nicolau A, Padua D, editors, *Languages and Compilers for Parallel Computing*, Lecture Notes in Computer Science 892, pages 141–154. Springer-Verlag, 1995.

[95] Blume W, Doallo R, Eigenmann R, Grout J, Hoeflinger J, Lawrence T, et al. Advanced program restructuring for high-performance computers with Polaris. Technical Report 1473, Center for Supercomputing Research & Development, University of Illinois at Urbana-Champaign, January 1996.

[96] Eigenmann R, Hoeflinger J, Padua D. On the automatic parallelisation of the Perfect Benchmarks. *IEEE Transactions on Parallel and Distributed Systems*, 9(1):5–23, January 1998.

[97] Calinescu R. A BSP scheduling tool for loop nest parallelisation. Technical Report PRG-TR-36-97, Programming Research Group, Oxford University Computing Laboratory, November 1997.

[98] Boulet P. Bouclettes: a Fortran loop parallelizer. In Liddell H, Colbrook A, Hertzberger B, Sloot P, editors, *High-Performance Computing and Networking 1996*, Lecture Notes in Computer Science 1067, pages 784–791. Springer-Verlag, 1996.

[99] Boulet P, Brandes T. Evaluation of automatic parallelization strategies for HPF compilers. In Liddell H, Colbrook A, Hertzberger B, Sloot P, editors, *High-Performance Computing and Networking 1996*, Lecture Notes in Computer Science 1067, pages 778–783. Springer–Verlag, 1996.

[100] Ierotheou CS, Johnson SP, Cross M, Leggett PF. Computer aided parallelisation tools (CAPTools) - conceptual overview and performance on the parallelisation of structured mesh codes. *Parallel Computing*, 22(2):163–196, 1996.

[101] Johnson SP, Cross M, Everett MG. Exploitation of symbolic information in interprocedural dependence analysis. *Parallel Computing*, 22(2):197–226, 1996.

[102] Ellmenreich N, Faber P, Griebl M, Gunz R, Keimer H, Meisl W, et al. LooPo - Loop parallelization in the polytope model. Technical Report, Department of Mathematics and Computer Science, University of Passau, http://brahms.fmi.uni-passau.de/cl/loopo/doc/loopo_doc.ps.gz, April 1996.

[103] McCormack J, Asente PJ, Swick RR, Peterson C. *X toolkit : the Intrinsics & Athena Widgets*. Silicon Press, 1990.

[104] Allen JR, Kennedy K, Porterfield C, Warren J. Conversion of control dependence to data dependence. In *Conference Record of the 10th ACM Symposium on Principles of Programming Languages*, pages 177–189. ACM Press, 1983.

[105] Cormen TH, Leiserson CE, Rivest RL. *Introduction to Algorithms*. The MIT Press, 1990.

[106] Tiskin A. Bulk-synchronous parallel Gaussian elimination. In Vasilev NN, Vershik AM, editors, *Representation Theory, Dynamical Systems, Combinatorial and Algorithmic Methods (Part 4)*, Zapiski Nauchnykh Seminarov POMI 258, pages 115-133. Russian Academy of Sciences, 1999.

[107] Aho AV, Hopcroft JE, Ullman JD. *The Design and Analysis of Computer Algorithms*. Addison-Wesley series in computer science and information processing. Addison-Wesley, 1974.

[108] Floyd RW. Algorithm 97 (shortest path). *Communications of the ACM*, 5(6):345, 1962.

[109] Tiskin A. All-pairs shortest paths computation in the BSP model, 1998. Unpublished manuscript. Available as a postscript document from http://www.dcs.warwick.ac.uk/~tiskin/pub/.

Index

MIX
Papier aus verantwortungsvollen Quellen
Paper from responsible sources
FSC® C105338

If you have any concerns about our products,
you can contact us on
ProductSafety@springernature.com

In case Publisher is established outside the EU,
the EU authorized representative is:
Springer Nature Customer Service Center GmbH
Europaplatz 3, 69115 Heidelberg, Germany

Printed by Libri Plureos GmbH
in Hamburg, Germany